Blockchain Applied

Blockchain Applied

Practical Technology and Use Cases of Enterprise Blockchain for the Real World

Stephen Ashurst and Stefano Tempesta

Foreword by Stylianos Kampakis, Phd, MSc

Routledge
Taylor & Francis Group

A PRODUCTIVITY PRESS BOOK

First published 2022
by Routledge
600 Broken Sound Parkway #300, Boca Raton FL, 33487

and by Routledge
2 Park Square, Milton Park, Abingdon, Oxon OX14 4RN

Routledge is an imprint of the Taylor & Francis Group, an informa business

© 2022 Taylor & Francis

The right of Stephen Ashurst and Stefano Tempesta to be identified as authors of this work has been asserted by them in accordance with sections 77 and 78 of the Copyright, Designs and Patents Act 1988.

Library of Congress Cataloging-in-Publication Data
A catalog record for this title has been requested

ISBN: 9780367677367 (hbk)
ISBN: 9780367677350 (pbk)
ISBN: 9781003132592 (ebk)

DOI: 10.4324/9781003132592

Typeset in Garamond
by Newgen Publishing UK

MIX
Paper from
responsible sources
FSC www.fsc.org FSC™ C013985

Printed in the United Kingdom
by Henry Ling Limited

For Anthony and Isabella

Stephen Ashurst

As a European man living in Australia, I'd like to acknowledge and respect the traditional custodians whose ancestral lands I am living upon here today. I acknowledge the deep feelings of attachment and relationship of Aboriginal peoples to their country and recognise that their culture and heritage is important to all peoples today.

Stefano Tempesta

Contents

Contents

Foreword

Blockchain is, alongside AI, the most revolutionary technology in computer science right now. Blockchain is often compared in importance to transformational technologies like the internet or the operating systems of the early 1990s that gave rise to the personal computer.

Blockchain is promising to provide a new infrastructure layer for many of our current systems, such as supply chains, financial transactions and healthcare. These are only some of the systems that are being disrupted by blockchain.

While many people in the public associate blockchain with bitcoin, the truth is that blockchain is way more than that. The challenge, however, is explaining what blockchain is and how it can be used to a wider non-technical audience, without diluting the core benefits that blockchain can offer. This is a difficult task, given that blockchain is a technology comprised of many interrelated components, from game theory to advanced cryptography to network theory.

This is where Stephen and Stefano do a great job. This book explains all the fundamentals of blockchain, from its inception, down to case studies in many different verticals.

Blockchain is fundamentally a technology that can transform society. The success of this endeavour depends on its being understood by business leaders, governments and society at large. Books like *Blockchain Applied* help disseminate this knowledge and explain blockchain in simple terms to all those who need it the most.

I hope that you will enjoy reading the book as much as I did, and that you will discover in its pages some case studies which you can apply in your own organisation. And, who knows? Maybe when you buy the new edition of this book, you'll pay for it using a cryptocurrency using a blockchain-backed system.

It's only a matter of time until blockchain becomes just another normal part of everyday life, like smartphones and the World Wide Web. This book will help you visualise this new world before it arrives and understand the myriad possibilities.

Stylianos Kampakis

PhD (Computer Science); MSc (Informatics); MSc (Intelligent Systems); BSc (Mathematics & Statistics); BSc (Cognitive Psychology); Diploma (Economics); Honorary Research Fellow, University College, London Centre of Blockchain Studies; Member, Royal Statistical Society; and Editor, Journal of the British Blockchain Association.

Preface

'Blockchain is a technology that has a potential to disrupt industries and ...'

We've all heard this statement over and over again. Does it ring true to you?

It's 2021, and Stephen and I have for several years really felt we wanted to tell the story of where blockchain has already impacted industries and markets, where distributed ledger technology has already been applied successfully and where it might go next, and hence here is this book: a collection of use cases where both of us, via our own independent journeys into blockchain, can relate to the reader 'real life' stories of customer transformation and success when blockchain solutions have been implemented.

The development of a blockchain-based solution is a process in a larger digital transformation that a business, enterprise or organisation embarks on. Blockchain is not brand new but is often seen as a challenger technology given its apparent complexity of implementation and for the mindset shift away from traditional governance processes that it forces.

Decentralisation, distribution, peer-to-peer networking, proof-of-work, consensus: these are all terms and aspects that most organisations, of any size, don't normally discuss in their IT strategy (let alone business) meetings.

But when we add blockchain benefits to the list with 'new' terms such as transparency, immutability, traceability, security for business processes, cost cutting, simplification and streamlining, then suddenly the attention of the organisation is secured and blockchain starts making a lot more sense.

Companies worldwide, with barely any variance among industry sector, geography or scale, have all faced the gloom and doom of digital transformation in some way. The majority of digital transformation projects fail, resulting in a waste of money and time. According to an Everest Group study in 2020, a whopping 73% of enterprises did not provide any business value whatsoever from their digital change efforts. Furthermore, 78% failed to meet their business objectives at all through change. Put another way, only 22% achieved their desired results.[1]

A study from *Harvard Business Review*[2] reports that the two big reasons for technology change failure are disagreement among top managers on the objectives of the transformation and the challenge (the study says 'inability') in moving from concept to a production project. We agree.

And this is why Stephen and I sensed there was a gap in the market for a book to position blockchain technology not just as a 'promised land' for resolving organisational IT challenges but as an appropriate solution.

In this book, of which we are proud that there isn't a single line of software code, we aim to bring better visibility on the benefits of adopting blockchain by showing examples of companies, enterprises and organisations that have done just that. These scenarios witness organisations that have agreed on the objectives of their transformation and were able to move from a blockchain proof of concept to 'live' solutions that truly add value to their business.

Our intention is to make blockchain 'real', and to help readers appreciate the contexts where blockchain does and can have a real value and where its adoption can and does really make a difference.

Not all business and technical challenges get benefits from blockchain, and blockchain is not necessarily a solution to all use cases. Blockchain is not a panacea, but for those organisations, businesses and enterprise where it is, the advantages are clear as you will read in the book.

Happy reading, and please do get in touch for comments and feedback.

Stefano and Stephen

Notes

1 https://enterprisersproject.com/article/2019/8/why-digital-transformations-fail-3-reasons.
2 https://hbr.org/2019/10/the-two-big-reasons-that-digital-transformations-fail.

Acknowledgments

Stephen Ashurst: As most writers do (I suspect), I owe a debt of gratitude to the authors who educated me.

Stefano Tempesta: Thanks to the Azure Blockchain product group at Microsoft, who have inspired me in my journey into blockchain technology since 2017, and specifically Mark Russinovich, Yorke Rhodes III and Marc Mercuri. Your business acumen and technical readiness is beyond normal!

I'd like to also thank Michael Desmond at the Microsoft *MSDN Magazine* for trusting me and giving me the first public space to write about the application of blockchain in the enterprise.

And last but never the least, Oren Alazraki, mentor and motivator in pushing me always beyond my limits. You are the reason why I became a Microsoft Regional Director, one of only 150 of the world's top technology visionaries appointed by Microsoft specifically for their proven cross-platform expertise, community leadership and commitment to business results, and the only Microsoft MVP ever in three categories: Azure, AI and Business App.

About the Authors

Stephen Ashurst: By day, Stephen Ashurst is an independent software writer and wealth tech consultant. By night, he is a fintech entrepreneur. Stephen did manage to get an undergraduate degree in PPE, but failed Bar School miserably. Seeing the light, he quit law and turned his attentions to the IT industry – a good move, for all concerned.

A resident of London, Stephen travels constantly for pleasure and work. But home is where the heart is. And so are family, friends, dogs and 3,000 books. Sadly, so is his kitchen, the site of varyingly successful cooking experiments.

Stefano Tempesta: Stefano Tempesta works at Microsoft in the Azure Confidential Computing product group to make the Cloud a more secure place for your data and applications. Additionally, Stefano is advisor to the Department of Industry, Australia, on the National Blockchain Roadmap, with focus on helping people gain and own their digital identity. Stefano is also co-founder of Power Community, a non-profit organisation whose mission is to empower communities around the world with better ICT processes for customer relationship management and customer service.

Awarded 'Gold Disruptor' by ACS (Australian Computer Society) in the ICT Professional of the Year category in 2019, and a member of G-20Y Association, a prestigious executive leadership development and business networking organisation, Stefano leads the Smart City and Technology Innovation committee.

Married and with two children, Stefano is currently based in Australia. A passionate traveller, a poor musician and an avid learner of new technologies and (programming) languages, Stefano is a British and Italian citizen, and speaks fluent English, Italian, and terrible Russian.

Chapter 1

The Blockchain Age

In the era of the internet, online transactions and smart contracts are the lifeblood of all internet activity for individuals and businesses, governments and software platforms alike.

The primary function of economies is to maintain a steady, secure and predictable flow of money transactions through foreign exchange transfers, payments and credit. Economic transactions are dependent on transparent and accurate records being kept within the central bank and banking system and via government agencies such as tax authorities and welfare benefits services.

Civil legal systems depend heavily on clarity of contracts between entities in order for transactions to be enforceable. Commerce, land and property, and investment agreements – to name but a few – require parties to access and adhere to the terms agreed, with close attention to be paid to detailed terms and dates.

The digital revolution unleashed by the internet is undeniable but has not yet reached its zenith. Process automation, machine-learning and artificial intelligence, distributed apps and matching engines are pushing forward changes in human transactions and are driving automation in every field – for example, healthcare and finance.

Where this journey of innovation takes us is still far from clear, but in order to ensure consistency and fairness, there will need to be a value-focused approach to transaction and contract management.

This book focuses, for the first time, on the real-world impacts that distributed ledger technology (DLT), also known as blockchain, will have

DOI: 10.4324/9781003132592-1

on transactions and contracts. We refer to this as the 'Blockchain Age', a real revolution in the way things work online.

But this is not a technology book. Our intention is to set out and explain the business potential of blockchain and to provide the reader with a comparison of the day-to-day practices of six industries and how they might be changed by their wholesale adoption of blockchain: (1) trade finance, (2) healthcare software, (3) retail savings and investments, (4) real estate and land registry, (5) central bank currency, and (6) fund management.

Our hope is that, by demonstrating how transactions and contracts are now, in the internet age, versus how they might be in the near future in the age of blockchain, we'll sketch out a new way of thinking and talking about distributed ledgers: how blockchains may be deployed to fix real-world constraints and dissolve obstacles to progress in key industries.

What Is 'Blockchain'?

In the information technology world, the new noun 'blockchain' is self-explanatory: a 'block' is a storage unit or space for digital information to be stored in a database; and a 'chain' refers to the various or string of database locations where these blocks of information are stored.

But what information do these blocks store within them? And how many blocks long might a chain be?

Blocks encompass specific information about digital/online transactions. Each block records a transaction amount, time and the date on which it took place. The details (but not necessarily the identities) of the transaction participants such as individuals, companies, legal entities and so on are also stored in the block by way of assigning a cryptographic hash or unique digital signature instead of revealing actual names.

Blocks are validated by all parties using one of the several different methods of consensus mechanism available, and blocks are then attached to the chain (note: the very first block in a chain is known as the 'genesis' block). New blocks are issued according to pre-set rules and, in some cases, based on a background activity known as 'mining'.

Blocks also interact with business rules about the transfer and status of certain information within each block, such as who owns what and when a transfer might take place and between whom. These rules, and the execution of them, are known as 'smart contracts': embedded processes in the operations of the blockchain that are automated.

Because blockchains are decentralised ledgers, there is no centralised location where a blockchain can be downloaded. New participants in a blockchain must install suitable software (such as Web3py for example, a Python library for connecting with the Ethereum blockchain network) on their laptop and then connect to the blockchain via the internet, *locally* on their own machine using software such as *geth* that will sync a blockchain to a laptop, or *hosted* (blockchain access that's provided by a third-party service). Once connected, there are clear links to where a participant may access the main blockchain itself and, usually, several test or sandbox instances of the blockchain for testing smart contracts etc.

On a day-to-day basis, new and existing blocks are linked together using cryptography, the science of constructing codes for data security and privacy. Therefore, by design, these blocks within a chain of databases cannot be modified or altered and are immutable.

In Bitcoin, a block has been designed to hold 1 MB of data, which would mean each block can store thousands of transactions within itself. By definition, blockchain technology is decentralised, meaning, for example, that the contents of each block are available for public viewing. Transparency is a key feature of blockchain.

Let's understand the history of blockchain technology and how it has weaved through countless innovations and upgrades to its place in our automated world today.

History in the Making: Blockchain Technology

The idea for blockchain technology was put forward by research scientists Stuart Haber and W. Scott Stornetta in 1991. They were the pioneers in the computer programming concept of *time-stamping* digital documents so that they could not be backdated or manipulated.

Blockchain technology was first configured and implemented as a practical solution in 2008 by a pseudonymous group of developers, Satoshi Nakamoto. They designed and developed the technology using *hash* encryption to uniquely timestamp blocks of data without surfacing the identity of the entity that performed the transaction.

This approach was highly innovative in that it did not require a central governing body to provide confirmation and verification. Therefore, blockchain is sometimes referred to in computer science as a *peer-to-peer trustless mechanism*.

This design was implemented as a core component of the cryptocurrency bitcoin. It multiplied the transparency of transaction details as the ledgers were made available to the public on the Bitcoin cryptocurrency network. The Bitcoin blockchain storage size recording all transactions that had occurred on its network reached 350 GB in June 2021.

The raging success and galloping growth of blockchain technology can be seen in the upward trend of the increment in the Bitcoin block file size today, which had surpassed 200 GB of storage space for Bitcoin in the first quarter of 2020.[1]

By 2014 various other approaches to decentralised ledger technology were initiated in addition to Bitcoin, which developed blockchain technology further and has created a 'Blockchain 2.0' wave of innovation.

'Bitcoin 2' saw the emergence of Ethereum and its cryptocurrency *ether*. Vitalik Buterin, the founder of Ethereum, believed that the uses of blockchain technology went far beyond simply recording transactions. Buterin created an innovation in blockchain technology that enables the construction, design and management of smart contracts on the Ethereum platform.

Smart contracts are blockchain-hosted automated computer programs that document, manage, verify and execute business rules, specifically the terms of legal agreements between parties. Smart contracts are directly written in code within blocks.

Smart contracts expand the range of blockchain functionality from transactional data storage to the automatic implementation of business rules and legal conditions on that data and reduce third-party oversight as the public structure of blockchain creates transparency and significantly lowers manipulation of data.

Following the breakthrough innovation of smart contracts, independent software developers and engineers have created and published applications that run inside the Ethereum blockchain known as *DApps* (decentralised applications). Thousands of such applications are now running in the Ethereum blockchain, offering smart contracts for telecom providers, power, energy utility platforms and financial exchanges.

To understand how blockchain technology works, let us look at the process flow of steps from the occurrence of a transaction to the recording of the data in the blocks.

Blockchain in the Real World

In parallel with the development of blockchain technology over the past decade or so, business and industry have also become highly integrated by deploying complex networks, vertical enterprise platforms and solutions that rely on data, transactions and business rules.

Most enterprises today are integrated with key partners and suppliers outside their organisational boundaries in multiple industries and are, in addition, required to engage with a multitude of government and regulatory agencies. The common currency between all these entities is *data*, and the requirement for people and processes to define, manage and secure that data is a vital part of the real-world activities of individuals, businesses and government.

But data in real-world infrastructure is exposed to risk from mistakes, hostile actors and competition. We are all familiar with the large-scale incidents that relate to data – leaks, hacks and even the legal exploitation of data for political and commercial purposes. Boards, founders and managers, therefore, are constantly looking for technological solutions which enable business-to-business (B2B) data integration to operate with fewer risks, greater security and better reputational outcomes than exist currently.

In addition, business data governance in complex; modern integrated networks require all participants (individuals, businesses and government) to adhere to contractual obligations and complex rules of engagement, for example data privacy and processing directives and laws. There's something of a mismatch when detailed agreements between parties are difficult to measure for performance and adherence in the real world and certainly not in real time. The emergence of peer-to-peer models makes enforcement of multi-party data agreements even more cumbersome.

Blockchain technology offers smart contracts as a powerful solution to the real-world active management of data in a secure, access-controlled and transparent way. Smart contracts enable modern, integrated businesses, their partners, suppliers and regulators to act together without breach, as smart contracts automatically execute business rules when the conditions are met.

The key attribute of a smart contract is its ability to streamline complex business rules between parties into a predictable series of automated or semi-automated activities. Since each smart contract is built with cryptographic security, it also renders the outcomes of the executed rules as highly secure, immutable data that can't be manipulated.

So the net effect of the smart contract is to build *trust*: all parties, having agreed to the business rules expressed in the smart contract, can have faith that the automation of the smart contract and the blockchain will execute exactly the outcomes agreed.

Smart contracts offer a considerable advantage for every industry where there are legal agreements in force. Smart contracts significantly reduce legal paperwork, mitigate against the risk of breach and reduce the need for non-automated reconciliations and manual errors. Smart contracts, being cryptographically secure, are immune to hacks and malwares as every data point recorded as a result of the smart contract's executing a rule is stored in all nodes of the blockchain by consensus.

Blockchain Forecasts

According to a Deloitte global survey on blockchain, business executives and leaders are recognising blockchain as a pragmatic solutions platform in this sometimes contentious, complex real world of enterprises, their suppliers, partners and regulators. Deloitte foresees a sustainable growth for the blockchain market in the next five years, with an expected growth of the global blockchain technology market to be 62.1 per cent between 2015 and 2025 compound annual growth rate (CAGR).

One of the survey respondent companies, Gartner, forecasts that

> The business value-add of blockchain will grow to slightly more than $176 billion by 2025, and then it will exceed $3.1 trillion by 2030. Today, blockchain paves the way to transact in a secure, immutable, transparent, and auditable way.[2]

Blockchain Applications

Blockchain is the foundation technology of digital ('crypto') currencies such as bitcoin, ether, and many others.

Blockchain and bitcoin are related in the same way that concrete is related to a road bridge: blockchain provides the infrastructure; bitcoin is the 'traffic' that moves back and forth across the bridge.

And while cryptocurrencies may or may not succeed in the future, blockchain is here to stay and has already become widely deployed in many business scenarios. We'll take a look at some recent examples below, and of course we'll take a detailed view of applied blockchain use case scenarios later in the book.

Blockchain in Distribution

Blockchain will, in the future, play a major role in the digital management and optimisation of analogue assets. Blockchain has the ability to deliver end-to-end asset tracking and provide authoritative trust for asset data, as well being a good way to provide a trusted asset-based data exchange.

From a technical perspective, blockchain is a transparent and verifiable distributed digital ledger – the ideal channel for distribution of physical assets.

3M is an American multinational conglomerate corporation operating in the fields of industry, worker safety, US health care and consumer goods. Using 3M's customised distribution blockchain, any 3M partner can track and audit their products throughout the distribution and supply chains. The blockchain-powered distribution solution provides 3M customers with the ability to authenticate the quality of their products but also gives them more control over their own supply chains, reducing cost, delivery risk and the incidence of counterfeit products.

Ultimately 3M's blockchain-based distribution solution increased revenue by minimising the cost of anti-fraud efforts, said Oscar Naim, lead software architecture specialist for 3M:

> We see blockchain on Azure as a way to link the physical and digital worlds … A simple label or number on a box is not a good enough identifier because no one knows if it was printed by the manufacturer or added later – plus it doesn't provide visual cues that are easy to identify.[3]

For 3M, blockchain-based technologies are also making their way from distribution services and into next-generation solutions in areas such as (1) trustworthy information exchange, (2) protection of the authenticity of a company's branding, (3) streamlined and automated contract management, and (4) the enablement of next-generation distributed business models like peer-to-peer exchanges.

While blockchain technology can be complex, the 3M example demonstrates that companies interested in innovation need to start learning more about blockchain-based solutions.

Blockchain in Sales Management

Blockchain has the potential to redefine the economics of the modern world. This is especially true of distributed peer-to-peer (P2P) business models.

Companies in a variety of different industries have demonstrated the value of blockchain, especially those organisations with a pre-existing P2P business model, firms with complex supply chains, service enablement companies (such as Airbnb or Uber) or companies needing the transparent storage of legal documents.

Blockchain has also been successfully deployed in professional sales. To replace a manual, spreadsheet-based system, Microsoft has adopted blockchain technology to track sales and royalty payments for Xbox games. When a consumer purchases a game from Microsoft Store, purchase information is immediately placed on the blockchain where game publishers have instant access to royalty information. Using the blockchain in this way has improved trust by making the royalty payment calculation process more transparent for publishers.

Companies also have to decide early on what type of organisation they want to create to support their blockchain. A consortium of participants can create a blockchain that is visible and accessible to just its members, allowing them to trust transactions.

A joint venture brings two or more companies together and uses the blockchain to establish trusted transactions and communications. An open-source organisation can use a peer-to-peer consensus process to determine if transactions should be included on the blockchain. Each business model requires an appropriate blockchain organisation.

Again, from a sales perspective, Microsoft looked for another way to use blockchain. In 2015, the company evolved from selling software to creating and selling cloud services, which required the firm to regularly vet partners' creditworthiness.

To speed those credit checks, Microsoft collaborated with Bank of America Merrill Lynch to automate the credit-assessment process and the issuing of standby letters of credit (SBLC). Microsoft benefited quickly from the move: the time to issue an SBLC shrunk to three to five days from three weeks or more. The solution reduced risk between parties, enhanced the transparency of audits and improved the predictability of working capital.

Blockchain Benefits

In emerging markets, blockchain can be integrated by governments and businesses to achieve transparency, sustainability, trust among peer-to-peer networks, and business process and data security as it offers the following functionalities:

1 **Increased accuracy in transactions**: Blockchain transactions are programmed over a wide web of computer networks that eliminates human error in the verification process.
2 **Economic efficiency**: Most enterprises rely on third-party transactions and services for their end-to-end processes. Blockchain eliminates the need for verification from intermediaries and therefore reduces the cost associated with them.
3 **Decentralised ledger**: Since blockchain encrypted data is stored across several networks of computers instead of a centralised location, it becomes impossible to hack the entire chain. Even if a single block were hacked, the entire chain spread over various networks will not be compromised.
4 **Time efficiency**: Central authorities require ample time to verify, approve and settle transactions, whereas blockchain is a distributed settlement system, updating blocks rapidly and without a single point of failure; and
5 **Data security**: Every transaction made on a blockchain network has to be verified consensually by the thousands of linked computers. Verified transactions are then added as a block in the chain. A unique hash is assigned to each block which cannot be edited or changed, making the entire chain secure and impenetrable.

Blockchain Challenges

Blockchain is not a panacea and has already plenty of unresolved uncertainties and challenges to its wider adoption, for example:

1 **Comprehension complexity and low awareness**: This is the core issue that industries and governments face. Senior executives and boardroom leaders have extremely limited knowledge on the concept and workings of blockchain technology. Most software industry professionals still regard blockchain with caution and are not aware of its potential to streamline business verticals and supply chains.

2 **Lack of uniform standards**: Since blockchain is a fairly new concept and has not yet been adopted widely across industries, there is a lack of industry-specific standards and interoperability. This could be addressed if common standards, protocols and methodologies are negotiated and agreed between interested parties; and

3 **Lack of regulations and legal framework**: Typically, with advancements in technology, regulations do not catch up as quickly. Once regulations are published, governance, compliance and adherence follow. As of today, in many countries for example, the validity of smart contracts is not yet recognised in court.

Blockchain Business Model Design

Businesses need to adopt modern practices and new technology in order to thrive and compete, as well as to develop their own efficiency and long-term sustainability.

Under four approximate headings of customers, infrastructure, business proposition and financial viability we see the following as relevant to how and where blockchain business model designs could be deployed.

1 **Customer segments**: Blockchain can be used to identify and access new customer databases by connecting to some or all network nodes;

2 **Stack complexity and risk**: Reducing the number of intermediaries and entities in a non-blockchain stack eliminates cost, complexity and risk for most businesses, something that blockchain is especially efficient at delivering;

3 **Client relationships**: With a vast expanse of client data stored in blocks, businesses do not have to rely on peers or intermediaries to benefit from better, data-driven client relationships. Authentic and fast retrieval of data can be conducted on an implemented blockchain;

4 **Value deliverables**: A business deliverable utilises resources such as finances, logistics and documentation to ensure premium quality

and value. Adoption of blockchain would reduce the time taken for processing the transcripts of the deliverables and thereby reduce the costs associated with the same;

5 **Governance**: Standardised regulations for blockchain will enhance governance and compliance by individuals and business and could provide better access to data by regulatory authorities for enforcement purposes; and

6 **Collaboration and consortium**: In the complex network of integrated industries today, a collaboration of blockchain data and smart contracts enhances trust and creates the opportunity for greater efficiency between an enterprise and its suppliers, partners and regulators.

The Future of Blockchain Technology

Although blockchain is sometimes spoken of as both a revolution *and* an evolution of database technology it is, in reality, neither. Blockchain is a reboot of ledger technology and concepts that haven't changed in several hundred years, but it's not necessarily 'new'.

To some people, blockchain is forever linked to Bitcoin and, on that basis, indivisible from cryptocurrencies generally. This is also not a fair – or even close – representation of what blockchain is and how it will be most commonly deployed in the future.

In reality, more and more individuals, companies and governments are realising that blockchain's many benefits might suit some – but not all – of their existing cumbersome and complex operating models and processes. In these cases, blockchain offers efficiency, security, transparency, immutability and the prospect of better governance of, and simpler access to, data.

In the future, it is predicted that by 2030 most governments around the world will create or adopt some form of virtual currency based on blockchain. In the future, next-generation blockchain technology will resolve many of the current limitations, such as scalability, privacy controls, toolset maturity and interoperability. And in the future, price-stable tokens regulated by monetary policies and backed by collateral will start to gain traction as they become more reliable as a means of exchange and as a store of value. Governments that have failed to create a successful cryptocurrency will turn to 'stablecoins' as their virtual currency of choice.

Blockchain has the potential to increase financial inclusiveness and reduce corruption by enabling transparency, and this will in turn help nations to bridge the poverty gap and income disparity parameters.

Once a sound base of common standards, governance regulations across all blockchain types, their useful markets etc. is in place, the scaling-up of blockchain is predicted. Blockchain's next generation will have the potential to restructure industries from finance, land and property, and energy to healthcare.

Notes

1 Andy Martin, 'Blockchain Business Model Design'. www.linkedin.com/pulse/blockchain-business-model-design-andy-martin.
2 Gartner, 'Gartner Predicts 90% of Current Enterprise Blockchain Platform Implementations Will Require Replacement by 2021'. www.gartner.com/en/newsroom/press-releases/2019-07-03-gartner-predicts-90--of-current-enterprise-blockchain.
3 Microsoft, '3M Explores New Label-as-a-Service Concept with Blockchain on Azure to Stop Counterfeit Pharmaceuticals'. https://customers.microsoft.com/en-au/story/blockchain-3m.

Chapter 2

Bitcoin: Blockchain v1.0?

Many people associate blockchain with Bitcoin. Although Bitcoin is probably the most prominent example of applied blockchain technology, there is certainly more to blockchain than cryptocurrency.

But inevitably, we cannot avoid writing about Bitcoin in the context of blockchain, not least because it's with Bitcoin and Satoshi Nakamoto, Bitcoin's mysterious creator, that everything started in 2008. Since the publication of *Bitcoin: A Peer-to-Peer Electronic Cash System*, Satoshi Nakamoto's white paper (https://bitcoin.org/bitcoin.pdf; see abstract in Figure 2.1), blockchain as we know it today took off.

Satoshi Nakamoto's identity remains unknown, and much speculated upon; but what's of greater relevance and importance is the breadth of innovation that blockchain technology brought into the digital world, addressing a few of its age-old problems with its novel solution: the decentralisation of transactions.

'Decentralisation of transactions' refers to the possibility of decoupling transactions from a central authority (a 'transaction', in computer science terms, refers to a 'programmable event'). In financial payment terms, for example, it means making and receiving online money payments without relying on a central authority, such as a bank or credit card provider, to approve the transaction.

Bitcoin works as a peer-to-peer (P2P) network where digital currency can be transferred between participants with no single entity solely in charge of approving transactions. But, as in any digital environment made up of bytes and files, data can still be copied and transferred to multiple other people and devices. For a digital currency, copying data is a problem,

DOI: 10.4324/9781003132592-2

Bitcoin: A Peer-to-Peer Electronic Cash System

Satoshi Nakamoto
satoshin@gmx.com
www.bitcoin.org

Abstract. A purely peer-to-peer version of electronic cash would allow online payments to be sent directly from one party to another without going through a financial institution. Digital signatures provide part of the solution, but the main benefits are lost if a trusted third party is still required to prevent double-spending. We propose a solution to the double-spending problem using a peer-to-peer network. The network timestamps transactions by hashing them into an ongoing chain of hash-based proof-of-work, forming a record that cannot be changed without redoing the proof-of-work. The longest chain not only serves as proof of the sequence of events witnessed, but proof that it came from the largest pool of CPU power. As long as a majority of CPU power is controlled by nodes that are not cooperating to attack the network, they'll generate the longest chain and outpace attackers. The network itself requires minimal structure. Messages are broadcast on a best effort basis, and nodes can leave and rejoin the network at will, accepting the longest proof-of-work chain as proof of what happened while they were gone.

Figure 2.1 **The abstract of the bitcoin white paper published by Satoshi Nakamoto in October 2018.**

as it could, in theory, seriously undermine the principles of ownership and spending of a digital currency.

Bitcoin addresses this 'double spending' issue by recreating, in the digital world, the same concept of scarcity of money as we have in the real world, making bitcoins the first applied blockchain use case in history.

The First Transaction

From the white paper shown as an extract in Figure 2.1, Bitcoin was born. The first block, the so-called 'genesis block', was issued on January 3rd, 2009.

The creation of Bitcoin's genesis block and the initial subsequent blocks in the Bitcoin chain slowly started to gather more supporters as time progressed. What happened to Satoshi after the creator mysteriously left Bitcoin in 2010, by which point he is credited with having mined close to 1 million bitcoins, remains unclear.

Since then, and in the teeth of the resistance of the financial establishment year after year, Bitcoin has steadily gained traction. But a large cohort of independent software engineers and political idealists started to believe the protocol which Bitcoin represents would revolutionise the entire monetary system on a global scale. And six years after Bitcoin block 0 was mined, the financial elites ceased their naysaying and began to attempt to commercialise Bitcoin in 2012.

Satoshi's breakthrough is more than just a fundamental paradigm shift limited to computer science. Bitcoin pushed forward a technology that is also peer-to-peer, open, secure and censorship-resistant, and was promoted by its adherents as the most deliverable type of electronic money ever created. Since the creation of the Bitcoin genesis block 10 years ago, the Bitcoin technological innovation has allowed us to think of a new way of storing and exchanging value that's potentially more democratic, accessible and transparent than anything we've experienced before.

With Bitcoin, transactions between individuals are conducted globally, on a permissionless basis and across hundreds of national borders without the need for any pre-existing trust and no centralised control.

The innovation Satoshi gave to the world in 2008, i.e. Bitcoin, is the planet's monetary system black swan and comes pre-equipped with a positive feedback loop. After 10 years, Bitcoin has survived the 'passing trend' phase and is now a permanent fixture in the world of money and payments.

Getting Started with Bitcoin

Bitcoin uses P2P technology to operate with no central authority or banks. Managing transactions and the issuance of bitcoins is carried out collectively by the Bitcoin network itself.

Bitcoin is open source, its design public; nobody owns or controls Bitcoin and everyone may participate. Bitcoin enables participants, individuals and businesses, to exchange value and transact in a different way than they normally do. Like the transfer of a fiat currency, such as US dollars, euros, British pounds sterling, Japanese yen etc., it's critically important that care is taken, exactly as would happen with real cash in the wallet in your pocket or bag. So, how does Bitcoin work?

New Bitcoin users need to install a blockchain-powered digital currency wallet on their computer or phone. There are countless digital currency wallets available on the open market, for example the Coinbase app.

On first use, a user will need to seed their wallet with fiat currency and buy any fraction of a bitcoin (one bitcoin can be divided into eight decimal

places, meaning there are 100,000,000 million Satoshis or fractions in
1 bitcoin). Buying a whole or fractional bitcoin will automatically generate
the user's first Bitcoin address (more addresses can be created on an as-
needed basis). It is possible to disclose a Bitcoin wallet address to others
to facilitate transfers between wallets. This is similar to how email works,
except it is recommended that Bitcoin addresses should be used only once
to prevent potential unwanted interference.

The entire Bitcoin network relies on its own proprietary underlying
blockchain. All confirmed bitcoin transactions are recorded on the Bitcoin
blockchain. Bitcoin wallet addresses are used by the Bitcoin blockchain
to record bitcoin transfers between participants. The integrity and the
chronological order of the Bitcoin blockchain are enforced by the integrated
Bitcoin blockchain cryptography.

A bitcoin 'transaction' is, in fact, a transfer of value between bitcoin
wallets that gets reported to, and included in, the updated Bitcoin
blockchain. Bitcoin wallets keep a secret piece of data called a private key
or seed, which is used to sign bitcoin transactions, providing a mathematical
proof that they have come from the owner of the bitcoin wallet. This private
key signature also prevents a bitcoin transaction from being altered once
it has been confirmed. All bitcoin transactions are broadcast to the Bitcoin
network and usually begin to be confirmed onto the Bitcoin blockchain
within 10–20 minutes as the result of a process called bitcoin mining.

Bitcoin Mining

Bitcoin mining is a distributed consensus process that is used to confirm
pending bitcoin transactions by including new blocks in the Bitcoin
blockchain. Mining enforces a chronological order for the Bitcoin
blockchain, protects the neutrality of the Bitcoin network and allows
different, distributed computers to agree on the state of the Bitcoin network.
In order to be confirmed, bitcoin transactions must be stored within a
Bitcoin data block that exactly fits very strict cryptographic rules that will be
verified by the whole Bitcoin network. These rules prevent previous blocks
from being modified because doing so would invalidate all the subsequent
blocks.

Bitcoin mining also creates the equivalent of a competitive lottery that
prevents any one actor on the Bitcoin network from too easily adding
new blocks consecutively to the Bitcoin blockchain. In this way, no group

or individual can control what is included in the Bitcoin blockchain or interfere or replace parts of the Bitcoin blockchain to roll back their own transfers, for example, and thereby potentially unfairly gain advantage.

Bitcoin Wallets

As in real life, a bitcoin wallet must be secured. Bitcoin makes it possible to transfer bitcoins anywhere in a very easy way and it allows bitcoin wallet owners to be in control of their own bitcoins.

Such great features also come with great security concerns. At the same time, Bitcoin can provide very high levels of security if used correctly. Whoever joins the Bitcoin blockchain network should remember that it is their responsibility to adopt good practices in order to protect their bitcoins in a well-functioning wallet.

Bitcoin Value

The current value of bitcoin is volatile. The price of a bitcoin can unpredictably increase or decrease over a short period of time due to its young economy, novelty and highly speculative nature.

Consequently, keeping hard-earned savings with bitcoin is not recommended and it must be noted that bitcoin is not any sort of investment – it should be used for speculative purposes only.

Bitcoin Transactions

It's also important to remember that any payment received with bitcoin can be converted to local ('fiat') currency. But bitcoin wallet-to-wallet payment transactions are irreversible. This means that a bitcoin transaction cannot be reversed, it can only be refunded from the wallet receiving the bitcoin back to the bitcoin wallet that initiated the transfer. This means extra care should be taken when making/sending or receiving bitcoin transactions.

In a bitcoin transaction, the Bitcoin network can detect typos and usually won't allow a bitcoin to be sent from a valid wallet address to an invalid address by mistake, but it is recommended that Bitcoin users apply local controls for additional safety and redundancy when making and receiving bitcoin transfers. Additional services might exist on the Bitcoin network and in wallet apps in the future to provide more choice and protection for both businesses and consumers who choose to make and receive bitcoin transfers.

A bitcoin wallet address is a unique identifier of 26–35 alphanumeric characters that represents a possible destination for a bitcoin transfer. Like email addresses, it is possible to send bitcoins to another wallet simply by using their address. However, each bitcoin transaction is identified by a different Bitcoin address, and most Bitcoin software and websites help with this by generating a brand-new wallet address for each bitcoin transaction.

Bitcoin Security and Privacy

Some effort is required to protect one's privacy with Bitcoin. All bitcoin transactions are stored publicly and permanently on the Bitcoin network, which means any Bitcoin participant may see the balance at, and transactions relating to, any Bitcoin address.

However, the identity of the Bitcoin user behind a Bitcoin address remains hidden to others on the network until information is revealed during a bitcoin purchase or transfer. This is one reason why Bitcoin addresses should only be used once.

Unconfirmed bitcoin transactions aren't secure. Bitcoin transactions don't start out as irreversible. Instead, each bitcoin transaction is updated with a confirmation score that indicates how hard it is to reverse it (see Figure 2.2). Each bitcoin confirmation score takes an average 10 minutes before being

Confirmations	Lightweight wallets	Bitcoin Core
0	Only safe if you trust the person paying you	
1	Somewhat reliable	Mostly reliable
3	Mostly reliable	Highly reliable
6	Minimum recommendation for high-value bitcoin transfers	
30	Recommendation during emergencies to allow human intervention	

Figure 2.2 Recommended confirmation transactions to secure a payment permanently.

committed to the whole Bitcoin network. If the bitcoin transaction pays too low a fee or is otherwise atypical, getting the first confirmation can take much longer.

Bitcoin: Still Experimental

Bitcoin is an experimental new digital currency that is in active development. Each improvement makes bitcoin more appealing but also reveals new challenges as bitcoin adoption grows. During these growing pains, bitcoin adopters might encounter increased transaction fees, slower transaction confirmations or even more severe issues – such as wallet hacks.

We should all be prepared for problems and consult a technical expert before making any major investments in bitcoin. At this stage, it is reasonable to say that nobody can predict bitcoin's future.

Bitcoin is not an official currency. That said, most national jurisdictions require payment of income, sales, payroll and capital gains taxes on anything that has value, including bitcoins. It is our responsibility to ensure that we adhere to tax and other legal or regulatory mandates issued by our government and/or local municipalities.

In conclusion, Satoshi Nakamoto's original Bitcoin paper is still recommended reading for anyone studying how Bitcoin works. Choose which translation: https://bitcoin.org/en/bitcoin-paper or explore the Bitcoin Wiki: https://en.bitcoin.it/wiki/Main_Page.

Bitcoin is Decentralised

Unlike traditional currencies, which are issued by central banks, bitcoin has no central monetary authority. No one controls it. Bitcoins aren't minted like US dollars or euros; they're 'mined' by individuals and increasingly by businesses using hundreds of computers all around the world running software that solves mathematical mining puzzles.

Rather than rely on a central monetary authority to monitor, verify and approve transactions and manage the money supply, bitcoin is enabled by a P2P computer network made up of its users' machines, akin to the networks that underpin BitTorrent and Skype.

Bitcoin Advantages

Bitcoin has several advantages over other current transaction systems, including the following:

- **Cost-effective**: Bitcoin eliminates the need for intermediaries;
- **Efficient**: bitcoin transaction information is recorded once and is available to all parties through the distributed Bitcoin network; and
- **Safe and secure**: The underlying Bitcoin ledger is tamper evident. A bitcoin transaction can't be changed after is has been made; it can only be reversed with another bitcoin transaction, in which case both bitcoin transactions are visible.

Bitcoin is actually built on the foundation of blockchain, which serves as Bitcoin's shared ledger. Think of blockchain as an operating system, such as Microsoft Windows or MacOS, and Bitcoin as only one of the many applications that can be run on that operating system.

Blockchain provides the means for recording bitcoin transactions, but this shared ledger can be used to record any transaction and track the movement of any asset whether tangible, intangible or digital. Bitcoin and blockchain are not the same thing. Blockchain provides the means to record and store bitcoin transactions, but blockchain has many uses beyond bitcoin. Bitcoin is only the first use case for blockchain.

Bitcoin Definitions

Bitcoin can be defined in various ways; it's a protocol, a digital currency and a platform. It is a combination of P2P network, protocols and software that facilitate the creation and usage of the digital currency named bitcoin.

Nodes in this P2P network talk to each other using the Bitcoin protocol. Note that Bitcoin with a capital B is used to refer to the Bitcoin protocol, whereas bitcoin with a lowercase b is used to refer to the bitcoin digital currency.

Before you go on with this chapter, please check your understanding of the concepts in Table 2.1 and Table 2.2.

Table 2.1 Terminology

Term	Link
Peer-to-peer network	https://techterms.com/definition/p2p
Bitcoin mining	www.investopedia.com/terms/b/bitcoin-mining.asp

Table 2.2 Learn more

Title	Author	Link
How Does Bitcoin Work?	Techquickie	www.youtube.com/watch?v=L-Qhv8kLESY

How Cryptocurrencies Work

Bitcoin is a digital or 'crypto' currency.

Most people are familiar with traditional payment mechanisms such as electronic money, bank wire transfers or credit cards. These forms of payment are traditional in the sense that they rely on a central authority, namely the bank or the credit card institution, to host a digital ledger of all their customers and the electronic transactions that are executed.

This in turn requires IT infrastructure to host that digital ledger securely and the software to run transactions. Who hosts that infrastructure, who controls the rules of performing monetary transactions? Is there trust that this infrastructure doesn't get compromised, personal data leaked or, even worse, currency gets lost? We do have to trust that the hosting authority takes all the necessary precautions to prevent attacks and any form of fraud.

To address – and indeed, improve upon – that need for trust, cryptocurrencies distribute the storage of transactional data to all currency holders who then keep their own copy of the ledger.

In order to make a transaction like, for example, 'Alice pays Bob 10 digital coins', the transaction is broadcast into the network for all members to see and record on their own private version of the ledger. After the transaction, how can the network get everyone to agree on what the correct ledger position is?

When Bob receives the transaction 'Alice pays Bob 10 digital coins', how can he be sure that everyone else received and believes that same transaction? That he'll be able to later use those 10 digital coins to make a trade with Charlie? How can Bob be sure that everyone else is recording the same transactions in the same order?

'Hashes' and Trust in Cryptocurrencies

Cryptocurrencies running on blockchain benefit from a distributed protocol for accepting or rejecting transactions and recording the order in which those transactions are processed. This ensures that all parties can feel confident all network members have the same protocol and therefore the same ledger as themselves.

In fact, trust is the problem statement addressed in the original Satoshi Bitcoin white paper. At a high level, the solution Bitcoin offers in respect of trust is to trust whichever ledger has the most computational work put into it, something called a 'cryptographic hash function'.

The general idea to introduce trust among parties in a cryptocurrency like bitcoin is to use computational work as a basis for what to trust, so that fraudulent transactions and conflicting ledgers would require an infeasible amount of computation to be generated.

This concept is at the heart of bitcoin and other cryptocurrencies. A hash function takes in any kind of message or file, and outputs a string of bits with a fixed length, for instance 256 bits. This output is called the 'hash' or 'digest' of the message, and it's meant to look arbitrary. It's not really random, as it always gives the same output for a given input. But the idea behind it is that when someone slightly changes the input, even a single digit in the transaction payload, the resulting hash changes completely. In fact, for the hash function in use in Bitcoin, called SHA256, the way that output changes on an even minimal variation of a byte in the transaction is entirely unpredictable.

How Hashes Work

The SHA (secure hash algorithm) is one of a number of cryptographic hash functions. A cryptographic hash is like a signature for a text or data file. The SHA256 algorithm generates an almost unique, fixed-size 256-bit (32-byte) hash. Hash is a one-way function; it cannot be decrypted back. That means that it's incredibly hard to compute it in the reverse direction, and to date, this has not been achieved.

There is no simpler method to find an input message so that the SHA256 hash of that message gives this exact string of bits rather than just guessing and checking. Attempts have been made to try to reverse engineer the desired input by digging through the details of how the hash function works, but no way has yet been found to do that. Interestingly enough, there's no proof that it's impossible to compute a hash in the reverse direction, yet a huge amount of modern security depends on cryptographic hash functions.

How can such a function prove that a particular list of transactions associated with a large amount of computational effort is genuine and, thus, can be trusted? Bitcoin makes the process of guessing this hash value interesting.

In Bitcoin, it requires lottery-sized odds to calculate and find a special number such that when this number is appended at the end of the hash value of the transaction, or list of transactions, and has been processed by the application of the SHA256 encryption calculation to the entire number, the first 30 bits of the output are zeros.

This is how hard it is to find that number. For a random message, the probability that the hash happens to start with 30 successive zeros is about 1 in a billion. Because SHA256 is a cryptographic hash function, the only way to find a special number like this is just guessing and checking billions of different combinations before finding the special one.

This clearly represents a large amount of computational work and that is what is called a 'proof of work' in the Bitcoin network.

Bitcoin Transactions and Hashes

Proof of work is intrinsically tied to the list of bitcoin transactions. If a single bitcoin transaction changes, even slightly, it would completely change the hash, so that another billion guesses would be required to find a new proof of work, a new number that, taken together with the hash of the altered list, creates a new number that also starts with 30 zeros.

Back to the cryptocurrency network: the core idea behind the original Bitcoin paper is to have everybody trust whichever ledger has the most work put into it. Bitcoin first organises a given ledger into blocks, where each block consists of a list of transactions, together with a proof of work, which is exactly this special number so that the hash of the whole block starts with 30 zeros.

In the same way that a transaction is only considered valid if it is signed by the sender, a block is only considered valid if it has a proof of work attached to it. Also, to make sure there is a standard way to order these blocks, a block has to contain the hash of the previous block.

Blockchains Build Trust

In that way, changing any block, or trying to swap the order of two blocks, would change the block after it, which changes that block's hash, which changes the next block, and so on.

That would require redoing all the work, finding a new special number for each of these blocks that makes their hashes start with the required leading zeros. Because blocks are chained together like this, instead of calling it a ledger, this is commonly called a 'blockchain'.

How Bitcoin is Different

This distributed ledger system based on a proof of work is how the Bitcoin protocol works, and how many other cryptocurrencies work. There are just a few details to clear up.

In Bitcoin's mining process, the goal is to be the first to find a hash value that is less than or equal to the target hash. This is typically done by brute-force guesswork of all possible numbers between 0 and 2 to the power of 31. This random number, called a *nonce* ('number only used once'), is 32-bits (or 4 bytes) long, and the difficulty of finding such a number is adjusted every 2016 blocks mined, or roughly every two weeks. This is to maintain an average 10 minutes for each new block to be mined in the Bitcoin blockchain network.

Bitcoin Rewards

All of the bitcoins in Bitcoin are derived, ultimately, from block rewards given to successful block miners. This reward mechanism was published as part of the original Bitcoin protocol and is public knowledge.

Bitcoin rewards were originally 50 bitcoins per block. Every 210,000 Bitcoin blocks, which is about every four years, that reward gets cut in half. As of 2019 the reward was set at 12.5 bitcoins per block, and because this reward decreases linearly over time, there will never be more than 21 million bitcoins in existence.

The Bitcoin Block Reward Halving Countdown website (www. bitcoinblockhalf.com/) shows the number of days until the number of bitcoins mined by miners per block will reduce from 12.5 to 6.25 bitcoins in the next bitcoin halving.

A bitcoin halving happened on block number 420,000 mined on July 9th, 2016. The bitcoin block reward went from 25 bitcoins to 12.5 bitcoins. The most recent bitcoin halving happened at block 630,000 on May 11th, 2020.

Bitcoin Transaction Fees

However, this doesn't mean bitcoin miners will stop earning bitcoins. In addition to the block reward, bitcoin miners can also pick up bitcoin transaction fees. The way this works is that whenever a bitcoin transfer is made, bitcoin transferors may optionally add a small bitcoin transaction fee with it, that will go to the miner of whatever block includes that bitcoin transfer.

The reason for this is to incentivise bitcoin miners to actually include the bitcoin transaction in the next bitcoin block.

Bitcoin Transaction Volumes

Another consideration concerns performance.

In Bitcoin, each block is limited to about 2,400 transactions, which many critics argue is unnecessarily restrictive. For comparison, Visa processes an average of around 1,700 transactions per second, and is capable of handling more than 24,000 per second. Slower processing on Bitcoin means higher transactions fees, since that's what determines which transactions miners choose to include in new blocks.

Before you continue with this chapter, please review the terms in Table 2.3 and Table 2.4 and consider some additional reading if required.

Table 2.3   Terminology

Term	Link
Cryptographic hash	https://en.wikipedia.org/wiki/Cryptographic_hash_function
Proof of work	https://en.bitcoin.it/wiki/Proof_of_work

Table 2.4   Learn more

Title	Author	Link
Bitcoin – Cryptographic hash function	Khan Academy	www.youtube.com/watch?v=0WiTaBI82Mc
Bitcoin – Proof of work	Khan Academy	www.youtube.com/watch?v=9V1bipPkCTU

Bitcoin: Reaching Consensus

Members of the Bitcoin protocol can be considered 'block creators'.

Block creators see the bitcoin transactions being broadcast to the Bitcoin network, collect those bitcoin transactions into a block, execute some computational work to find the special number that makes the hash of this block start with 30 zeros, and then broadcast out to the Bitcoin network the new Bitcoin block they've found.

To compensate a block creator for all this work, a special bitcoin transaction is added at the top of each new block. This special bitcoin transaction is used to transfer a reward to the block creator.

The process of creating new blocks is called 'mining', since it requires a lot of work, and it introduces new bits of currency into the economy. Cryptocurrency miners create blocks, broadcast those blocks to the rest of the network, and get rewarded with new digital coins for doing so. From a miner's perspective, each block is like a lottery game, where everyone is guessing numbers as fast as they can, until one lucky individual finds one that makes the hash of the block start with the required zeros, and gets rewarded for doing so.

Bitcoin Consensus Explained

The way the Bitcoin protocol works for someone using this system is that instead of watching for single bitcoin transactions, they watch for new blocks being broadcast by bitcoin miners, updating their own private copy of the digital ledger.

A Bitcoin node is typically connected to up to eight other Bitcoin nodes, to which it broadcasts a new block.

By 'gossip', each Bitcoin node propagates that block to the entire Bitcoin network. There may be a situation when two distinct blockchains with conflicting transaction histories exist. The Bitcoin network prefers the block with the longest bitcoin transaction history, i.e. the one with the most work put into it, as the reliable branch. If there's a tie, the Bitcoin network waits until an additional block is added that makes a branch longer.

So even though there is no central authority, and everyone is maintaining their own copy of the Bitcoin blockchain, if all participants agree to give preference to whichever blockchain has the most work put into it, this mechanism of proof-of-work and block broadcasting represents the way to arrive at a form of decentralised *consensus*.

Bitcoin: Trust and Consensus

But why does this make for a trustworthy system? To answer this question and understand at what point Bitcoin members can trust that a payment is legitimate, it's helpful to walk through what it would take to introduce a fraudulent transaction in this system.

If Alice wants to fool Bob with a fraudulent block, she might try to send him one that includes a bitcoin transaction with her paying him 100 digital coins, but without broadcasting that block to the rest of the network. That way everyone else thinks she still has those 100 digital coins. To do this, she'd have to find a valid proof of work before all other miners, each working on their own block. That could indeed happen, and in this case, Alice would win this 'miniature lottery' before anyone else. But Bob will still be seeing broadcasts made by other miners, so to keep him believing the fraudulent block, Alice would have to do all the work herself to keep adding blocks to this special fork in Bob's blockchain that's different from what he's seeing from the rest of the miners.

As per the Bitcoin protocol, Bob always trusts the longest chain he knows about. Alice might be able to keep this up for a few blocks if just by chance she happens to find blocks more quickly than all of the rest of the miners on the network combined. But unless Alice has close to 50% of the computing resources among all miners, the probability becomes

Table 2.5 Terminology

Term	Link
Gossip protocol	www.btcwires.com/round-the-block/what-is-gossip-protocol/
Bitcoin confirmation	https://en.bitcoin.it/wiki/Confirmation

Table 2.6 Learn more

Title	Author	Link
Gossip protocol	Pico Labs	www.youtube.com/watch?v=WrBf9kg-_ZY

overwhelming that what all the other miners are working on grows faster than the single fraudulent blockchain that Alice is feeding Bob. Eventually Bob will reject what he's hearing from Alice in favour of the longer chain that everyone else is working on.

This implies – accurately – that bitcoin traders do not necessarily trust a new block immediately. Instead, they wait for several new blocks to be added on top of it, precisely for six blocks. After that, if no other longer blockchains exist, everybody can trust that this block is part of the same chain everyone else is using. And with that, trust is reached by consensus among the members of the network.

Before you continue with this chapter, please review the terms in Table 2.5 and Table 2.6 and consider some additional reading if required.

Bitcoin as Capital Investment

Bitcoin has started a revolution with the introduction of the very first fully decentralised digital currency, and the one that has proven to be extremely secure and stable from a Bitcoin network and protocol point of view.

As a currency, bitcoin is quite unstable and highly volatile, albeit valuable. This has also sparked great interest in academic and industrial research and introduced many new research areas.

Since its introduction in 2008, bitcoin has gained massive popularity and notoriety and it is currently the most successful digital currency in the world, with billions of dollars invested in it. Its popularity is also evident from the high number of users and investors, increasing bitcoin price, everyday news related to bitcoin, and the number of start-ups and companies that are offering bitcoin-based online exchanges.

Bitcoin Bubble?

Bitcoin has raised itself into public consciousness over the last few years and has captured the attention of some of the world's biggest investors and traders.

The bitcoin price has soared to highs in excess of US$50,000, causing many to fear an investment bubble. Capital investment firms have branded the rise of bitcoin and cryptocurrencies a 'once-in-a-generation' opportunity and called on people to grab it with both hands, despite being described as one of the most extreme market events in the monetary trading field. Glen Goodman, in his book *The Crypto Trader*, writes that 'Crypto is the Wild West of trading, and that means the risks, as well as the rewards, are greater'.[1]

The bitcoin and cryptocurrency sectors are, however, still recovering from a deflating of value that impacted the market throughout 2018, with many major cryptocurrencies losing around 90% of their value.

Bitcoin and most other major cryptocurrencies soared throughout 2017, with bitcoin rising from under US$1,000 per bitcoin to almost US$20,000 in under 12 months. The sudden downturn experienced by bitcoin in 2018 was labelled 'crypto winter' for its debilitating effect on the industry, with many newly founded crypto businesses forced to cut costs and fire staff to survive the turbulence. According to Goodman,

> A multi-billion-dollar market has arisen from nothing in less than a decade. Huge fortunes have been made. Some, of course, have been made and then lost almost as quickly, as with any new market, there are dramatic ups and downs, but many more will be made in the future.[2]

Bitcoin's Value Prospects

The wider cryptocurrency market is now worth some US$270 billion globally, with bitcoin by far the largest cryptocurrency by both usage and value, making up around US$150 billion of that.

Bitcoin investors are meanwhile watching closely the so-called bitcoin halving event, where the number of bitcoins awarded to miners for mining new bitcoin blocks will drop from 12.5 bitcoins to 6.25 bitcoins. The start of the year-long countdown has caused some analysts to predict a return to bitcoin's all-time highs could be imminent.

Should I Own Bitcoin?

But what does it mean to 'own' a bitcoin?

You may have heard about the concept of a digital wallet. A bitcoin wallet is loosely the equivalent of a physical wallet, but it's meant to store bitcoins. The wallet doesn't actually store any digital value or token. Rather, it contains one or more cryptographic keys, which allow the owner to spend the bitcoins allocated to it in the Bitcoin blockchain network.

A bitcoin wallet shows the total balance of all bitcoins it controls, and it initiates transactions towards another node in the network. This is different from how credit cards work, as in a card circuit it's the merchant that initiates the payment instead.

If you are considering owning bitcoins, there are two main approaches to consider. First, you can simply buy bitcoins from an exchange, using fiat currency such as a bank transfer or a card payment. Alternatively, you can enter the business of mining bitcoins and earn your own. Be wary, mining is an expensive business.

If you are considering owning bitcoins for a purely financial investment, also do keep in mind that bitcoin price is highly volatile. The price of a bitcoin can unpredictably increase or decrease over a short period of time due to its young economy, decentralised nature, and the fact that it's not backed by a government or a stable currency.

Consequently, keeping your savings with bitcoin is not recommended at this point. Bitcoin should be seen as a high-risk asset, and you should never store money that you cannot afford to lose with bitcoin.

Bitcoin Basics

There are also a few traits of bitcoin that are worth considering before making any investment:

- Bitcoin payments are irreversible.
- Bitcoin transactions are not anonymous.

A bitcoin transaction cannot be reversed, it can only be refunded by the person receiving the funds. This means you should take care to do business with people and organisations you know and trust, or who have an established reputation. For their part, businesses need to keep track of the payment requests they are displaying to their customers.

A bitcoin wallet won't let you send money to an invalid address by mistake, but it's best to have controls in place for additional safety and redundancy. Additional services might exist in the future to provide more choice and protection for both businesses and consumers, for example to protect your privacy with Bitcoin.

All bitcoin transactions are stored publicly and permanently on the network, which means anyone can see the balance and transactions of any Bitcoin address. However, the identity of the user behind an address remains unknown until information is revealed during a purchase or in other circumstances. This is one reason why some people use Bitcoin addresses only once.

It is also important to consider that bitcoin is still an experimental new currency that is in active development. Each improvement makes bitcoin more appealing but also reveals new challenges as bitcoin adoption grows. During these growing pains, fees may increase, transactions may take longer to get confirmed, or the value of bitcoins may vary dramatically. Keep in mind that nobody can predict bitcoin's future.

And if you are considering bitcoin for business purposes, please check your government tax system and regulations. Bitcoin is not an official currency, but you may still be required to pay income, sales, payroll, and capital gains taxes on anything that has value, even if a transaction has occurred in bitcoins. It is your responsibility to ensure that you adhere to

Table 2.7   Terminology

Term	Link
Bitcoin wallet	https://en.bitcoin.it/wiki/Wallet

Table 2.8   Learn more

Title	Author	Link
What Is A Bitcoin Wallet?	The Cryptoverse	www.youtube.com/watch?v=AD-vWx3oA84
How to Get a Bitcoin Wallet	Wealth Hacks	www.youtube.com/watch?v=cy8Je44_k2c

tax and other legal or regulatory mandates issued by your government and/
or local municipalities.

Notes

1 Glen Goodman, *The Crypto Trader* (Harriman House, 2019), Preface.
2 Ibid, Introduction.

Chapter 3

Blockchain 2.0 and Smart Contracts

Blockchain is the technology behind modern-day cryptocurrencies like bitcoin, Ethereum, Ripple, and many others. It is not wrong to say that 'blockchain technology is related to cryptocurrencies in the same way cement is related to a building' because it works as a foundation to provide the required technical proficiency for a wide range of solutions. Today, these blockchain solutions are helping various industries transform the way they work for the better. Some examples of this technology application are

- Secure exchange of sensitive medical data;
- Fast and secure cross-border transactions;
- Collection of advertisement insights;
- Fast insurance claim processing;
- Anti-money-laundering tracking platform development;
- Supply chain monitoring system development;
- Logistics monitoring system development;
- Decentralised e-voting mechanism development;
- Real-estate processing applications;
- Government record management;
- Personal identity management;
- Robust cybersecurity; and
- Smart contract applications.

DOI: 10.4324/9781003132592-3

It is clear that blockchain technology will stay for a long time because it has made an impact in almost every vital industry. Hence, this technology is not just limited to cryptocurrencies. For example, as mentioned before, blockchain technology can help in the development of a supply chain monitoring system. Let's consider the example of 3M. The technology will allow any 3M partner to track and audit products via the company's customised distributed blockchain. This solution will assist 3M customers authenticate their products' quality and have more authority over the supply chains. As a result, the occurrence of fake products will decrease.

The technologies based on blockchain are making a lot of difference today and helping companies in multiple ways, such as secure exchange of business data, tracing consumer behaviour, faster payments and much more. The technology is complex, but corporations are interested in investing in this technology and exploring more about its wonderful capabilities.

Blockchain technology will incorporate the future for digital management and optimisation of analogue assets for detailed tracking and authoritative data exchange, along with the development of a credible and shared platform of trusted data. From a technical point of view, blockchain is a transparent and decentralised public ledger that will transform the way individuals and organisations think about enforcing contracts, exchanging assets and sharing information. Since it is a distributed digital ledger, it does not rest with a single provider or entity but rather is distributed through a network of computers.

Businesses all across the globe are using this technology as a common data layer to launch a new category of applications that will help to share business processes and vital data across multiple organisations for

- Eliminating waste;
- Improving the operation's efficiency;
- Reducing the risk of theft and fraud; and
- Creating new revenue channels.

Blockchain possesses diverse potential and characteristics that can revolutionise the modern economy with the help of distributed peer-to-peer models for businesses. The technology also features an intelligent cloud feature that can encourage companies to operate in an entirely different way in their respective industries and provide a competitive edge to the early adopters.

It should also be remembered that blockchain is an emerging technology that is still in the development phase and experiencing metamorphic changes. Hence, business executives should get themselves prepared to expect some turbulence and false starts in the initial stage of putting the technology into service. While being prepared for the challenges, it is also necessary to come up with plans that will work for blockchain.

Some of the leading businesses like Apple, Microsoft and Alphabet have already adopted this technology in their operations and proved to the rest of the world how it is helping them to scale gigantic growth. Also, it is not just about growth, but enhanced user satisfaction. Let's take the example of Microsoft to understand better. Microsoft adopted this technology in 2018 to eradicate the need for time-consuming reconciliation and reduced the access time to royalties data for Xbox game publishers from 45 days to just a few minutes. The blockchain technology provided the company with interconnected self-balancing ledgers and, as such, there was no need for manual reconciliation. Also, the process of royalty calculation became more transparent, which further elevated trust.

Companies are also required to make an early decision in regard to the type of organisation they intend to establish for supporting their blockchain. An association of various entities can develop a blockchain that is accessible to only its members so that trustworthy transactions can take place. In a joint venture, two or more companies join hands and can create a blockchain to allow trusted transactions and information exchanges between them. A peer-to-peer consensus procedure can be used by an open-source organisation to evaluate whether the transactions should be counted on the blockchain. However, Microsoft adopted a different way.

The company evolved its operations in 2015 from selling software to developing and selling cloud services, which required Microsoft to make a careful examination of partners' creditworthiness on a regular basis. To boost the speed of such credit checks, the company decided to join hands with Bank of America Merrill Lynch to automate the process of credit assessment and get the standby letters of credit (SBLC) issued as quickly as possible. This collaboration helped to reduce the time of issuing SBLC from three weeks or more to only three to five days. This blockchain solution also diminished the risk between parties, improved the transparency of the audit, and escalated working capital predictability.

Smart Contracts

Today, smart contracts are defined as codes that are kept on a blockchain and are executed automatically if the predetermined conditions are met. The definition of the term 'smart contract' was first coined by Nick Szabo, a legal scholar and computer scientist in the early 1990s, who also invented the virtual currency Bit Gold a decade before bitcoin was invented. He defined smart contracts as 'automated transaction protocols that execute the terms and conditions of a contract'.[1]

The definition of smart contract was changed by 2014 when a new blockchain network called Ethereum was founded. The founder of Ethereum, Vitalik Buterin, defined the term smart contract in the following way:

> A smart contract is a computer program that directly controls some kind of digital asset … The smart contract approach says instead of a legal contract, immediately transfer the digital asset into a program, the program automatically will run code, validate a condition, and determine whether the asset should go to one person or back to the other person, or whether it should be immediately refunded to the person who sent it or some combination thereof.[2]

The meaning of smart contract has been further expanded and its latest definition has already been stated above. However, to establish better clarity of the term, this chapter also focuses on the subcomponents of smart contracts in the later sections.

How Smart Contracts Work

To start with, it should be remembered that smart contracts cannot necessarily be classified as enforceable legal contracts in a court of law. However, smart contracts are capable of solving some of the basic social problems that are involved in a traditional exchange or commerce. So, what is the problem in traditional exchange or commerce? Well, it is a *social problem of opportunism.* The party that has already transferred their assets puts themselves in a vulnerable position to the opposite party's opportunism. In this case, the second party may simply depart from the exchange with the assets of both parties. For Thomas Hobbes, an English philosopher who lived in the seventeenth century, the social problem of opportunism was the reason behind failed commerce and poor social relations. In his work *Leviathan*, he described the problem thus: 'For he that performed first has no assurance the other will perform after, because the bonds of words are too weak to bridle men's ambition, avarice, anger, and other passions, without the fear of some coercive power'.[3]

Smart contracts can help in the elimination of the social problem of opportunism as these contracts offer an escrow structure for the assets from both parties involved in the exchange. As such, the assets will be dispersed only if both the parties in the exchange have made necessary contributions. Also, no human intervention is required to execute the escrow because a smart contract can do this job all by itself.

The behaviour of a smart contract is dictated by its code and this code operates on a decentralised blockchain network having robust and honest execution. Hence, it is the only code that will describe what will happen. The code includes the rules of interaction that have been agreed upon by both parties in the exchange. There is no involvement of any other party in smart contracts, and there is no way that any of the parties can leave the exchange with the assets of both the parties because of the escrow mechanism as well as code. Hence, a smart contract is a great way to successfully address the opportunism problem.

The legal enforceability of a smart contract is restricted in many different ways. First, such contracts have control only over those digital assets that have been represented on the same blockchain where the smart contract lies. In most cases, these digital assets are cryptocurrencies, but they can also represent physical assets from the real world, such as a token representing real estate titles.

However, a smart contract is enforceable and secured only if the transfer of digital assets is part of the contract. In the case of the transfer of physical assets, they do not get any benefit of security and enforceability from the smart contract and have to rely upon other mechanisms like courts. For example, if the transfer of a token representing a piece of land is taking place through a smart contract, then the owner of such land would be dependent on an external system like a traditional legal system.

Another aspect of smart contracts is that maximum blockchains allow for only the consensual transfer of the digital assets. As such, it is difficult to render the contracts enforceable without an escrow.

If one of the parties to a contract has promised to execute an action at a particular time in the future, then it might provide an advantageous position to that party to break the promise when the time to perform the action actually arrives. Incentivising the parties to execute their promises is one of the core responsibilities of a legal contract, even if it is not beneficial. In the case of smart contracts, however, only consensual transfers are allowed to take place, which eliminates the possibility of smart contracts forcibly acquiring the digital assets from the users in the first place. Smart contracts can exercise control only over those digital assets for which such a contract has been catalogued as the owner or has been exclusively granted the power to transfer. Hence, future obligations cannot be enforced by a smart contract in the same way a legal contract can.

For instance, if payments are not secured up front, then there is no means to impose future payments. Currently, the system for honouring wages doesn't exist in smart contracts. On the other hand, it's possible to write down a code that can automatically withdraw money from an account. This system can be easily omitted by pulling out all funds from the account, discarding it, and creating a new one. Since the identity of the blockchain owner is kept anonymous, it's not necessary that the new account created will be connected to the old one, allowing the account holder to avoid the agreed-upon commitments.

Last, an individual executing a smart contract on a blockchain can't make a direct call to the world outside. A smart contract accesses information regarding the outside world only when a new blockchain transaction appeals to the smart contract. For example, if a smart contract is on an insurance basis that is to be paid out when there is any property damage due to extreme weather conditions, the smart contract has to be aware of the current weather conditions. Thus, the smart contract is dependent upon an outside source of information, known as an 'oracle'. An oracle has immense power because it has the ability to direct the outcome of the contract. When the oracle is not biased and still has a singular entity, then by communicating with the smart contract, the oracle can be halted, by disrupting the most powerful aid of blockchain called 'censorship resistance'. System design has been implemented to make an effort to solve alleged oracle complications by incentivising the various oracles to produce another copy of the same data, which is used as a proxy of the original one that has the true information about the world.

Similar to legal contracts, mandatorily smart contracts are incomplete and will not cover all potential consequences. However, legal contracts depend upon the judiciaries and laws to resolve unexpected actions. Currently, a smart contract can't be compared to any non-digital option. Nonetheless, smart contracts can be written explicitly, based upon decentralised conflict resolution mechanisms. If the contract is involved in conflict, then the contract can take the output of conflict resolution services into account and then continue further.

Presently, smart contracts are rudimentary, but they're already being used by many industries for various purposes such as securing cryptocurrency trading, establishment and exchange of decentralised financial products, and in the prediction industry.

As smart contracts enable the secure exchange of digital assets between anonymous entities without any human intervention, it is fast and cheap compared to the human set-up (which is costly and slow for regular computation). Moreover, it can be imposed on agreements across the world, while the legal system struggles to deal internationally with efficiency. In the set of private ordering systems, smart contracts are a new tool and ensure expansion of the sphere of exchange and cooperation in places where legal prosecution can't reach.

Smart contracts have successfully lowered the risk of collaboration; now the cooperative world can achieve much more.

A Smart Ledger: A Single Truth Source to Build Trust

Think of a ledger you know, such as an Excel spreadsheet. Blockchain is also like a spreadsheet but it has some key differences. First of all, it can't be changed, which means that the data, once stored, can't be replaced. Only a new transaction – such as the amount credited to clear out the debits – can be listed in it. Second, the blockchain spreadsheet is secured cryptographically. Thus it provides the user with good confidence that the data stored can't be tampered with. Third, these spreadsheets can be shared with various parties. Lastly, the blockchain spreadsheet is operated through a mechanism – a consensus algorithm – that regulates what should be settled in the spreadsheet with agreement among the users.

In addition to the ledger, many blockchains also administer smart contracts. This represents the business process in the form of code; it extends the opportunity to share attestable data as well as attestable processes among several parties. The organisation can add contracts that would specify how their business will be executed, boost conflict resolution, scale up accountability, and provide end-to-end transparency to help users make better decisions for the business.

Good for Business, Good for Society

The solution powered by blockchain can capture information about the product supply chain participants, which serves other purposes as well. The blockchain data can act as a source of information and through this data one can get the location of the product (e.g. ice cream) origin, including all the details about the cow that gave the milk and from where the vanilla was sourced.

A blockchain is capable of registering the declarations of the supply chain shareholders, consumers and producers, and it also assures that the farm uses only sustainable and fair-trade methods. Since the blockchain can also be implemented to represent the business flow through smart contracts, it can automatically enforce, define and monitor the agreement among the supply-chain associates. For example, if goods are dispatched for the final recipient, smart contracts can trigger payments automatically. If there are any disputes, then the contract manages how the claims can be directed among the participants.

Automated blockchain enforcements and triggers might potentially help the entire world avoid the humanitarian calamity caused by transactions such as the milk scandal in 2008 which claimed 300,000 victims, discourage forced child labour, and control the ISIS threats regarding poisoning the food supply from Europe.

Internet of Things (IoT) Technology Empowering the Supply Chain

The collaboration of blockchain and the internet of things (IoT) offered a new path to enforce and monitor compliance in the whole supply chain. Let's go back to the ice cream company. Ice cream is one of several kinds of products – such as milk, medicine and meat – that must be stored in a safe environment if it is to be consumed safely. Ice cream must be refrozen, because otherwise it will melt during transportation, making it unsafe for consumption and putting consumers at risk. There is evidence that transport company partners are not aware of the problems and are mostly unwilling to inform the company or customer about the bad condition of the product, as it may cause financial liability for them.

Here, a solution powered by a blockchain is provided with sensors that can convey information regarding humidity and temperature in the smart contract. If the reading of humidity and temperature exceeds the acceptable range, compliance problems can be notified through the smart contract. All the parties can mutually agree to implement blockchain as the only source of truth and, as such, the ice cream company would be informed about the products in real time. As a result, the technology will allow us to pull the product out of the supply chain and make the party accountable when they violate the transportation terms in the agreement.

The application of IoT sensors to the blockchain can serve the pharmaceutical industry to tackle safety problems such as counterfeit drugs. On an annual basis, counterfeit drugs have a value of about US$200 billion in the industry. In the developing economies, one-third of drugs are counterfeit and 30% of them don't have active ingredients. Therefore, companies like 3M are introducing solutions powered by blockchain that can deter and detect health issues and handle the bottom-line concern.

Trusted and Legitimate Digital World

Organisations can seize the power of blockchain technology by introducing many of its attributes together. Consider a scenario where John, a driver from Seattle, provides ride-sharing services. He is an amazing driver with a great reputation with customers. Now, John wants to invest in a high-end vehicle for offering high-tier services but he doesn't have enough capital. He needs to show a driver's license as proof for insurance or a loan.

Presently, all banks, car manufacturers, government agencies and insurers are adopting digital services and capabilities in parallel. Car manufacturers using the smart economy approach are recognising the number of millennials buying cars, and are analysing alternative car models for leases and sales. They are introducing smart contracts for ride-sharing businesses to approve loans to qualified drivers.

If John, using the smart contract, applies for a car lease from the manufacturer, then the application for the smart contract evaluates multiple circumstantial reputation sources such as:

- The government confirms John's identity.
- The transportation department attests that he currently has a driving license to drive the type of vehicle provided.
- The testimonials from the ride-sharing service assure that he is employed and verify his salary.
- The testimonials from the ride-sharing service also confirm his driving reputation, which includes value, number of rides, reviews, etc.
- The bank verifies his wealth and payment ability.
- The auto manufacturer guarantees the vehicle and its service history.

An algorithm is built based on the data provided and a proposal determined for John. With a low score, he will be provided with a lease based on a smart contract at a reasonable rate. With a good score, he will be offered a vehicle at no cost with a loan having specific terms that would allocate the percentage of fare he will pay directly to the loan server or manufacturing company. With an exceptional score, he will be provided with a no-cost car, with tolls and fuel coverage, and he would need to pay all these through a fare percentage.

John also needs to have insurance for the new car. The insurance company is given access to the vehicle servicing history, his employment details and driving history for custom insurance. Except for lease payments, smart contracts can be connected to payment being made proportionally to manufacturers from the fares after the ride service delivery. The company operates based on information provided in the incorruptible ledger, thus the efficiency and speed of all kinds of transactions are enhanced.

For public safety, riders and regulators of the car service are satisfied that the ride will be secure. Transparency and evidence reveal that John has no criminal background, has a good history in the driving community, has a valid driving license, hasn't exceeded the allowable driving hours, and overall has a positive driving reputation. Thus, car manufacturers can trust that the vehicle will remain safe and will be maintained well. The government can access synchronised blockchain data from the ride-sharing service for real-time audits to reduce administration costs and ensure compliance.

The Boundaries are No Longer Barriers

Billions of dollars have already been invested in blockchain, and some genius minds across the world are engaged in understanding how it can reinvent industries and organisations. The power of blockchain has led businesses and brands to rethink existing trading models. They are re-evaluating opportunities that would have seemed non-viable earlier and analysing the opportunity frontiers to benefit society.

A new smart economy is being built globally to boost trust on digital platforms. The boundaries are no longer barriers and there are infinite opportunities, with new possibilities and directions. It requires an evolving and future-driven mindset for activating progressive changes. The organisation reinventing its brand with agility will rise above the competition to unlock new business space that will be viable commercially and will thrive in the digital age.

It might be disappointing that smart contracts have a misleading name. They are not smart, nor in the form of legal pages where individuals need to sign at the end.

A smart contract is a piece of code based on business logic and simplifies three basic functionalities:

1 It stores the rules;
2 It verifies the rules; and
3 It can be shared with everyone on a blockchain.

Smart contracts include rules for the completion of whole transactions without having the required number of digital coins for payment. Smart contracts support various transactions along with the monetary one. The rules coded can be applied to any transaction taking place over the blockchain. This evolution of blockchain technology is known as blockchain smart contracts – Blockchain 2.0.

Defining Smart Contracts

Let's begin with what smart contracts exactly are. They are software applications run over a blockchain system that impose rules to let the parties securely execute transactions of money, exchange property, or something valuable. With smart contracts, you don't need to talk to a middleman for your transactions.

Blockchain supports transactions without any broker or intermediary. There is no involvement of a government corporation, escrow agent, or any lawyer. Transactions are executed and completed automatically with the help of validation technology, using a computational system to check that the block of a transaction or a transaction is correct. The smart contract consists of code segments that are executed for processing transactions, whether it's an IoT transmission, financial transaction, digital signature, and so on.

This is the primary difference between smart contracts and regular contracts. The services provided by a broker or lawyer frequently attract a payment. Moreover, there is always a wait to get services from them. Smart contracts automatically execute the transactions between the defined parties on the blockchain, and the best thing is that they define the conditions for transactions as well as prosecuting them. In summary, smart contracts include the rule code and verify whether the right conditions are applied or not.

For example, Alice wants to buy a car, but she can't buy it directly from the car manufacturer. A dealer is mandatory as an intermediary between the seller and the customer. Alice can easily make payment for the car using the traditional digital system, through credit card or bank transfer. For this condition, Alice needs to have enough funds in her bank debit or credit account. The dealer needs to create an agreement that has to be signed by both parties, check whether the payment is made successfully, take out his commission, and verify whether Alice has a valid driving license and new car insurance before she drives it home. In addition, Alice also pays credit card and bank fees. Alice can believe the dealer that the car is working properly, or if she bought a brand new car, the car manufacturer will provide a warranty for it. The whole process requires a number of days or even a few weeks.

Let's execute this whole process on a blockchain network, and Alice will use cryptocurrency and blockchain technology to buy her new car. Now, she can directly make a deal with the car manufacturer. She can store the amount required to buy her car in a smart contract until she gets the car delivery. The car manufacturer would provide the dealer service itself in the local market. Blockchain does not replace intermediaries. It makes things work better. In this case, the dealers are not able to authorise any financial transactions, they are just allowed to deliver the car from manufacturer to customer. The car dealer needs to provide Alice with the key to her car on the specified date; once she is happy with the deal then she would release funds for the payment.

The dealer doesn't need to be concerned that Alice might change her mind or even leave without paying, as the transaction fund is already transferred to some sort of common account. On the other hand, Alice doesn't have to worry about paying up front, and the dealer will get the payment only after Alice gets the keys.

This is how smart contracts work. They set rules for processing the transaction and enforce terms and conditions accordingly, thus having the trust of both parties. Put simply, smart contracts work upon if-then-else clauses and get the benefit of high security as the data is recorded in a blockchain. No party can tamper with the data stored without notifying the other. If either of them tries to access the code to change the rules of the contract or for block mining, both parties need to validate the modification in the smart contract.

How Smart Contracts Impact your Life

There are various applications in smart contracts for transaction verification. This includes contract conditions for validation, financial services, credit enforcement, property law, insurance premiums, and many more. Simply, smart contracts have the potential to solve disputes that were impossible to solve before.

In Finland since 2015, prepaid cards have been provided to refugees in the country. The identity card details are stored in the blockchain network. The refugees are able to open a bank account without any ID proof or passport and can obtain government benefits to live a decent life. Even more interesting is that with smart contracts, they can borrow digital currencies from the network, so they not only live a decent life, but they can also receive credit and can thrive from business.

Diaspora is a decentralised social network of artists that uses no text – only images are shared. Artists play here, look for new concepts, get together, and make beautiful art. Smart contracts are implemented to ensure payment is done fairly, and to make sure the artwork is not plagiarised or stolen. The most interesting thing in this project is that more than 150,000 artists from 50 different countries have unveiled their creativity to create something new. Just imagine if we channelled this intelligence and creativity to other practices for solving problems around the world.

The progress humankind has achieved from the beginning to this information age is nothing in comparison to what humankind can attain by sharing knowledge by using the same distribution technology platform.

The alliance of blockchain and IoT has the potential to replace the traditional management of the supply chain by implementing a smart contract that is transparent and decentralised. IoT devices are used to record and transmit data to each level of the supply chain; this information is updated to an IoT hub, which accumulates these data streams in storage for further analysis.

Smart contracts on blockchains work on rule-based intelligence to validate data provided and update it to other stages of the supply chain in a completely transparent and trusted manner. For example, logic, terms, and conditions can be coded in smart contracts for the verification of correct processes to execute transactions of products among the different levels of the supply chain.

Why Smart Contracts are Desirable

Smart contracts are a great innovation in blockchain technology as the use of them enables the automation of transactions of value (goods, services, currency) among parties. Think of smart contracts as software applications that run over the decentralised network of blockchain and have a single purpose: validate conditions set in the code of the contract and authorise or reject the transaction associated with it. Because this layer of software in a blockchain network runs automatically, it doesn't require human intervention. Technically, this means there is no end user pressing a button on some user interface to run a smart contract. Execution is triggered by a specific event happening in the network.

The automation of execution of a smart contract removes the supervisory overhead, thus making smart contracts an essential feature of blockchain technology for creating trust between parties using machines (computer power) rather than human judgement.

Substantially, once conditions set in a smart contract are met – goods reach their destination at the expected level of quality, or the dealing parties agree over the exchange of cryptocurrency – then transactions of value are carried out automatically. Completed smart contracts represent a sort of digital receipt that authorises the progress of a goods supply chain to the next stage, for example, or a cryptocurrency payment to reach the beneficiary. Behind this, a blockchain digital ledger stores, in an immutable way, all transactions and the instances of the executed smart contracts, which, as mentioned, are the receipt of completion of a transaction.

For instance, an airline can provide insurance services to its customers by integrating smart contracts in its booking system, and release funds automatically on money claims based on verifiable events such as flight delays or lost baggage. Or, in a supply chain, when a cargo shipment arrives at the entry port, the content of the containers is verified whether it's been properly stored and has remained unopened throughout the journey; only at that point, when these conditions are met, the shipping bill will be automatically issued.

Smart contracts are also a medium to transfer digital tokens as a representation of a unique physical asset, such as a painting, or a book or gold, etc. Tokens can have a fixed supply, constant inflation rate, or even a supply determined by a sophisticated monetary policy. The Ethereum blockchain implements the ERC-20 token standard to allow for seamless interaction with other smart contracts and decentralised applications on the Ethereum network. However, it is important to understand that not every smart contract is a digital token. As Martha Bennett, principal analyst at Forrester Research, reported: 'you can have smart contracts running on Ethereum that trigger an action based on a condition without a token involved'.[4]

Smart contracts can also be employed to process transactions of cryptocurrencies. Once the payment is confirmed, the cryptocurrency can be exchanged between seller and buyer automatically, without requiring an additional action for processing the payment.

Bennett pointed to the fact that most of the businesses operating on a blockchain network don't use tokens. They define rules for token allocation in smart contracts as well as conditions for the transaction to be valid. In Bennett's words, 'that still doesn't mean the token is the smart contract – it all depends on how the token has been constructed'.[5] This is key to appreciate: tokens don't necessarily have to be about economic value. A token is simply an authority you hold which provides you a right over an asset: if you own a token, you own the rights to access or sell the asset it's associated with, even if there is no associated economic profit.

From this description, you may be realising that smart contracts are not really smart or have any legal implications. Smart contracts only consist of business rules coded into software that is used to validate a transaction. Quoting Bennett:

> People often ask what makes smart contracts different from
> business rules automation software or stored procedures. The

answer is that conceptually, the principle is the same; but smart contracts can support automating processes that stretch across corporate boundaries, involving multiple organizations; existing ways of automating business rules can't do that.[6]

In other words, as the code of smart contracts runs openly when an event occurs in the blockchain network, rules are not only applied to the entity who coded the smart contract but also to the other parties allowed on the blockchain. 'In other words' – Bennett writes – 'they're code that does what it's been programmed to do. If the business rules have been defined badly and/or the programmer doesn't do a good job, the result is going to be a mess'.[7] Even if designed and programmed correctly, a smart contract is not really smart per se, as all it does is function according to coded computer instructions.

Translation of the rules for business into software code doesn't turn a smart contract automatically into a legally imposed agreement between the parties involved. Some initiatives have been taken which aim to legalise smart contracts, but at this time, there is no agreed standard of smart contracts yet. An open question that Bennett asks: 'What happens if the software has bugs and yields bad results? Is the resulting loss now also legally binding?'.[8] Good question…

As we have seen before, smart contracts include rules to automate the transaction process. Good programming is important for the correct processing of the validation rules, as well as the accuracy of data entered into the smart contract also being essential. Once you record the rules in the contract and store it in the blockchain digital ledger, it becomes unalterable. After the contract is created, neither the programmer nor the user can modify it. So, if the data recorded in the blockchain is not accurate, then smart contracts can't work correctly on it.

This opens a big challenge of injecting data from external sources. 'With blockchain, it's garbage in – garbage forever', Avivah Litan, vice president of research at Gartner, titled her blog post. 'The truth and legitimacy of the data on the distributed ledger is not at all guaranteed by blockchain'.[9]

The mechanism for entering data into a blockchain is known as an 'oracle', that is, a single point of contact between the external data and the smart contract. Oracles can be based on the hardware or software. For example, a hardware-based oracle is the RFID sensors inside a cargo container which transmit location information to the smart contract holder. A software-based oracle is an application that feeds flight delays or lost baggage information through an Application Programming Interface (API). In this latter case, for example, the smart contract would receive the information necessary to process an automatic refund to holders of travel insurance issued on the blockchain. It goes without saying that it is essential that the smart contract receive correct data from the outside source for the insurance holder to trust the insurance provider.

The blockchain might be decentralised among thousands of nodes while smart contracts are not. Smart contracts execute over a single node. The blockchain nodes have no transparency to show how the smart contract actually works. Any alliance of companies that are part of the blockchain network has to rely upon an oracle in which information is being recorded in the smart contract.

If your organisation is a part of a blockchain confederation, for example for a supply chain, there is no means of knowing what's happening in the smart contract. There is no approved testing method. Essentially, it is necessary to take the word of the organisation processing over the servers on which the smart contract and oracle reside that the information fed into the blockchain is accurate.

Litan insisted: 'You have to go to one source, one table, one oracle for that data. There are no standard processes to verify the data is what it says it is and it's coming in properly. It's the central point of failure'.[10] Then she added 'It's not mature yet … I have talked to companies participating in a consortium and asked how do you know what the smart contract is doing and they say they don't. If you have a contract running your life, wouldn't you want to know what it's doing?'.[11]

Because oracles transmit data from any source, there is no authentic trustworthy data that can be verified before reaching a blockchain network, according to Sergey Nazarov, CEO of ChainLink, an oracle start-up that uses various external sources for oracle data. Nazarov wrote that the data might get 'benignly or maliciously corrupted due to faulty web sites, cheating service providers, or honest mistakes'.[12]

Assuming for a moment that quality of data can be ensured, the problem to resolve, says Nazarov, is still in the nature of regular contracts, as either party involved in the exchange may initiate the transaction while the other one decides not to complete the payment. This, as you can imagine, could lead to lengthy and expensive legal battles.

Regular contracts can't be enforced by technology the way a smart contract can. A smart contract is said to be deterministic as it can always be enforced when the events related to its conditions occur. Smart contracts

depend on specific events to occur for them to be activated, events that
are triggered by factors external to the smart contracts themselves, such
as IoT telemetry data being collected from devices installed in vehicles or
industrial equipment in a supply chain process, for instance.

For example, ChainLink built a smart contract for a media-based business
organisation in which fees are paid in reserve form to a search engine
optimisation (SEO) company until URLs for new articles arrive and maintain
ranking in the search engines for a particular period of time. Fee payments
were held in a smart contract, before being released to the search engine
optimisation firm at satisfactory completion of work. This could be assessed
automatically based on the search engine rank reached by the specific URL,
thus validating the condition in the smart contract to process the payment.

Developing smart contracts has traditionally being a task for software
engineers, attracting complexities that programming languages and tools for
blockchain bring as the market matures.

Nowadays, we see more people able to define the basic rules of a
smart contract, even with no software coding.. Bennett said, 'we're even
beginning to see tools that allow business people to pull together the basics
of a smart contract. That's only the beginning, though, as some companies
have already discovered it can be a challenge to ensure that every network
participant runs the same version of a smart contract'.[13]

Benefits of blockchain technology, such as the ability to code verification
on conditions and trigger actions accordingly, enable efficiency of business
processing. Companies can automate, and thus optimise their business
lines, introducing automated controls, process verification, and basically
trust between all the parties involved. In the enterprise ecosystem, it
has accelerated trade, reduced cost, avoided error, mitigated error, and
enabled data integration, and the incorruptibility of blockchain has added
value. That's why for any enterprise it is important to adopt smart contract
platforms to build a solution on the blockchain. Blockchain 1.0, introduced
by Bitcoin, is not able to meet enterprise requirements.

Contrary to what many believe, smart contracts were not invented by
Ethereum and introduced in what the industry calls 'Blockchain 2.0', or
Enterprise Blockchain. This second blockchain evolution indeed launched
a programmable tier which enabled coding for controlling and verifying
the logic in blockchain depending upon the workflow. But the concept of
smart contracts was introduced in the 1990s by Nick Szabo, an American-
Hungarian cryptography expert. Szabo was the first person to work on
securing the exchange of data flow, introducing the idea of automating the

encryption and decryption of information. He published an article in 1996, *Smart Contracts: Building Blocks for Digital Markets*, which several people consider a pioneer of modern automated workflow practices.[14]

Szabo worked with manufacturers to automate their productivity pipeline and deliver products on demand more efficiently. The process needed to involve no humans. He implemented what we can now consider the very first smart contracts, whose code was able to read the conditions to elaborate on the incoming demand for products and activate operations on relevant machines to increase or decrease productivity accordingly.

In their initial form, smart contracts used to include instructions for simple data verification and process automation.; Now, with the advent of distributed networks, and the increasing need for automation in the enterprise, the adoption of smart contract s has become a key element of enterprise blockchain solutions.

Smart contracts operate based upon agreed conditions; code is implemented to automatically verify the input data and then execute the actions according to the conditions mentioned in the contract itself. These conditions are considered as the clause of the contract. The following properties of a smart contract represent its foundation as a mechanism to create trust among parties without human involvement:

1 Everything is automated, without any human manipulation.
2 The data stored in the digital ledger is immutable.

As smart contracts represent a new 'rule enforcement' paradigm, they execute automatically to validate and govern the business processes they are attached to, without asking for permissions of any user operator, or needing someone to interact with a user interface to trigger the validation itself. In addition, the conditions set in a smart contract are immutable and deterministic in the ledger, making a smart contract the proof and accuracy of data once entered.

But in this automated and controlled world, is there space left for humans? All control is shifted to coding in smart contracts; there is no requirement for human intervention. Engineers produce code for all rules and actions to be performed to control the process. The question arises here: What is the legal effect of smart contracts? What is the responsibility of the software programmer, because they don't have appropriate knowledge about the rules and regulations of business or law for conducting business internationally on a blockchain network? Should organisations trust their software developers to set up the rules of the contract properly and execute tasks without any conflict?

For example, the service gets disabled automatically if payment is not made on time. If strict rules are in place, after the grace period, services for gas or electricity would get cut off when the customer fails to make payment within the given time period. Would the code include the personal problems of customers which may cause payment delay? What would happen if the consumer is facing a problem in the payment platform, which is totally apart from the system which shuts down the services? In such cases, smart contracts do not seem to be smart enough, as they lack manual interpretation of rules. Researchers and studies have looked at the convergence of AI technology with blockchain, which might acquire some level of intelligence to handle problematic situations in the future.

Smart contracts and blockchain have brought real benefits to businesses; they have improved operation speed, reduced the cost of handling disputes, and automated the verification process. But automating and enforcing conditions and actions still depends upon coding by a programmer who is specialised in this domain, and there is a chance of accidental error in the code which runs the smart contract.

These are called 'bugs' in the software reserved on the blockchain, which is irreversible until a strategy is devised to fix and update the contracts if all parties involved agree to the modification. In an alliance network, the central host platform itself fixes bugs and controls the deployment of new versions of contracts. Confirmation of new contract rules is required from all the parties included in the alliance, but it's easier to clarify the new rules with all network parties rather than verifying it in a public blockchain network; it's optional to join in the decision-making process, although identity remains anonymous and there is not the security of having peers within the network.

There is an emerging trend of creating snapshots of rules and data versions in the existing blockchain network, also known as a fork. Forking means the divergence in the blockchain network, whether it's permanent or temporary. Simply, forking takes place when a blockchain breaks down into different branches. It may happen because of any change or software change in the smart contract.

According to the type of change, the fork can be classified as a soft fork or a hard fork. A hard fork means there is a permanent divergence from the earlier version of the blockchain; the nodes working on previous versions would not be accepted by the new version. A hard fork is also known as a radical change protocol that invalidates the previously valid transactions. The forked chain transactions will become invalid for the older chain. To get into the new forked chain one needs to upgrade all nodes with the latest version of the protocol.

A soft fork takes place when the modification in software protocol remains compatible with the old version also. The new forked chain has to honour and follow both old and new rules. The initial chain will run in line with the old rules. Thus, companies can select the blockchain solution according to the required forking strategy, whether the new rules are compatible with old rules (soft fork) or new rules are not compatible with the new rules (hard fork).

Who can take advantage of smart contracts? There are various businesses interested in this technology and many enterprises have already adopted blockchain automation processes in their business for experimentation. The shipping transportation and retail industries are already operating at an advanced stage of mature blockchain and IoT solutions for document verification and supply chain.

Through an automated control system the sensor collects the data and uploads it to 'IoT data hubs' which analyse and process the huge information stream; shipping containers are getting the authority to load or unload goods, and even activate the required industrial machinery when materials are available for processing. Factory advantages are clear: it reduces the waiting time while processing goods at different levels of the supply chain and optimises the resources.

Another example is the insurance field. Thanks to a tracker which tracks the real-time location of a vehicle, the information about the time operation can be collected in series, thus introducing a more competitive time in the industry.

Notes

1 Nick Szabo 1994 'Smart Contracts'. www.fon.hum.uva.nl/rob/Courses/ InformationInSpeech/CDROM/Literature/LOTwinterschool2006/szabo.best.vwh. net/smart.contracts.html.
2 Vitalik Buterin, *A Next Generation Smart Contract and Decentralized Application Platform*. Ethereum White Paper. https://blockchainlab.com/pdf/ Ethereum_white_paper-a_next_generation_smart_contract_and_decentralized_ application_platform-vitalik-buterin.pdf.

3 Thomas Hobbes, *Leviathan*, Chapter 8. https://courses.lumenlearning.com/suny-classicreadings/chapter/thomas-hobbes-on-the-social-contract/.

4 Martha Bennett, Andras Cser, Jost Hoppermann, Charlie Dai with Pascal Matzke, Michael Glenn, Ian McPherson, 'Predictions 2018: Be Ready to Face the Realities Behind the Blockchain Hype', *Forrester*, November 2017.

5 Ibid.

6 Ibid.

7 Ibid.

8 Ibid.

9 Avivah Litan, 'With Blockchain, it's Garbage In – Garbage Forever', October 23, 2020. https://blogs.gartner.com/avivah-litan/2020/10/23/with-blockchain-its-garbage-in-garbage-forever/.

10 Avivah Litan, Martin Reynolds and Lydia Clougherty Jones, 'Managing the Risks of Enterprise Blockchain Smart Contracts', Gartner Research, February 2020.

11 Ibid.

12 Steve Ellis, Ari Juels and Sergey Nazarov, 'ChainLink: A Decentralized Oracle Network', September 2017, https://link.smartcontract.com/whitepaper.

13 Martha Bennett, Andras Cser, Jost Hoppermann, Charlie Dai with Pascal Matzke, Michael Glenn, Ian McPherson, 'Predictions 2018: Be Ready to Face the Realities Behind the Blockchain Hype', *Forrester*, November 2017.

14 Nick Szabo, 'Smart Contracts: Building Blocks for Digital Markets', *Extropy* 16 (1996). www.fon.hum.uva.nl/rob/Courses/InformationInSpeech/CDROM/Literature/LOTwinterschool2006/szabo.best.vwh.net/smart_contracts_2.html.

Chapter 4

The Next Generation of Enterprise-Ready Blockchain

In 2017, Microsoft Corporation released the Confidential Consortium Framework (CCF) open-source research project, a framework to build secure, highly available, and performant applications that focus on multi-party computing and data.[1] This is one of the first types of innovation to adopt blockchain technology for the advancement of the enterprise. Presently, the protocol of blockchain technology needs complicated development in order to fulfil the security and operational requirements of enterprises. The Confidential Consortium Framework reduces these complications when it is integrated into blockchain networks; many critical requirements are addressed which are needed for commercial adoption such as distributed governance, fast transaction speed and confidentiality. These functionalities open up even more complicated blockchain scenarios of real-world industries – such as logistics, supply chain, financial services, retail and healthcare – thus blockchain is proving that it has the potential to transform business digitally. Mark Russinovich, chief technology officer of Azure at Microsoft, said,

> Blockchain is a transformational technology with the ability to significantly reduce the friction of doing business … Microsoft is committed to bringing blockchain to the enterprise. We have listened to the needs of our customers and the blockchain community and are bringing foundational functionality with the Confidential Consortium Blockchain Framework. Through

DOI: 10.4324/9781003132592-4

an innovative combination of advanced algorithms and trusted execution environments (TEEs), like Intel's Software Guard Extensions (SGX) or Windows Virtual Secure Mode (VSM), we believe this takes the next step toward making blockchain ready for business.[2]

Key advantages of the blockchain network-integrated framework are

1 High-speed transaction as it supports thousands of transactions per second;
2 Data confidentiality is managed easily without degrading performance; and
3 A comprehensive, industry-first distributed governance model for blockchain networks that establishes a network constitution and allows members to vote on all terms and conditions governing the consortium and the blockchain software system.

Vice president of Software and Services Group and general manager of Platforms Security Division at Intel, Rick Echevarria said

We are thrilled to work with Microsoft to bring blockchain to the enterprise. Our mutual customers are excited by the potential of blockchain. Intel is committed to accelerating the value of blockchains powered by Azure on Intel hardware, by improving the scalability, privacy, and security of the solutions based on our technologies.[3]

The design of the framework will be compatible with any ledger protocol and can be operated on any operating system, cloud, and hypervisor which is compatible with TEE. The very first implementation consists of Hyperledger Sawtooth, R3 Corda, Ethereum, and J.P. Morgan Quorum. David E. Rutter, CEO of R3, said

The R3 Corda platform was built for enterprises. We designed it with the financial industry from the ground up to solve real business problems, but we also knew it had to be deployable and manageable in today's complex IT landscape. No other distributed ledger technology platform is as interoperable or easily integrated and partnering with Microsoft is another milestone in our mission to facilitate a world of frictionless commerce.[4]

The technical white paper and its descriptions are accessible for entrepreneurs and developers who want to learn about the framework. Microsoft launched the codebase for the framework on GitHub. It's an open-source project which will be executed with partners, customers, business communities and blockchain technical consultants for the advancement of the blockchain technology foundation.

For more information about the Microsoft technical white paper and technical demonstration, you can visit www.aka.ms/cocoframework.

Releasing the Confidential Consortium Framework for Blockchain Networks Integrated Enterprise

Blockchain is transformational automation with the potential to expand digital transformation beyond the barriers and improve company processes with partners, customers and suppliers. A growing number of enterprises are adopting blockchain because of its secure and transparent platform for business owners to digitally track assets beyond the trust boundaries, and for business partnerships it offers new opportunities for company collaborations and introducing new business strategies.

Microsoft launched this framework to introduce blockchain in the enterprise – and is working with the blockchain community, customers and partners to develop and advance it, in order to meet all enterprise requirements. Their mission is to guide organisations to level up in this new business era where multi-party scalable computation can be executed securely and provide services to improve business processes, whether they are a retailer, health provider, global bank service provider, or any type of organisations with a need for an immutable digital ledger technology.

Enterprises are implementing blockchain technology to fulfil business requirements; they have also realised that various existing protocols of blockchain are still not able to meet the enterprise's key requirements such as confidentiality, governance, performance and required processing efficiency. Because the existing blockchain systems were built to function in public scenarios involving anonymous identity with maximum transparency, the transactions committed are posted clearly and openly, each of the nodes in the network has the ability to execute any transaction, and an intensive computational algorithm is applied with common consent. These safeguard the integrity of blockchain networks and complement company requirements such as confidentiality and scalability.

Efforts are required to improve the existing blockchain protocols or to showcase new protocols to fulfil the general requirement for enterprise trading. But one attribute will be improved at the cost of another attribute – for instance, confidentiality is enhanced at the cost of lower performance or greater complications.

Simplifying the Blockchain Adoption for Enterprises

As reported before, the Confidential Consortium Framework is an open-source research project which allows confidential and high-scale blockchain networks to meet key enterprise requirements at scale.

This framework has been designed by Microsoft to achieve confidentiality of consortiums, where actors and nodes are declared and controlled explicitly. According to the requirements, the framework offers another way for constructing ledgers, provides scalability to enterprises, ensures enhanced confidentiality, and distributed governance is given without compromising inherent security and mutation.

By taking advantage of the existing protocols of blockchain, the trusted execution environments (TEEs) such as Windows Virtual Secure Mode (VSM), Intel SGX, cryptography, and distributed systems, the Confidential Consortium Framework allows blockchain network-integrated enterprise to deliver

1 Rapid database speed for throughput;
2 Business-specific, richer and flexible confidentiality models;
3 Support for non-deterministic transactions; and
4 Distributed governance executed by the network policy management.

By providing these functionalities, the model presents a trustworthy foundation to the existing blockchain protocols that are integrated to provide complete ledger solutions, opens up the high-scale and broad scenarios in industries, and has the capability to transform business digitally.

Microsoft explored the system potential of various industries, including supply chain, financial and retail services. In the words of Tom Racette, vice president, Global Retail Business Development, Mojix,

> Being able to run our existing supply chain Dapp code much faster within the Framework is a great performance improvement that will reduce friction when we talk about enterprise Blockchain readiness with our retail customers. Adding data confidentiality support without sacrificing this improvement is what will enable us to lead the digital transformation we are envisioning with Smart Supply Chains.[5]

Whether a customer is building an end-to-end finance solution for trade, implementing blockchain to ensure high security, or holding smart contracts for enterprise to drive businesses efficiently, the Confidential Consortium Framework fulfils all the requirements of the enterprise. Microsoft is the only company providing cloud services that provide on-premises consistency and hyper-scale public cloud service while giving entry to the Azure ecosystem for a wide variety of apps which will be created based on a layer of shared data in the blockchain.

An Open Approach

From the design perspective, the framework is open and compatible with all blockchain protocols. Microsoft has started integrating systems with Ethereum and revealed that Intel, R3, and J.P. Morgan Chase are committed to integrating enterprise Quorum, Hyperledger Sawtooth, Corda, and ledgers respectively. This is the first stage only. Microsoft is looking forward to analysing integration opportunities with different ledgers in the future. Joseph Lubin, founder of ConsenSys, said, 'Confidential Consortium Blockchain Framework represents a breakthrough in achieving highly scalable, confidential, permissioned Ethereum or other blockchain networks that will be an important construct in the emerging world of variously interconnected blockchain systems'.[6]

Mark Russinovich believes that the system will be able to achieve maximum benefits from the contributions of the talented open-source communities that are driving innovations in the blockchain industry today.

The project was initiated as a joint partnership between Microsoft Research and the Azure product groups, but it has already received benefits from the recommendations made by a plethora of partners and customers. Launching the codebase is a means to achieve development far beyond the goals incorporated by the joint collaboration of Microsoft Research and Azure.

The Confidential Consortium Framework would be appropriate from a design perspective with all ledger protocols and can be accomplished on premises and in the cloud, over any hypervisor and operating system which supports a suitable TEE. The team is designing with this flexibility in order to enable community integration with the framework along with the other protocols, try it on any hardware, and accommodate it to enterprise requirements that haven't been thought of.

The eagerness of industry for blockchain is growing; while blockchain technology will take time to achieve the confidence of enterprise, the team is focused on accelerating enterprise adoption and development in collaboration with the community.

To learn more about CCF, you can visit the technical white paper (http://aka.ms/cocopaper) and a demonstration on YouTube (http://aka.ms/cocodemo).

In the tech world, blockchain technology is gradually becoming a common terminology. Still, many people believe that blockchain technology is applicable to only cryptocurrencies. But that's not the reality. When blockchain technologies increase in enterprise, people will recognise the versatility of this technology.

Blockchains in enterprises are empowering large industries with an equal security level, easy to control and use, fundamentally evolving the business course.

Blockchain will stay; many businesses have already started to appreciate the new adoption of this technology. While many are critical, vendors and start-ups are constantly working to develop it. Thus, it has pushed enterprise to adopt the technology at a faster rate than expected. Is there anyone who doesn't want to secure their position in the future blockchain industry?

Define Enterprise Blockchain

Enterprise blockchain is a network of blockchain which can be integrated and implemented for enterprise purposes. These enterprise blockchain technologies are specifically equipped to operate all the demands of the organisation at the enterprise level.

At a rapid rate, blockchain is getting integrated into the corporate ecosystem. New projects in this sector will soon dominate the industry. Enterprise blockchain networks will disrupt the typical old business strategies and will soon take over as lead technology in the global enterprise market.

Blockchain is able to handle the demands of organisation-level businesses. The long history of blockchain revealed its capabilities. Around the globe, many projects are running over blockchain and this technology is perfect for global utilisation.

Enterprise blockchain is implemented by enterprises to increase impact on consumers. Popular brands such as Amazon and IBM are utilising many blockchain projects and also working with the existing blockchain platform.

What is Promoting the Blockchain Revolution Worldwide?

The answer is clear – the API (Application Programming Interface) economy. The API economy is growing enormously and many organisations are implementing this technology for the advancement of their business. Even though blockchain technology is advancing rapidly, it is still not able to match the growth rate of the internet.

Presently, enterprises need to manage huge amounts of data as well as maintain fast transaction speed across the world to keep their businesses growing. Thus, various challenges arise with security, transparency and complex issues.

Security: The enterprise architecture is centralised, meaning hackers can take advantage and hack easily into devices, applications and users' accounts. Existing technology is not able to provide the minimum required level of security.

Transparency: There is no visibility point from where the organisation can track their services to customers. This negatively impacts the business and increases problems with counterfeiting.

Complexity: The global enterprise requires cooperation in the workplace and needs to keep pace with several intermediaries. Managing all these increases overall costs and creates complex issues.

Every year enterprises take hits of over US$7.5B due to counterfeiting. This estimation is just for the USA! Across the globe, product suppliers need to pay off interest of up to 30%, which increases the product or service price for consumers. Even if the manufacturer delivers a budget-friendly product, consumers are not able to get all the benefits.

In this tragic situation, the sinking economy can be saved with blockchain technology. Enterprises can get back the lost trust of their consumers by integrating with these technologies.

Now, the growth of API data is a new currency, and with the integration of enterprise blockchain solutions, organisations can finally breathe a sigh of relief.

Is the Opportunity Vast?

If we look into traditional practices, institutions such as corporations, banks or the government have to manage risk factors. Now, organisations can finally implement blockchain to eradicate the uncertainty, which will ultimately decrease costs.

This transformation will affect the world economy in a major way. The future lies in the programmable economy. The enterprise blockchain solution will take the lead in the market and is expected to generate an annual business value of over US$175 billion by 2025, rising to US$3 trillion by 2030![7]

Is Enterprise Blockchain Ready?

Still, blockchain technology is in an immature phase. Although the tech world is familiar with the entire concept, the majority of organisations are not aware of how the technology works. The technology it is improving, though, and enterprises are striving hard to overcome the primary challenges.

Assessing platforms, organisations are consistently searching for a platform through which they can solve all their complex issues. Blockchain is a type of transformational network, but enterprises still want something even more specific, especially for industrial purposes. Although big enterprises want to build their own networks, the true value can be achieved when many blockchain networks work together.

Enterprise blockchains can become the right partner to cover the loophole between data management and organisations. Many such projects have already been deployed in the industry and enterprises are impatient to get integrated with blockchain. Let's get into the next section to understand the situation in depth.

The Blockchain Technology Features for Enterprise Utilisation

In this section, we will get into particular blockchain technology features which add value to an enterprise. Enterprise blockchain solutions can truly shake up the industry and bring innovation at scale.

Peer-to-Peer Network Ensured by a Decentralised System

Decentralisation is one of the most important features of enterprise blockchain systems because it solves the issues of centralised authority and single point of failure on computing and storage needs. The traditional client-server model has become outdated and expensive to run.

The Working of Client-Server Structure

In a client-server network, everyone uses a common centralised server. Anyone can connect, send to the server, and send a query to access the information. Nowadays, this is exactly how the internet works. For example, if you are searching something on Google, you need to enter a query for Google's servers, and it will provide you with relevant results.

The relationship between the client and server is known as the client-server network system. But in this structure, there are some significant problems.

Everyone is dependent on the server, and if anything goes wrong, everyone in the loop will experience a breakdown of service equally. For example, if a server is not available for any reason, no one will be able to access it.

Most crucially, servers often deal with clients' personal information. If somehow a hacker gets into the server, they can steal sensitive data.

Therefore, the organisation works on networking architecture to its systems by massive spending on anti-cyber-attack schema to secure it from hackers.

To the Rescue: Blockchain's Decentralisation is Coming

Blockchain is a decentralised network and it doesn't deliver a client-server system. Without the interference of a central authority, users can take advantage of peer-to-peer connectivity. Since there is no central server, there is no chance of failure issues at a single point. Hacking has become difficult because control depends upon the clients in the network. It's free of all issues of the client-server system and enterprises can readily trust the system.

Eradicate Corruption with Immutability

What is meant by immutability? In the case of blockchain, it means once the data block is recorded in the ledger, no one can alter or change it. So, there is no way of tampering with the information.

Enterprises need to deal with cyber-attacks as well as internal corruption. Altering the data for one's own advantage is one of the major ways in which corruption occurs. But if enterprises use the blockchain ledger system, no one can use it for their own gain by changing the data in it. Thus, big industries can get rid of corruption.

But how does blockchain do it? To create immutability, the blockchain implements a hash function that encrypts the information present in the block. Hashing always produces a result of a finite number. Whatever the input is, it will deliver a fixed-length random number. It becomes quite difficult when you are dealing with a huge number of different information lengths. Every next block in the blockchain consists of the hash function of the earlier block.

Consequences of an Attack

Let's take an example where John tries to alter the information stored in a block. If he attempts to make any alterations to the block, it changes the hash function of the block, which then alters the hash function of the immediate next block in the queue. When the data and hash function of one block are changed, it will change the characteristics of other blocks also. Therefore, the entire chain of blocks will be disturbed if there is any attempt to make alterations. But it is not possible to change the characteristics of the chain of the blocks. The blocks are immutable, and nobody can execute any alterations in the information stored in the blocks without breaking the chain. When zero-knowledge proof is added into the blockchain, it will render the technology more robust.

Improved Transparency Boosts Responsibility

With the help of blockchain technology, users can experience the advantage of complete transparency. So, if someone says that blockchain technology is transparent, what do they mean? In the case of a public blockchain, any person on the ledger can see the history of other node transactions. But if you think it's easy to see what everyone else is doing on the network, then you are not entirely right.

While the transaction history of a person stays visible, their identity remains covert; only the public address of the individual, rather than the name or any other kind of identification, is visible to everyone.

However, this doesn't mean that a person will get up to mischief by hiding in the shadows. If it is possible to detect the public address of an organisation on the network, then it is also possible to search for it and check how the organisation is executing transactions on the network. Therefore, enterprises have no other option but to be responsible and not participate in any dark activities.

Tracking Products

When products are offered to customers, the success rate for delivery is not always 100%. There have been many cases of counterfeit products infiltrating the product shipment process. In order to prevent this, organisations and consumers can now track the products until the shipment arrives at the customer. This allows the parties to properly navigate the problem if something goes wrong and then implement the necessary actions accordingly.

Organisations are asked more and more to show transparency in their supply chain, to avoid consumers not trusting the brand and its products, if, for example, the origin or ingredients are questionable. With blockchain technology, transparency and trust can be maximised, which will help to build a wider consumer base.

Good Savings because of Cheaper Costs

It is easy to integrate blockchain technology in the service and many vendors have already done so. In comparison to other traditional practices, blockchain technology as a service (BaaS) in the operations helps to save a lot of funds in the long run. Let's find it out why this is so.

If you intend to build your own blockchain network, you will have to take care of some complex situations such as

- Understanding how the technology functions;
- Building the network without any faults or errors; and
- Recruiting an efficient team of professionals who can build and maintain the network.

These requirements will cost an organisation a lot more than BaaS solutions. Also, the development of a blockchain network can deflect an organisation from its core goals and activities. Hence, it is best to integrate blockchain technology in the form of a BaaS solution instead of developing your own network.

There are lots of ways through which blockchain technology can help to reduce the costs of an organisation.

To start with, organisations typically use a client-server network. A typical client-server network is beleaguered by vulnerability and temperament issues and in order to deal with them, organisations end up spending a lot of funds on security software each year. However, with blockchain technology, enterprises have everything from one source and there isn't any need to invest additional funds in security protocols.

Finally, through these enterprises, we can send or receive a large amount of money quickly. The company need not depend upon any intermediate party or need to wait for funding.

Financial Institutions Cutting Cost

Financial institutions such as banks have to deal with different issues. Every year US$1.6 billion is spent just on Know Your Customer (KYC) regulations. For financial enterprises, this is a burden.

With blockchain, they can easily have the information required for KYC regulations. To open a bank account, the bank asks the customer for simple identification information and can get other information directly from the network. To open a new account at a different bank, instead of repeating the whole process, the bank can access the KYC information directly from the previous bank. Thus, a huge amount of money can be saved in the long run.

Financial institutions can implement blockchain for the smooth compilation of internal branching. They can also grant their technology to other banks for future benefits. For financial enterprises, adopting blockchain is the right move.

Efficiency is Enhanced with Faster Networking

Fast networking is one of the best features of blockchain. This new integrated feature of the enterprise system can transact within a few minutes. In the beginning there was a major issue in blockchain technology because as the network grew larger, transaction speed drastically slowed down. However, enterprise blockchain technology can sort out all demands of the enterprise. The transaction speed is also maintained well.

In the banking system, transaction processing requires three to five days. It is still very hard to make a payment in a short time period. When closing any major contract or getting funds for a new project you might get delayed because the bank needed too much time for transaction processing. But a blockchain-based system transaction can be executed within a few seconds! This can truly save money, for example, if you are dealing with a million-dollar project and you can transact the amount within seconds! Isn't this delivering faster output than the typical business?

It not only streamlines processing, but it also increases the efficiency of the overall business of enterprises. Enterprises can deliver this fast transaction facility to their customers to gain more attention in the market.

How Businesses use Blockchain

There are various indications to show blockchain technology is affecting the business space.

Blockchain for Customer Relationship Management

The combination of blockchain technology and customer relationship management (CRM) systems offers to significantly improve workflows and build trusted networks with partners to extend relationships with customers. Each time a business interacts with customers, blockchain extends traceability, trust and transparency as well as breaking down the barriers for the business and data sets. Let's see how blockchain technology helps companies enhance their CRM system.

Blockchain technology would help companies to get 360-degree views of consumers. As blockchain technology has distributed network architecture, the data set is broken down. Rather than creating multiple copies, a single set of records is accessed for all applications, and data redundancy by various systems can be reduced. Thus, companies can become more responsive and reduce data redundancy. CRM-based platforms can compose more detailed and contextual information about the customers and products, hence feed the blockchain network with rich information.

Security is improved, as in the blockchain, the potential cryptographic tools protect the code. The data stored once are immutable or irreversible. The data can't be tampered with or erased.

The quality of data understanding regarding customer activities has been greatly improved; blockchain decentralised systems deliver the business space a deeper insight into the real-time customer's expectations and preferences.

Data accuracy and quality are improved. In any ecosystem, data integrity is important when a system is updated as it has a risk of human error. Integrating with other technologies such as blockchain SRM solutions, the internet of things can help companies to have a better understanding of data, without any human intervention.

Blockchain Network for Customer Experience

According to research, 72% of consumers and business buyers expect that blockchain technology will transform companies within the next few years. This can be done by:

■ Providing a secure ecosystem. Blockchain increases the security of business–consumer interactions, thus companies gain more trust. For customers, the safety and authenticity of goods in the supply chain can be checked. As they share data and transact, now everyone involved can be more confident that their data won't be compromised or misused due to viruses, breaches or malware.

■ Making real-time transactions. Blockchain allows us to record and access transactions by the parties involved in near real time – thus transforming the speed of customer service.

■ Providing customised experiences. Scott Likens, emerging technology leader at PwC, said, 'Since blockchain enables consumers to selectively and securely share their data, they'll likely feel more confident in doing so – enabling companies to customize products and services'.[8]

■ Blockchain is helping companies to earn loyalty in many ways. Examine how to run customer loyalty programmes on the blockchain network: because this technology can connect different loyalty programme schemes and create points for exchanging information, customers can collect and store points conveniently in their digital wallet and use them to perform transactions – a streamlined process to encourage engagement. According to Joshua Q. Israel Satten, blockchain partner at Wipro Limited,

Of course, it's not just B2C that will be affected. I believe blockchain's also poised to revolutionize B2B, in particular, creating trusted networks and processes between businesses so the partner ecosystems can be activated in a wholly optimized and automated way.[9]

Productivity of Blockchain

By adopting blockchain solutions, companies can ensure more productivity over time. This technology has the power to build more accurate and reliable systems, and reduces record redundancy, data loss and potential administrative errors.

The shared ledger is beneficial especially for the effective alliance of smart contracts. Financial services companies, and those in the legal profession and supply chain sector have already deployed smart contracts; the software programs can be integrated into a shared ledger to simplify and automate business arrangements and processes. With predefined triggers, terms can be automated without depending upon the expensive intermediary parties to negotiate the deal.

For example, a company can create invoices which can get paid automatically when the truck delivers goods to the distribution centre, or distribute dividend certificates to stockholders after the profit reaches a fixed level.

Since, on the blockchain, smart contracts can execute mechanical tasks automatically (processing payments, confirming data, enforcing contracts, and much more), employees can get additional hours for completing more tasks. Satten says,

> Blockchain can have tremendous benefits for the employee experience. If an organization's enterprise architecture harnesses DLT and smart contracts, and makes use of customized web-based applications alongside customized UIs, it can massively cut down on the overall number of systems used. At the same time, it can automate processes, better secure its information and reduce errors. That means employees get an improved user interface with more digitization and operations interoperability, which can significantly impact productivity.[10]

Fundraising by Blockchain

Blockchain technology – in the version of initial coin offerings (ICOs) – can simplify fundraising for organisations as an option for capital funding and traditional debt offered by private equity firms, venture capital firms and banks.

This type of reach is based upon tokenisation. Here, the digital tokens are built on a blockchain network and are implemented as an alternative means to denominate value – for instance, used in substitute for money.[11]

The tokens can be represented as tangible assets, which can be applied to a wide range of business processes. In the real estate sector, there are various innovative uses such as trading and tracking tokenised assets. The tokens can be enabled for 'fractional ownership' or allow the real estate owner to split their property and sell off equal stakes.

For ICOs, an organisation sells off a fixed number of digital tokens in public. Some start-ups have raised a significant amount by building and selling their own digital assets – the tech company EOS successfully raised US$4.2B in 2017.[12]

How Blockchain will Disrupt Industries

Some of the most common uses of blockchain consist of the following sectors:

1 Financial services. Many start-ups are disrupting the traditional work-force and deploying blockchain to develop the target application, for example, multiple intermediaries required for processing transactions, such as cross-border payment exchange, stock exchanges, and money transaction services. Sandra Ro, CEO of the Global Blockchain Business Council, says

> Their goal is to reduce complexity and cost. There's also a major focus on developing blockchain solutions to counter fraud and ensure the integrity of data. Obviously, all of this has been a big wake-up call for banks and other financial institutions. As they try to understand these developments and their potential impact, we're seeing them invest in blockchain. They're setting up internal teams, investing in startups, and creating common initiatives to understand the potential and search for use cases that can be implemented with minimal risk.[13]

2 Healthcare. Healthcare start-ups are analysing means to implement blockchain to share medical records in a secure way, safeguard sensitive data from breaches, and provide patients more control of and access to their information.
   – Companies are seeking to build blockchain-based healthcare solutions which can provide, for example, anonymous data sets for research organisations, and new means to defend against counterfeit drugs.
3 Food. Several organisations are analysing blockchain solutions in which industries collaborate by implementing new models for business. For example, IBM has launched a food safety solution based on blockchain with Walmart to bring together retailers, distributors, processors and growers.[14]

– By creating and sharing the permanent record of the food system, the organisation hopes it will be easy to trace products from the farm to distributors. Thus, contaminated food can be investigated quickly. Walmart and other partners now have more efficient ways to verify the food origin and provide understanding about pathways and conditions through which food products travel. Such an environment of accountability and transparency helps build trustworthy relationships with consumers. According to Andrew Conn, Director of Product Design, Emerging Technology at Salesforce,

We're going to see a lot more of this type of cross-cutting action across industries, where companies rally round blockchain technology to create a common data model that can deliver more value to the customer, I believe we'll get to a place in the near future where we'll have many different industry coalitions or 'partner ecosystems' of this type competing against each other, each with the customer at the center.[15]

When Blockchain is Good for your Business

For the blockchain defenders, there are challenges; for instance, its development has been accompanied by various levels of promotions and many analysts point out that it's not certified. Certainly, it's true that this technology would not provide a solution for each and every business problem. It requires initial research, because it's a complex technology, and knowing how to integrate it with the existing technology stacks and processes.[16]

To take advantage of the technology, companies need to understand which business problem they want to resolve and how they can use this technology to sort out the issue. Shira Rubinoff, cybersecurity and blockchain advisor, says

If companies focus on specific use cases that pertain to them and their market position, they can determine whether they should invest in the technology or not, However, companies do need to understand very precisely what problem they are looking to solve and whether blockchain is in fact the correct vehicle to get it done.[17]

Six Questions to Verify whether Blockchain is a Good Option for your Business:

1 Do you want to figure out a business issue, rather than an integration issue? Mistakenly, blockchain is seen as an integration technology, but that's not its core potential. If integration is your target, it is better to implement an API, web service, or Enterprise Service Bus (ESB).

2 Do business processes need inherent irreversibility? This is the foundational property of blockchain, so determine whether the feature would help you to achieve the objective or would inhibit it.

3 Do you want to transact value objects from one entity to another? Analyse whether immutability would benefit your business. Also, does your business need consensus? If yes, then you can get the advantage by using blockchain.

4 For business purposes, do you need to transfer information among organisations? To manage trust across different levels of organisations you can deploy blockchain. It can simplify the business process among the upstream and downstream partners.

5 Rather than targeting a few parties, do you want to stick to an ecosystem? Examine whether the issue you want to resolve significantly has two shareholders. Integration is the best way to target a handful of parties. Blockchain is the right option to target a particular ecosystem.

6 Do you have the right strategy to adopt and get engaged with partners? Without the collaborated adoption of blockchain, the impact of your business would be limited.

Research shows that 22% of IT leaders have identified blockchain applications for their organisations and are actively working on the blockchain project. Those who have already mapped the abilities of blockchain to enhance their businesses are not wasting further time.[18]
  According to Sandra Ro

> Blockchain can drive profound change across a range of industries and sectors, reimagining the way we do so many things, right now, for example, the technology is poised to disrupt how we manage health records, fight voter fraud, and distribute welfare, to name just a few areas. The possibilities are endless.[19]

Power of Trust

Even in its early days, the power of distributed ledger technology has been used to provide potential financial services.

At its core, the financial services industry needs to establish trust across multiple parties for the exchange of value. Organising the exchanges has enormous risks and responsibilities; such issues are elevated in platforms with a high volume of traffic, performing millions of critical transactions per day. Having the technology to guarantee trust among parties with no or minimal human intervention has the potential to change this sector and scale process automation.

Distributed ledger technology (DLT) delivers a combination of distributed systems and advanced cryptography, enabling the transfer of immutable data recorded on the ledger among the counterparties. This ledger avails the companies of a transformative platform to organise settlement and trade of digital assets; it helps to insure, securitise, transfer, and finance businesses.

This foundational and potential application has been growing in the marketplace; companies are exploring DLT for smooth cross-organisational partnerships, to remove the requirement of error-prone audits and to build transformative business strategy by using the real-time vision of customers.

Firms are considering enhancing DLT-powered solutions through 'smart contracts', a set of software instructions that allow business users to set terms and conditions to transfer value only when such T&Cs are agreed by all parties. This is a further step towards introducing trust in the process automation.

While trust can be misguided, blockchain is providing the ability to ensure trust over the untrusted parties, which can potentially rebuild the fundamentals of financial service providers.

Firms need to analyse DLT's core power and most impactful use cases in order to put this theory into action.

1 Corda – The technology created by R3, along with a huge alliance of financial companies, is an open-source platform granted for DLT applications. It is slightly different from the rest of the ledgers; for example, data is transferred to different points to ensure the privacy of transactions and limit viewability.

2 Quorum – As an Ethereum fork, it was developed by J.P. Morgan to fulfil the requirements of financial service-providing firms. Granted with

private and public transactions, and private transactions are required to be confirmed by all nodes without revealing the transaction details.

3 Hyperledger Fabric – Initially launched by the Linux Foundation and now sponsored by IBM and other companies. An authorised blockchain is created around modularity and flexibility. Channels manage the privacy – the chain can only choose the participants who can share and access the distributed ledger.

The Power of an Immutable Asset

Although there are several subsets of the DLT group, all with unique use cases and unique strengths, they have three major benefits:

1 Reduced risk;
2 Reduced cost; and
3 Improved customer experience.

Reduced Risk

With isolated processes and legacy technology causing resistance against complex and developing industry regulations, presently companies are struggling hard against both fraud and error. Frequently, outdated solutions usually consist of manual testing of risky tasks such as auditing and validating the trade information. Isolated data forms are quite dangerous, since a conflict may take place between the differently created versions of the original data.

Distributed ledger systems can resolve such issues. With the consensus method, the data is reunited to ensure that multiple organisations accept the agreement and smart contracts are conditionally formatted to confirm the key data sets more rapidly and dynamically than manual processing. To safeguard, real-time access to authentic data can enable the regulatory system to verify submission with high confidence.

Reduced Cost

Eradicating the major risk factors from financial service organisations saves cost in its own way; the cost of regulatory fines and fraud put a huge burden on firms.

But companies can reduce costs by eradicating the intermediary third party while dealing with multi-party processes and for value transactions by creating conditional smart contracts correctly and securely to automatically execute the transfer of assets, to avoid the involvement of intermediary monitoring. DLT's accuracy can secure the settlement payment while still working to improve the quality of risk evaluation, to efficiently boost trade-off.

Improved Customer Experience

Operations based on DLT can drive more positive experiences for customers. With a specified, verified copy of the original data, the claim can be handled efficiently and quickly, reducing the involvement time of customers, and ensuring correct disbursement.

Banks are not the only organisations that are gaining advantage by reducing the amount of fraud. DLTs safeguard data storage and collection, which keep customer data secure and is important for the current digital era.

Concepts such as digital lockers – which can keep crucial documentation while providing accessibility to limited parties – allow customers to interact with companies securely without making personal trips.

Putting Blockchain into Action

Although financial institutions are cautiously adopting the comprehensive strengths of blockchain, interest is growing in one of the major applications: digital asset transaction scenarios.

Depending on its services, an organisation may have various use cases along with the defensive supply chain of digital assets. It gives a broad range of applicability while processing asset transactions.

1　Commercial and retail banks create and issue digital assets by implementing blockchain to track processes from performance and provenance of underlying due for collateralised debt obligations (CDOs) to physical commodity flow for security.
2　Commercial banks are financed with responsibility for expanding credit for purchased assets and want to process the finance trade smoothly by

distributing a common data structure among the credit providers, KYC, and corporate customers.

3 The clearinghouse and exchange settlement for trade or post-trade is transforming the trading system into smart contracts to transfer digital assets efficiently between parties. Smart contracts verify trade terms and ownership, as log records on a blockchain are immutable.

4 For processing asset claims and insurance, brokers work with corporate customers and banks to transform the policy terms into code, to accurately collect the pertinent data to set the premium process. Due to immutability, the broker needs to adjust the premium with new information. This reduces the expenditure of corporate customers, and removes the claim processing burden and brokers' reconciliations.

5 The regulatory bank's concessions are automating and securing compliance processes that are driven out from the accurate data sources, so reduce both risks of error and cost while auditing compliance with authority such as MiFID II, Basel III, and Dodd-Frank.

Notes

1 www.microsoft.com/en-us/research/project/confidential-consortium-framework/.
2 https://news.microsoft.com/2017/08/10/microsoft-announces-the-coco-framework/.
3 Ibid.
4 Ibid.
5 https://azure.microsoft.com/en-au/blog/announcing-microsoft-s-coco-framework-for-enterprise-blockchain-networks/.
6 Ibid.
7 www.industry.gov.au/sites/default/files/2020-02/national-blockchain-roadmap.pdf, p. 6.
8 www.salesforce.com/ap/blog/2020/03/apac-what-is-blockchain-technology.html.
9 Ibid.
10 Ibid
11 See https://medium.com/coinmonks/asset-tokenization-on-blockchain-explained-in-plain-english-f4e4b5e26a6d.
12 See www.ft.com/content/69abdb66-666c-11e8-b6eb-4acfcfb08c11.
13 www.salesforce.com/ap/blog/2020/03/apac-what-is-blockchain-technology.html.

14 See www-03.ibm.com/press/us/en/pressrelease/53013.wss.

15 www.salesforce.com/ap/blog/2020/03/apac-what-is-blockchain-technology. html.

16 See https://hbr.org/2017/01/the-truth-about-blockchain?referral=03759& cm_vc=rr_item_page.bottom; https://hbr.org/2018/06/what-blockchain-cant-do.

17 See www.salesforce.com/uk/blog/2018/04/decoding-blockchain-what-it-is-and-what-it-isnt.html?d=7010M000001yv8PQAQ&nc=7010M000001yv8UQAQ.

18 www.salesforce.com/blog/enterprise-it-trends/?d=7010M000001yv8PQAQ& nc=7010M000001yv8UQAQ.

19 Sandra Ro, www.salesforce.com/ap/blog/2020/03/apac-what-is-blockchain-technology.html. See also www.zdnet.com/article/welfare-payments-in-australia-could-be-delivered-over-blockchain/; https://venturebeat.com/2016/ 10/22/blockchain-tech-could-fight-voter-fraud-and-these-countries-are-testing-it/.

Chapter 5

Governance and Security

Blockchain technology is offering promising opportunities to advance digital transformation and recreate how companies do business across the globe, including the operational challenges faced by governments. Policymakers are at the initial stage of evaluating blockchain and its powerful use cases in regulatory sectors such as transportation, healthcare, financial services, manufacturing, and retail.

As companies are rushing to analyse blockchain applications, the blockchain environment is becoming dynamic and diverse. Start-ups like Project Ubin (with the Association of Banks in Singapore and the Monetary Authority of Singapore), Digital Identity ID2020, and MiFID II Data Reconciliation (with Barclays, UBS, Credit Suisse, and others) shows how blockchain has evolved from cryptocurrency transaction technology to a wide platform for digital payment. However, it's not exempt from risks. Businesses are adopting blockchain technology to protect code and data as blockchain's architecture delivers cybersecurity features that are not available in traditional technologies and ledgers. While it can't eliminate security risks, blockchain provides benefits of in-built resistance to cyber-attacks. Before enterprises deploy blockchain, they should identify and understand the risk factors.

Blockchain Networks Security

One advantage of blockchain is its in-built flexibility to tackle cyber-attacks. While it's not protected from all types of cyber risks, the unique structure

DOI: 10.4324/9781003132592-5

of blockchain provides cybersecurity power which is not available in legacy technologies or in traditional ledgers.

- Blockchain's distributed architecture improves the resiliency of the entire network which protects it from getting exposed or compromised from a single point of failure.
- Blockchain's consensus mechanism elevates the efficiency and integrity of the overall shared ledgers because it is a prerequisite to have consensus between the participants in the network for validating the new blocks. The possibility that a hacker might corrupt the ledger is reduced.
- Participants also get to experience improved transparency on the blockchain network which makes it almost impossible to corrupt the network via malware or any other manipulative actions. The blockchain network might also contain more than a single layer of security, not only at the network level but at the individual participant level as well.
- Last but not least, the blockchain is hosted on cloud platforms like Microsoft Azure. Cloud technology offers robust cybersecurity protections because of the access controls of the platform.

There are lots of cybersecurity features present in blockchain technology which makes it quite complex for someone to tamper, compromise, or manipulate something on the network, but like any other technology, it is prone to some cybersecurity threats including those threats that occur because of human errors. Human errors can also contribute to the possibility of a cybersecurity threat and these errors include software coding errors or errors that come from faults in the information security practices of the network's participants. Blockchain technology is also prone to identity-based threats where the attackers manipulate the consensus mechanism that has been activated by establishing control over the maximum number of blockchain nodes.

In order to reduce these risks, it is necessary to employ reliable and robust cyber risk management protocols.

Types of Blockchain

When developing a cybersecurity program for blockchains, it is important to take a wide range of structural considerations into account. The records fed into the blockchain are immutable and such immutability prevents any kind of tampering. The immutability also constructs an auditable record, although special programming might be needed to restore the integrity of the blockchain if any fraudulent transaction has been introduced into the blockchain. The participants in the blockchain network have some roles and responsibilities that require an attentive governance structure for achieving an efficient balance of security and access.

So, on a broader scale, there are two types of blockchain: permissioned and public blockchains.

A public blockchain is like an Ethereum blockchain or a Bitcoin blockchain that permits an individual having technological proficiency to

- Access and view the ledger;
- Propose a new block's addition to the ledger; and
- Validate the transactions by implementing the established protocols.

An individual who has installed certain software is allowed access and can also participate in the transactions by utilising the blockchain.

The public blockchain makes use of the consensus mechanism for establishing trust between the participants who are not aware of each other's identity. However, it has more to offer, including the following:

1 **Proof-of-work**: It utilises a system of rewards for establishing constructive behaviour. This is done by requiring the participants to compete for gaining the rights that can allow them to publish the subsequent blocks by solving comprehensive puzzles and challenges.
2 **Proof-of-stake**: It utilises a system of penalties as well as the participants' amount at risk in the blockchain for evaluating the rights to publish the next blocks.

The public blockchain follows the structure of administrative governance, but it works without any central authority.

Permissioned blocks, on the other hand, restrict access to the ledger to only trusted parties or certain people who must participate by using their authentic identities only. A single party (like a private blockchain) or a consortium of companies (like a group of banks) can also develop permissioned blockchains. These blockchains are dependent upon the governance structure for controlling access, enforcing the rules and responding to incidents, including cyber-attacks.

Since there are some trust factors between the participants, the permissioned blockchains utilise less intensive or less comprehensive mechanisms. For example, a proof-of-authority model might enable the participating nodes to publish new blocks either on a rotating basis or at will, dependent on verification of supporting rights. Traditional features for security can be incorporated in the permissioned blockchain, such as a cloud platform which controls accessibility and manages security features which are customised for a specific blockchain.

From a cybersecurity perspective, both permissioned and public blockchains have favourable characteristics, along with a consensus mechanism, encryption and ledger distribution. The blockchain depends upon the deployed encryption at various points of the network. First, the accessibility rights of participants are controlled by engaging private/public key encryption. Second, in the blocks, the transactional data is encrypted with a cryptographic hash mechanism. Third, with the help of cryptographic hash functions, the data blocks are linked together in chronological order, thus the ties of the data block with the earlier and consequent blocks are secure and attempts to tamper with the data in the blocks would alter the hash values. Thus, cryptographic hashing defends against any change in the data within the blocks without changing the history of all chained data blocks. Because of this type of encryption, attackers need to change the whole blockchain in order to target a specific transaction.

Blockchain Protection

Earlier we identified that blockchain network features have various abilities to reduce the risks to cybersecurity; they can identify, prevent and withstand various kinds of cyber-attacks that mostly target financial institutions.

Distributed architecture: The permissioned blockchain has distributed architecture which minimises the cyber-attack's effect. The distributed network has implicit operational resilience features as single-point failure is not possible here.

Consensus validation system: The consensus system consistently checks the integrity of all transactions over the ledger and validates the new data in blocks.

Encryption: The accessibility rights of participants are secured with private/public key encryption or a cryptographic asymmetric key. The linked blocks are encrypted through a combination of digital signatures and cryptographic hashing.

Transparency: Blockchain offers transparency between the participants that makes it tough for hackers to release malware within the network in order to gather information or to transmit data to another database handled by a hacker.

Still, risks exist.

External data and endpoint risk: Only the information ingested and consumed by blockchain is secure. The traditional off-chain system from where the transactional data is taken to construct representational data on the blockchain is not necessarily secure. Importing such information from the off-chain system may cause endpoint risk. The connection between the external world and on-chain data is represented by cryplets, maintaining integrity on the blockchain network.

Identity-based attacks: These have the ability to take over all the network nodes and can disable the distributed system protection and consensus validation in the network. This risk factor can be reduced by using a trusted cloud-based multi-tenant directory and management service to certify people's identities.

Quantum computing: Quantum computing is a long-term risk, gaining attention in industry as it attacks the computational power and compromises or weakens the cryptographic algorithms being used on blockchains and IT systems. Before adopting security protocols, update them to ensure the viability and success of the network.

When a technology emerges in the industry it naturally brings hidden risk factors. However, the companies operating on the blockchain are led by blockchain developers who are working with start-ups and seasoned industrial veterans.

Regardless of personal experience or company size, blockchain developers who are developing financial solutions for the industry need to conduct development and design with high sophistication to avoid security threats.

Developers must incorporate Security Design or Security Development Life Cycle (SDLC) principles and must integrate these principles into their working culture. The hardened libraries and security controls can be used to safeguard critical information regarding code, software and testing. To satisfy the SDLC standards, the blockchain code must undergo and pass rigid QA testing; to verify the security process, the security control of the application must be tested before launch and execute security testing by identifying and fixing bugs.

The intensity and complexity of cyber threats are continuously evolving; blockchain-like technologies can help withstand the risk from cyber threats and can protect the sensitive information of consumers and the integrity of IT systems. Blockchains offer cybersecurity characteristics and have similar risk factors which impact IT systems and have exclusive features, which help to evaluate industry and regulators.

In-Built Security

The distributed structure of a blockchain system favours business continuity and in-built security in the network itself by removing single points of failure. The peer-to-peer type of network delivers redundancy naturally in nodes. An exact copy of data and code is shared with each and every node, and as long as a node is up, it will execute business continuously.

A distributed and decentralised system doesn't go without its challenges, specifically in data and code synchronisation among all nodes involved. A consensus mechanism for the digital ledger is adopted to enhance the overall integrity and robustness of distributed information. To validate data in new blocks it is necessary to reach consensus to reduce hacker interruption or manipulation of data shared in nodes by compromised network contributors.

The blockchain participants are also provided with improved transparency, which makes it difficult to corrupt transactions through manipulative actions or malware. Finally, with cloud platform-hosting blockchains, like Amazon AWS, the IBM cloud, or Microsoft Azure, the access control, malware shields, anti-virus software and traffic management provide greater protection against cyber-attacks.

However, although blockchain technology has various in-built cybersecurity advantages, like other technologies it is still subject to many security risks, along with the risks due to human errors, including coding errors in the software of smart contracts, participants flaws in security practices, or lack of encryption key and identity protection. Identity-based cyber-attacks may seize control of the majority of nodes in a blockchain network, thus corrupting the consensus mechanism. To reduce these risks some cautious cyber-risk practices are required.

Table 5.1   Terminology

Term	Link
Distributed networking	https://en.wikipedia.org/wiki/Distributed_networking
Cloud computing	https://en.wikipedia.org/wiki/Cloud_computing

Table 5.2   Learn more

Title	Author	Link
What is Distributed Networking?	The Audiopedia	www.youtube.com/watch?v=moHwispmzUo

The blockchain network has distributed topology which provides resistance to cyber-attacks and business consistency. Transparency makes corruption of code or data difficult, and the vendor's security is provided by the public cloud host.

Before getting further into the chapter, it is recommended to understand the concepts in Table 5.1 and Table 5.2.

Typical Security Traits

When considering the protection of data and source code stored in the blockchain, critically the blockchain network topology must be considered. In permissioned blockchains, accessibility to the digital ledger is limited to certain trusted people, whose identity is verified up front. Public blockchains like Ethereum and Bitcoin permit everyone to join the network and contribute to transactions. Anyone having general software can access the network and can validate transactions of blocks in the blockchain. Thus, permissioned blockchain provides better access to control and governance than public blockchain. This blockchain network topology is evolved in private contexts or as an output of a deal between the alliance of different parties who are known to each other. When the participant identity is known then it becomes easy to impose security features on all contributors, like privileged roles and access control like transaction validators.

Permissioned blockchain delivers enhanced protection of data and code, but in public blockchains, there are some security aspects that are applied to the network topology.

- Blockchains are added with blocks that are immutable. Immutability resists record auditing or tampering.
- Participants' responsibilities and roles also include governance of the system, whether it is achieved through common consent by proof of work in public blockchains or for forming sustainable consensus in the network of permissioned blockchain.
- In addition to consensus and immutability, in a cybersecurity context both permissioned and public blockchains allow the sharing of data, code and various encryption forms.
- By using the asymmetric cryptographic public/private key pair the participants are managed. The transactional data in blocks is hashed and blocks are chained in sequence by referring to the consequent block. Thus, the entire chain becomes immutable, as any alteration in data in a block would change the hash value, and the whole sequence of blocks will be altered. Thus one needs to modify all the hash values recorded in the entire blockchain. Practically, this is an impossible mission!

There are three blockchain types, private, public, and consortium. Accessibility depends upon permissioned or permissionless, which depends upon the way identities of users are managed.

Before getting further into the chapter, understand the concepts in Table 5.3 and Table 5.4.

Table 5.3　Terminology

Term	Link
Blockchains and distributed ledger technologies	www.google.com/url?sa=D&q=https://blockchainhub.net/blockchains-and-distributed-ledger-technologies-in-general/&ust=1604562240000000&usg=AOvVaw1g2e21A1KqJaktiMn8tWFM&hl=en
Types of blockchain	https://devopedia.org/types-of-blockchains

Table 5.4　Learn more

Title	Author	Link
Different Types of Blockchains Explained	Blackwolf	www.youtube.com/watch?v=EiPQWJsLPPk
Public vs Private Blockchain – Bitcoin and Ethereum vs HyperLedger and Quorum	Altcoin Buzz	www.youtube.com/watch?v=NIPTUVIrU7M

Determine Cyber-Attacks

As explained earlier, blockchain systems provide in-built features to reduce cybersecurity risks and to avoid cyber-attacks.

As mentioned, the risk still exists. Attacks based on identity can impact overall major nodes of a network and threaten the consensus validation. This risk factor can be reduced by using a trusted cloud-based multi-tenant directory and management service to certify a person's identity. Businesses don't manage data and code in isolation in the blockchain network. The third-party endpoints and data from external sources are also risk factors, as only the information ingested and consumed by blockchain is secured.

A risk of corrupted data exists with 'off-chain' systems, which provide external data necessary to validate transactions, for example, customer documents, records, orders, invoices, addresses, etc.

Technology like oracles and confidential computing are solutions that are growing as trusted platforms to connect the external world to on-chain data, providing mandatory information integrity on blockchain networks. In the future, quantum computing will be used to improve the computational platform to negotiate the presently used cryptographic algorithm on blockchain platforms.

To adapt the cryptographic systems' security protocols, it must be upgraded with the latest technology to defend the network adequately.

The intensity and complexity of cyber threats are evolving continually. Blockchains deliver significant protection for cybersecurity, with some features being unique in this technology. Businesses are attracted by the in-built security protection features that blockchain networks offer, and are keener to migrate existing systems to blockchain-based solutions to improve their security.

Cybersecurity risks impact IT systems and apply to blockchains networks also, as they're not protected from denial of services, code vulnerabilities, or data or funds theft. It is important to identify these critical challenges. The common range of cyber-attacks on blockchain networks includes:

■ Malware or malicious software compromises data or code, by placing corrupted software or information on a network.
■ Attacks that target the software application execution in order to grab sensitive information, like authentication credentials.

■ Denial of Service (DoS) attacks that generate a huge volume of data and traffic to targeted applications in order to overload the system to disrupt the operations permanently or temporarily.

■ Man-in-the-middle attack means an unauthorised party is introduced in between the trusted party and the user to intercept or steal the data.

■ Ransomware attacks, which block the access of institutions to their own data unless the owner pays the hackers.

■ Keys theft to seize access to the encrypted data. The majority of blockchain attacks are executed to steal the cryptographic keys from the participants of the network and mostly don't attack the blockchain network itself.

Learn the key concepts of different kinds of cybersecurity threats, consisting of external data sources and endpoints, identity-based attacks, cryptographic key thefts, ransomware or denial of service, software inefficiencies and vulnerabilities, information theft, and man-in-middle attacks.

Before getting further into the chapter, please get familiar with the concepts in Table 5.5 and Table 5.6.

Table 5.5   erminology

Term	Link
Cryptography	https://en.wikipedia.org/wiki/Cryptography
Denial-of-service attack	https://en.wikipedia.org/wiki/Denial-of-service_attack
Ransomware	https://en.wikipedia.org/wiki/Ransomware
Multi-factor authentication	https://en.wikipedia.org/wiki/Multi-factor_authentication

Table 5.6   Learn more

Title	Author	Link
Real-World Blockchain Applications – Cybersecurity	Blockgeeks	www.youtube.com/watch?v=WvrmgR5gpvA
Quick Look: Blockchain for Cybersecurity – Microsegmented Network Access Control	RSA Conference	www.youtube.com/watch?v=vkrZxRZnu0A

Network Protection

Notwithstanding the significant in-built cybersecurity features of blockchain, efficient cybersecurity programs are important to protect the network and companies from cyber threats. The list in Table 5.7 includes the recommendation for protecting organisations from cybersecurity risks and all possible ways to safeguard the blockchain network.

Table 5.7   Cybersecurity risk protection recommendations

Cybersecurity Risk	Protection Recommended
Identity-based attacks	The trusted cloud-based directory, as well as identity management services, can help to reduce the risk. The identity management service certifies the personal identity of individuals who want to participate in the blockchain network. The service is able to identify any threat entity trying to take unauthorised control over the nodes on the network. A multi-factor authentication system if used will add an extra layer of security during the authentication procedure.
External data sources and endpoints	The blockchain network is secure as long as the information has been ingested and consumed within it. If an interaction has been made with an external system, then it would pose the threat of data corruption, but this can be minimised if only a small amount of data has been fed into the digital ledger along with the maintenance of the complete records in off-chain line-of-business systems. A level of trust is provided by oracles in the external data sources which are not liable to any consensus validation of the blockchain platform. Confidential computing is another smart solution that provides a better guarantee of the data quality that can be encrypted at any stage, and before joining the blockchain network, the data is validated.
Cryptographic key theft	It is essential to maintain confidentiality, integrity, trust and availability of crypto keys for accessing the data in the blockchain. The requirement to protect the nodes, as well as their identities in the network, can be fulfilled by a robust key management service.

(continued)

Table 5.7 Continued

Cybersecurity risk protection recommendations

Cybersecurity Risk	Protection Recommended
Software vulnerabilities and inefficiencies	Human errors in coding can bring cybersecurity risks to the blockchain network. There is no software in the IT industry that is completely free from all kinds of defects and any defect can generate a path to compromise and jeopardise the smart contracts in the blockchain network. ISO/IEC 27034-1:2011 has outlined the principles for secure software development life cycle that are appropriate because they explain the implementation of security through: • Design principles. • Reliable quality assurance program. • Robust security testing. • Ignorance of coding processes that have been rushed. • Production schedules are important for minimising defects in coding.
Denial of service or ransomware	In order to have robust protection from ransomware threats and DoS, it is best to have the blockchain network hosted in a public cloud network because cloud service providers offer built-in monitoring and control of traffic, protection from viruses, and filtering of malicious packets at the firewall level.
Man-in-the-middle and information theft attacks	The robust protection of the data exchanged between the parties can be achieved if the data at rest, in memory, and in transit has been encrypted while in use by the application. An extra layer of security is added through confidential computing because it detects and authorises the parties that were involved in the information exchange, and defending the code as well as data in a reliable and honest execution environment that is completely encrypted and cannot be accessed by any external system like an operating system, cloud host, or hardware.

Blockchain network cyber-threat prevention is not significantly different from regular network security protocols including

- Identity management;
- Secure software development practices; and
- DoS protection.

So, before you proceed further with this chapter, it is advisable to heck your knowledge and understanding of the topics in Table 5.8 and Table 5.9.

Table 5.8   Terminology

Term	Link
Identity management	https://en.wikipedia.org/wiki/Identity_management
Confidential computing	https://azure.microsoft.com/en-au/blog/introducing-azure-confidential-computing/
Blockchain oracles	https://blockchainhub.net/blockchain-oracles/

Table 5.9   Learn more

Title	Author	Link
Confidential Computing	Microsoft Research	www.youtube.com/watch?v=SUS3Zzko3eM
What is Blockchain Oracle?	George Levy	www.youtube.com/watch?v=S_1cWBWsS_I

Table 5.10   Learn more

Title	Author	Link
Using Blockchain Technology to Boost Cyber Security	Yuliia Horbenko	https://steelkiwi.com/blog/using-blockchain-technology-to-boost-cybersecurity/
Can Blockchain Fix Cybersecurity?	Maria Korolov	www.datacenterknowledge.com/security/can-blockchain-fix-cybersecurity

Conclusion

The evolution of blockchain technology continues, but at the same time it is necessary for cybersecurity controls (that help to eliminate security risks) to also evolve at the same pace. The operation, deployment and architecture of a blockchain affect the in-built cybersecurity risks of networks and regulate the controls and position them to resist cyber-attacks.

Key elements to be considered are the types and number of participants over the network; the diverse trustless identities that can contribute in-network; the power of encryption protocols, consisting of design, robust process of consensus validation, cryptographic hash mechanism; the range of assimilation with the external data; sensitivity of transactions or records in the digital ledger; and the ability to pinpoint malicious, erroneous and fraudulent data and code.

Table 5.11 Additional resources

#	Title	Link
1	ISO/IEC 27034-1:2011	www.iso.org/standard/44378.html
2	Digital Identity ID2020	https://blogs.microsoft.com/blog/2018/01/22/partnering-for-a-path-to-digital-identity/
3	MiFID II Data Reconciliation	www.google.com/url?sa=D&q=https://www.ubs.com/global/en/about_ubs/media/global/releases/news_display_media_global.html/en/2017/12/11/news-release-MiFID-II.html&ust=1604630400000000&usg=AOvVaw1nqAus9QMcKtMdc3gXt25G&hl=en
4	Project Ubin	www.mas.gov.sg/schemes-and-initiatives/project-ubin

The application of cybersecurity controls and principles, derived from industry regulations and guidance, for the blockchain system is important for an effective cybersecurity system. The final summary includes the following controls and principles.

1 Control access to the information systems: involve controls for authenticating and authorising access and the contribution of individuals in network activities.
2 Software developers conduct threat modelling to analyse threats and place mitigation action properly to reduce risk.
3 Encryption of documents: any digital asset and records, while data is in transit form, at rest, or in use by external applications and smart contracts.
4 Methodologies and systems detect actual and attempted attacks or intrusion in the blockchain system, involving system detection powered by machine learning.
5 The software development life-cycle application is implemented for secure practice which adheres to the industry's recommendation for protection against cybercrimes.
6 Regular audit practice is executed to evaluate cybersecurity risk administration, law compliance, corporate policies and regulations.
7 Responsive programs that determine actions to be executed when doubtful action is detected, along with data leakage, unauthorised access and code execution.

The application of all cybersecurity standards and instructions will protect the blockchain from any cyber-attacks.

Chapter 6

The Convergence of IoT, AI and Blockchain

What is the status of blockchain today? In PwC's survey of 600 executives across 15 territories in 2018, 84% of them mentioned that their organisations are involved with blockchain technology.[1] Companies are experimenting in the lab; maybe they are developing concept proofs. No one wants to be left behind; everyone is discussing blockchain.

It's easy to understand why. Being a damage-proof ledger, well-designed, and distributed blockchain cuts off intermediaries, increases speed, reduces costs, and enhances reach. It also offers traceability and transparency for several business strategies. Gartner determined that blockchain will produce annual business worth more than US$3 trillion by 2030. By the same year 10–20% of the global economy will operate based on blockchain-based systems.[2]

How Blockchain Is Developing Business

There are various indications that blockchain is essentially changing the business landscape. Here are a few significant business shifts:

- Tokenisation – the virtual or real asset represented on blockchain – is expanding to finished goods, raw materials, membership rights, income-producing securities, and much more. Now everything you do for businesses can be represented by blockchain.

DOI: 10.4324/9781003132592-6

■ Initial coin offerings (ICOs), where an organisation sells a fixed number of digital tokens in public, are channelling billions of dollars within blockchain platforms. It is a classic alternative for capital funding provided by private banks, equity firms, and venture capital; in the first five months of 2018, ICOs were able to raise US$13.7 billion. To date, the largest ICOs have been very different to each other, and included EOS.io, a blockchain protocol based on the namesake cryptocurrency EOS; Hdac Tech, an internet of things platform backed by Hyundai; and Huobi Token, a South Korean crypto coin for exchange.

■ Enterprise software systems, which are potential tools for organisation operations such as human resources, customer relationship management, and finance, have started integrating blockchain. For example, Oracle, Salesforce, and SAP have all declared their blockchain initiatives. In the future, most of the core business will be incorporated and executed on blockchain platforms. Using blockchain technology to plan for enterprise resources will allow organisations to execute processes smoothly, enhance data integrity and simplify data sharing.

■ New territory and new industry leaders are emerging. In 2017, Gartner found that 82% of blockchain applications were reported for financial services, but by 2018, the use cases in this sector dropped to 46%. The respondents of the PwC survey still see financial services to be the future or current driver of blockchain, but also need to check the potential of industrial products, utilities, energy and healthcare. Moreover, the business centre of gravity is shifting in Europe and the US. According to the PwC survey, presently the US is most advanced in blockchain development, but within 3–5 years China will be the leader.[3]

What Is Holding Blockchain Back?

Blockchain development becomes more difficult when intermediate parties participate. For example, a multinational company builds blockchain to administer the intercompany process for treasury management and transactions. The organisation might be struggling with multiple enterprise resource planning (ERP) systems, processes and inconsistent data. Instead of implementing a central ledger for each and every subsidiary, a distributed single ledger would eradicate the requirement of settlement. Companies are analysing how they can use digital tokens to represent other assets and cash to streamline the transactions of units within the business. Instead of wasting time with bank transfers, emailing each transaction, and currency conversions, they can conduct a tokenised transfer in real-time through smart contracts, and enable users to track the transactions.

No doubt, a company developing a blockchain itself has to confront problems relevant to data harmonisation, internal buy-in and scale. Still, the company can impose a set of rules of the blockchain; the same can be done with an ERP system. Generally, companies which are investing in blockchain technology for themselves will not realise much return on investment. The benefits can be best derived when different industrial participants get together to work on a shared platform. When third parties are invited to engage in business then an individual can't decide on the rules themselves.

PwC survey respondents raised concerns such as lack of trust between the users (45%), regulatory uncertainty (48%) and strength to bring together networks (44%). All these issues are presenting obstacles for blockchain adoption.

Why It's Tough to Believe Blockchain

According to the blockchain definition, it should induce trust. In reality, organisations are encountering trust issues for every process. The user needs to have confidence in the technology itself. For every growing technology, doubts and challenges exist across blockchain speed, reliability, scalability and security. There are concerns about the potential lack of control and standardisation with other blockchains. The trust gap in the blockchain is because of a lack of understanding.

Right now, most executives are not clear what blockchain is, and it's changing all facets of business. However, it's a use case that has gone beyond Bitcoin; even the current hype and focus across ICOs refer only to the potential conflict. Blockchain is playing the role of mutual change agent – as a new means of digitising assets into tokens, as a new infrastructure form, consisting of cryptocurrency – it's not easy to explain. With other emerging technologies, users can see a drone flying or try goggles to see virtual reality. But blockchain is a technically abstract phenomenon behind the scenes. Building trustworthy relationships in the blockchain network is a challenge. Maybe it's ironic that the technology is built to reach a consensus for design standards and rules.

Take payment mechanisms and systems in banking. In the existing system, everyone is running the system by rules, but they don't agree with how blockchain-based alternative models should be created and operated. Particularly, there is a lack of regulation on how different blockchain networks interoperate with each other. Most of the regulators are still approaching terms and conditions of cryptocurrency and blockchain. Many sectors have started studying and reviewing the problems, specifically regarding financial services, but the comprehensive regulatory ecosystem is still unsettled.

You have selected your doctor because she has a similar interest in technology and does not disappoint at all. She also has a brand new AI-inspired assistant, and the smart assistant is proficiently trained enough to accumulate a huge amount of medical periodical data to date. An AI can do this job easily but not a human. The doctor cannot remember the millions of data points but her AI assistant can. The doctor will not be able to stay up to date with the latest medical breakthroughs and discoveries but the AI assistant can.

When I was at my last medical check-up, I reported to the doctor a back pain issue. With the help of the AI assistant's advice, the doctor prescribed me back pain relief medicine from Big Pharma. The AI also noted that my blood pressure was on the higher side as compared to the previous year and prescribed hypertension pills from Big Pharma on that analysis.

Now at this point, I had started wondering who rendered the training modules and data for the neural network that helped train the AI assistant. Was it the pharmaceutical company – Big Pharma? If this company was the only one that was providing the training data to the AI assistant, then I would have some doubts regarding the objectivity of smart AI based on the assistant. Why should you believe in the data sourcing from any AI bot without gathering knowledge about the authenticity and integrity of the training data?

You wouldn't be blamed for thinking that the example is a little bit over the top. The example is over-construed, but what I am trying to explain here is that we should all think more about the amount of trust and faith that we invest in data these days, especially when we think from the perspective of IoT, AI and Cloud lens. How can we put faith in the data that has been generated via IoT sensor readings, AI-based recommendations and various other sources?

In this chapter, a detailed insight has been provided about how blockchain can improve the implementation of the latest technologies like Cloud, AI and IoT by filling the gap of a missing factor of trust so that enterprises can understand and implement the use of this technology in operations at a wider scale. On the other hand, the blockchain business network also has the advantage when implementing this technology into modern platforms based on blockchain and applications. It is a win-win situation.

Blockchain and Artificial Intelligence Together

Two technologies, blockchain and AI, are on the bucket list of almost every Chief Information Officer out there because these two technologies can form a powerful duo to re-shape industries. These two technologies bring a lot of influential benefits, but they also have some challenges when it comes to the adoption of these technologies. It is also not wrong to say that all the information about these modern-day technologies might not yet be known, and as such, the idea of combining AI and blockchain may be understood by some people as brewing an advanced version of IT pixie dust which would be something to look forward to. However, there is a practical way also to think about this collaboration as a sensible and efficient blend.

Currently, AI is ready to serve the objective of establishing a robust centralised process. The end-user should have trust in the central authority for providing a trusted business result.

Blockchain can serve the trust as well as the confidence of the users if the following three important elements of AI are decentralised:

■ Data
■ Models
■ Analytics

By decentralising these three elements, users will have the trust and confidence that they need to completely adopt and use the business processes based on AI. Now, let's have a further look into how blockchain is determined to escalate AI by providing data, analytics and models.

Your Data Belongs to You

Most of the leading and remarkable AI technology services across the globe are centralised, such as Facebook, Amazon, Apple, Google, Alibaba, etc. However, all of them have faced certain challenges with the element of trust among their target user base, who are excited about this technology but at the same time are also cautious. The question is, how can an enterprise provide assurance to the audience that its AI model has not crossed the boundaries?

Assume that such AI services are capable of providing a 'forensic report' that has been verified by an independent third party so that it can be proved to the users how and when the users' data is being used once such data has been ingested into the system. It can be further imagined that the data can be used only if the users have provided permission.

The blockchain ledger system can also be put to use for fulfilling the needs of digital rights management. The users' data would be licensed to the providers of AI under their own terms and conditions. The ledger would serve the purpose of an access management system where it will store the evidence and permissions through which a business would be able to use the users' data.

Trusted and Reliable AI Models

Let's take an example where blockchain is being used as a means to render trusted data and training models for machine learning. In this instance, a fictitious case could be created that would answer the question whether a fruit is a banana or an apple. The system of question and answering that we develop is recognised as a model and this model has been developed through the process known as training. The objective of training is to build a precise model that would answer the queries correctly most of the time. To train a model, we would need to accumulate the data to train on. That data could be anything such as the colour of the fruit (in the form of light's wavelength) or sugar content (in the form of percentage).

With the help of blockchain, you will be able to track the origin and source of the training data. You will also be able to see the audit trails of the proof by which the prediction was made whether a specific fruit is labelled as an apple versus a banana. An enterprise can also provide evidence that it is not 'mixing up' the books by marking the fruit more often as an apple if that fruit is the more expensive of the two.

Elaborating AI Decisions

A law has been adopted by the European Union which requires that if any decision has been made by machines, then the same should be readily explained. Failure to do so will attract various penalties and fines that could cost enterprises billions of dollars. The European Union GDPR (General Data Protection Regulation) has included a right that allows collecting explanations in regard to the decisions that have been made by the machine or algorithm. The enterprise also has the right to leave out some algorithmic decisions altogether made by the AI.

A huge amount of data is produced every second. This data is more than the human's ability to assess and use as the foundation for drawing relevant conclusions. But AI applications have the ability to assess and analyse extensive data sets along with many variables while connecting those variables with their relevant tasks and objectives. As such, AI continues to be accepted in multiple industries as well as applications, and many entities are relying upon the outcomes that the technology has to offer, although it is important that any decision that has been made by AI is verified for authentication by humans.

Blockchain is capable of establishing a clarification about the origin, understanding, transparency and explanations of the outcomes as well as decisions provided by AI. If the outcomes and decisions of AI are recorded through the transactions on the blockchain, then the in-built characteristics of the blockchain make the auditing of such outcomes or data points much simpler. Blockchain technology is an important medium that can introduce the trust element to the transactions in the network. Hence, the application of blockchain technology into the AI decision-making process could be the core element required for establishing the transparency necessary to completely trust the outcomes and decisions produced by AI.

Blockchain and the Internet of Things

There are billions of intelligent and connected devices that are part of the internet of things (IoT) today. The anticipated rise of billions more devices puts us at the threshold of a revolution and change across the electronics industry as well as other areas.

With the progress and growth in IoT, various industries are now capable of collecting data, drawing insights from such data, and then making smart decisions based on the analysis of such data. Hence, a lot of trust is placed on the information collected. However, the truth that needs to be investigated is where such data has been sourced from, and should we rely upon such data (that has not been validated yet) to make decisions and execute transactions?

For example, does the weather data honestly originate from the censor in the Pacific Ocean, or did the shipping container not exceed the agreed limit of temperature? There are lots of IoT use cases but all of them have the common issue of trust and reliability. This is where blockchain can help.

If blockchain and IoT collaborate, then real trust can be incorporated in the collected data. The core idea is to provide the devices with an identity (at the time of their development) that can be validated throughout the lifecycle of such devices via blockchain technology.

There is a lot of potential and a bright future for IoT in the capabilities of the blockchain ecosystem that are dependent upon the device identity protocol as well as reputation systems. The device identity protocol can allow each device to have a public blockchain key of its own and transmit the response messages as well as an encrypted challenge to other devices. As such, it is guaranteed that the device stays within the control of its assigned identity. Along with that, a device that has an identity can create a history that can be easily tracked by blockchain technology.

The business logic of blockchain is represented through smart contracts and whenever a transaction is proposed, then such smart contracts would be executed automatically within the regulations and guidelines that have been established by the network. Smart contracts can play an important role by rendering automated coordination as well as authorisation for the transactions. The underlying idea behind IoT was to offer the data and collect actionable information at a suitable time.

For example, the concept of smart home is a modern-day innovation and almost anything can be connected to it. If something goes wrong with IoT, then the IoT devices would still be able to execute actions like ordering a new component. There is a need to administer and manage the actions that have been executed by IoT devices and this need can be fulfilled easily by smart contracts.

In a continuing experiment in Brooklyn, New York, there is a community making use of blockchain to feed and record the generation of solar energy which allows buying the surplus credits of renewable energy. Residents own a device which has an in-built identity and it is used to create a reputation with the help of its history of records and exchange. With the help of blockchain, people will be able to accumulate their purchasing power more easily, distribute their maintenance burden, and have trust that actual solar production is being recorded by the devices.

As IoT is evolving along with its growing adoption, it will become essential to independently manage the devices as well as actions executed by such devices. Smart contracts and blockchain together will be able to apply such capabilities to IoT.

New Technology's Nexus

Blockchain technology is at the nexus of other modern-day technologies like AI, Cloud and IoT. Blockchain has the capability of bringing the missing factor of trust which these other modern-day technologies lack. It should be noted that the only way to gain trust is through the users' diversity.

As opposed to the databases that have only a single administrator, blockchain technology allows incorporating a diverse set of administrators for 'management and observation' of the data so that no single administrator can purposely or accidentally alter or delete the data. Once the administrators have arrived at a consensus, then the data is secured within the blocks that are linked to one another. Thereby, a tamper-resistant ledger is formed.

When modern-day technologies like IoT, AI and Cloud make use of blockchain for tracing the origins, permissions and proofs associated with the data used and issued from the systems, then the element of trust in the data is rapidly scaled. This trust factor makes it possible for AI, IoT and Cloud to be accepted without any danger of information being compromised. As a result, a new age of the application and adoption of such technologies is underway to influence the daily lives of people for the better.

'In data we trust … well, after you add a little blockchain', as said by Jerry Cuomo, IBM Fellow and vice president blockchain technologies at IBM, is correct in every essence.[4]

However, we should know that not every organisation is ready to take advantage of the benefits that blockchain technology has to offer. Hence, let's have a look at some of the trends that will continue to impact blockchain and many other similar technologies.

We need to first accept the fact that blockchain technology is one of the most sustained technologies in the last five years. As the value of this technology continues to rise, there would be a sense of frustration for it measured by many factors. One such factor is the belief that blockchain technology is a universal solution to a variety of problems in various industries.

There have been many early pilot projects, that were too centred on reflecting the validity of the blockchain. However, current projects are analysing the implementation of blockchain technology for solving vital problems and add value to services delivered by businesses. Instead of investigating whether the technology will work or not, people have begun to ask the right question: 'What can be done to make blockchain technology work for me?'

The Shift of Blockchain Development towards Practical Applications

When blockchain technology first came into this world, its use was primarily focused on the cryptocurrency ecosystem. It is not a wrong approach to technology, but it is not beneficial to many enterprises and businesses.

Organisations have started to see a more practical path for adopting blockchain-based solutions instead of just cryptocurrency use. Some industries have already started to embrace this technology so that they can take the maximum benefit of this approach.

There are several industries like healthcare insurance, banking, logistics and many more that are observing the implementation of this technology for a plethora of practical uses. Some of the useful and practical applications of blockchain technology include

■ Shipment tracking
■ Data security
■ Record keeping

However, often these uses or solutions are not blockchain technology but centralised databases.

Acceptance of Technology will Continue to Rise

Fintech enterprises across the globe were the first ones to adopt blockchain technology for cryptocurrencies. However, later on, it was realised that the technology has a lot more to offer to this world besides just digital currencies. The technology has started to gain relevance and be implemented in a number of industries because such industries have discovered the practical use case for a technology that can be used in various forms.

Blockchain technology has been used as the foundation for the development of tamper-proof clearing and settlement systems. The technology has an application in smart contracts and is also used for accelerating digital transactions.

The agricultural field is an area that has been successful in adopting blockchain technology to its advantage. The use of blockchain technology has also been observed in logistics and supply chains for tracking the origin of the material, information and various other resources.

The medical industry has also used blockchain technology to establish data transparency in the record-keeping process. Many other industries are navigating the practical uses of this technology so that they can improve their services.

The Expected Rise in Employment

An extensive range of applications and rapidly growing diversification will provide employment opportunities for developers. The number of corporations taking advantage of blockchain technology is increasing and because of this, the demand for developers is expected to rise exponentially.

In the current job market, employment in the blockchain industry is one of the fastest-growing fields. Even the freelance market has recognised blockchain, increasing the demand for skills in this technology.

Stablecoins to Gain More Prestige?

Investors and consumers all across the globe are searching for an alternative investment not having the same volatility as bitcoin. The search can end at stablecoins. There are many countries that are making necessary investments and conducting comprehensive research and development for making their own stablecoin.

As stablecoins increase, it will become necessary for many regulatory bodies to develop certain guidelines important for cryptocurrencies.

Government Agencies to Integrate Blockchain into Operations

Data management is not a challenge only for private-sector establishments. All those government agencies and bodies that are required to administer an extensive amount of information will find the solutions based on blockchain technology an attractive option.

The data systems that are currently being used by government agencies and bodies are distinct from each other, hence, implementing the blockchain-based solution will be very useful in simplifying the operations of government.

In 2020, the Department of Industry, Science, Energy and Resources of Australia published the National Blockchain Roadmap[5] to define the country's progress towards a blockchain-empowered future. The roadmap sets out a strategy for governments, industry and the academic world to capitalise on opportunities and address challenges. The roadmap not only identifies the current and future opportunities for blockchain but also proposes signposts towards a blockchain-inspired future, by describing a number of businesses applying blockchain, including agricultural supply chains, trusted credentials in the education sector, and transferable financial checks. Stefano Tempesta, one of the authors of this book, was a member of the working committee on the application of blockchain technology to digital identity and credentials.

A key outcome of this paper is the realisation that Australia has the ability to capitalise on the current potential of blockchain. The learning from investment in blockchain projects in recent years can be extended domestically and internationally, and can be summarised as having the following fundamentals in place:

- Effective, efficient and appropriate regulation and standards;
- The skills and capabilities to drive innovation; and
- Strong international investment and collaboration.

Getting these basics right for Australia's maturing blockchain industry – as well as for any other country which wants to follow a similar trajectory – will ensure Australia is well positioned to take advantage of the valuable business opportunities and the jobs and growth this technology can enable.

As with any emerging, disruptive technology – the paper goes on – blockchain and its uses will need regulatory frameworks that are fit for purpose. Challenges include obtaining and maintaining trust among parties, ensuring the security and integrity of data inside blockchain systems, and identifying participants with a balance of privacy and transparency. The paper also advocates for tech-neutrality, that is, ensuring that no single technology player has monopoly or preference over government blockchain systems. A final issue is making sure that smart contracts obtain legal status recognition, a topic that we've already touched on in Chapter 3 of this book.

More About Supply Chains

It would be good if the entire supply chain had the information quickly available for use by manufacturers, supply chain designers and procurement to improve the productivity of their processes and reduce the risk of supply chain breakdown. The implementation of blockchain technology will promote a system rich with benefits like

- Transparency
- Visible supply chain
- Effectiveness and productivity

However, it is important to have the capacity planning to ensure the success of any manufacturing operation. Capacity planning is a process in which the production capacity required by a factory to fulfil the dynamic demands of its target users is determined. The variation between the demands of the consumers and the production capacity of enterprise results in incompetency.

It happens because of unfulfilled deliveries that lead to dissatisfied and unhappy customers. The objective of capacity planning is to reduce such problems for manufacturing entities. In order to raise the use of the manufacturing systems' capacity, it is important to evaluate the overall equipment effectiveness (OEE).

Most companies collect OEE through manual methods which are not appropriate because it leads to poor data that further affects the decision-making process. However, with the coming of the industrial internet of things (IIoT), it will become much easier to monitor machine performance. It will also become easy to analyse the environmental changes and navigate the opportunities that can help to improve OEE. The advancements of the cyber-security in IIoT software and hardware merged with cloud computing have allowed this technology to act as a secure and reliable solution. It will also help to calculate manufacturing unit capacity in real time to achieve more effective planning. Customers will also be able to change their production requirements either in the upward or downward flow within a matter of a few seconds and immediately observe the effects on delivery dates.

However, this also means that the AI system would be able to use the data for planning the manufacturing cycles and routing of components on the basis of the machining capability and capacity of the manufacturer. As a result, one order will be spread over different suppliers if the delivery is needed urgently.

Developing an innovative platform that would combine various technologies like blockchain, AI and smart contracts will eliminate all resistance to a production system that can be scaled up instantly for meeting any production requirements.

Dynamic Supply Chains

The use of a transparent and decentralised smart contract system will disrupt the entire supply chain management architecture. Rule-based intelligence can be used by smart contracts for executing supply chain functions. Blockchains extend the support for the construction of trusted code that can be embedded into the system securely. The same can be used by the participants for specifying the terms and conditions of their transactions, which would ultimately create a smart contract.

Smart contracts can have a similar level of detail as a traditional purchase order. The quality accreditation will be implemented in the current methods, but will have the extra feature of being able to automatically execute tasks like negotiating prices.

Commercial partners will be able to monitor and analyse the time of deliveries, quality status, as well as costs, and then create as well as negotiate all the transactions automatically.

If it is combined with Industry 4.0 smart devices, it will mitigate costs and magnify efficiency by encouraging the machines to establish communication directly with each other, i.e. M2M (machine to machine), without any centralised control structure to slow them down. The manufacturing decisions will be made automatically, which will allow factories to make big leaps not only in efficiency but also in flexibility.

To understand better how a smart contract functions, we can take the example of an aerospace manufacturer that has issued a smart contract in favour of a marketplace; such a contract would also include the exact terms and conditions for a part/component that is to be produced from only aerospace-grade aluminium. Apart from this, the company also included the CAD model by defining the delivery and payment needs. Any supplier will be able to bid for the contract if they have the right credentials as well as machinery capable of manufacturing the required component.

If the timescale of delivery is not satisfactory, then the contract will allow the automatic distribution of the requirements across various qualified suppliers for achieving the target delivery date. As such, it will allow the buyers to scale up the manufacturing systems for fulfilling their needs.

Wrapping it Up

Under- or overestimating demand results in lost revenues for any manufacturer and this holds true especially for small-scale production units. Lost revenue can happen in the form of lost sales because of

- Poor delivery performance;
- Under-utilised assets;
- Substandard quality; and/or
- Stagnant inventory.

The inability to be flexible is the core reason behind the inefficiency in any production system. If the monitoring of machines is improved, or the energy usage is controlled, then it will help suppliers to boost productivity as well as the flexibility of any particular machine. Similarly, improving the overall performance of the system and good planning will result in the production of more products by using the same quantity of assets, which would improve productivity as well as flexibility.

Production plans all across the globe should rely upon machine learning, automation, blockchain and many other forms of AI for meeting the growing global demand and revolutionise the way factories execute orders, perform production and control quality.

Just imagine that you are now able to boost your manufacturing operations in a way that is similar to how the cloud services like Microsoft Azure and Amazon Web Services boost their capacity for fulfilling the demands on websites or eCommerce portals within a fraction of a second.

To develop a brighter future for manufacturing systems, it is essential to have intelligent and decentralised adaptive manufacturing.

Notes

1 www.pwc.com/gx/en/industries/technology/blockchain/blockchain-in-business. html.
2 Ibid.
3 Ibid.
4 www.linkedin.com/pulse/data-we-trust-well-after-you-add-little-blockchain-jerry-cuomo/.
5 www.industry.gov.au/data-and-publications/national-blockchain-roadmap.

Chapter 7

Trade Finance Use Case

Money makes the world go around, the world go around, the world go around. Money makes the world go around, of that we both are sure ...

Sung by Liza Minelli, words by Red Ebb/John Kander[1]

Source: www.eib.org/smes

Summary

This entire chapter is a use case, a case study. At the end of this chapter you'll be able to

- Understand and have an overview of trade finance (also known as procure to pay or 'P2P') and how that relates to blockchains;
- Know which industries use trade finance;
- Define the trade finance key legal entities and actors;

DOI: 10.4324/9781003132592-7

- Know about the different types of trade finance deployments;
- Compare blockchains in trade finance to current solutions;
- Get an understanding of a specific trade finance use case (a case history or caselet);
- Understand the positives and potential negatives in the trade finance use case; and
- Understand the likely future direction of trade finance.

Chapter Overview

Trade finance, or procure to pay (P2P), is the name given to the activity by which businesses and organisations in the private and public sectors source, order, invoice, purchase, pay for and reconcile the delivery of raw materials, commodities, machinery and goods in their supply chain. Trade finance may also refer to the procurement of services, but professional services (for example, management consultancy, legal and accountancy services) are usually bought and delivered via specific contracts known as service agreements and underlying 'statements of work'.

Trade finance is a day-to-day task for most organisations. It's a vital part of business management and administration. When trade finance is efficiently organised and runs smoothly, there are significant benefits available to the organisation: for example, reduced project delivery risk with fewer supply chain reconciliation breaks; better cash flow forecasting; and more satisfied suppliers who, for example, might as a result be paid sooner. When poorly executed trade finance goes wrong, on the other hand, this is a threat that may interrupt and disrupt key activities of the organisation with all that that implies.

The question that most managers face, therefore, is not 'can you afford to have a formalised trade finance system and operating model in your organisation?' but rather 'could your organisation afford to have a significant procurement or trade finance failure?'

Understanding trade finance is critical for all organisations.

- In this chapter we will examine the trade finance use case and smaller 'caselets'.
- The chapter will explain the main features, challenges and benefits of trade finance for managers and administrators.

- This chapter will cover typical trade finance supply chain entities and actors such as buyers, third-party suppliers, banks and finance providers, and professionals such as accountants, auditors and lawyers.
- The chapter will also include a detailed look at how blockchain provides a robust, efficient and cost-effective improvement to current trade finance deployments, and what this means for managers and executives.

Trade Finance in More Detail

Put simply, trade finance is the act of buying goods and raw materials from one or more suppliers, using finance or credit.

Trade finance is, in the majority of cases, an enterprise-level operation carried out inside the organisation. It's often confidential, given the sensitivity and timeliness of the procurement decisions required, especially for larger enterprises. However, because trade finance interfaces with one or many external suppliers, there are inherent complexities and challenges outside the organisation that have an impact too.

Trade Finance Software

Trade finance is usually configured and administered via integrated software systems and a dedicated operating model managed by trained staff or specialist external partners. In cases where trade finance is outsourced, there are additional complexities arising. These obstacles are typically offset in terms of the total cost of ownership. For the smallest organisations trade finance may be done on an ad hoc, case-by-case or project basis, sometimes via end-user computing such as an internal spreadsheet, emails and a cash ledger.

It is worth remembering that trade finance software systems may be purchased from third-party vendors or, less commonly for smaller firms, designed and built in-house. Trade finance systems may be hosted by an organisation on premises or via private or public clouds.

Trade Finance Policy

We will explore the different economic rationales for each trade finance configuration in this chapter. Every organisation will have varying policies over control of its trade finance data, security and access that will also play a large part in determining where and how a trade finance system is deployed, and we'll explore that too.

We find examples of trade finance with a credit element in industries such as construction (especially house construction and civil engineering for roads, railways and infrastructure in general), hospitality, vehicle/ automotive, shipping and aerospace manufacturing, fast-moving consumer goods (FMCG) and retail.

Governments, whether local, national or in a military context (and also non-governmental organisations, NGOs) use trade finance systems and operating models to streamline their own procurement and to align with the practices, processes and trade finance-related value chains of private-sector partners and suppliers.

Trade Finance in the Real World

Trade finance solutions will, in some instances, span multiple jurisdictions, currency areas, customs boundaries and time zones, as well as being used by organisations that are themselves multinational. This only adds to the complexity of systems and operating models.

Multiple factors, both macro and micro, increase business requirements for the design, use and deployment of trade finance systems and operating models. Alongside complexity are the other negative effects of user or system errors, whether negligent or deliberate, for example fraud, unavoidable delays, the increased risk in both delivery risk and operational activities, and non-trivial breaks in the supplier value chain.

Most trade finance breaks are not caused by failures in the trade finance system or model. More frequently, breaks are caused by the day-to-day activity of staff and trade finance actors, whether internal or via a third party. Some of these negative issues will be examined in more detail later in this chapter.

The Role of Banks in Trade Finance

Banks, and the finance function more generally, are drivers for greater efficiency and accuracy in the trade finance value chain.

Since the creation of money, it has been the role of banks and other providers of credit to pay and settle 'bills of exchange', an instrument or fungible security in the form of a corporate promise to pay or 'I owe you'

(IOU). In trade finance, banks (rather than the procuring organisation itself) are sometimes the counterparty directly paying a supplier against delivery, for example via a pre-arranged line of credit. Direct payments like these introduce additional and specific trade finance risks to the bank itself, as, for example, a fraudulent or non-existent delivery of goods or materials might not be apparent to the bank until after an invoice payment has been made by it on behalf of the organisation.

Blockchains in Trade Finance

Permissioned blockchains, the non-anonymous versions of distributed ledger technology (DLT, another label for blockchain), offer a compelling potential solution to some of the complexities and issues in trade finance. As we have seen in the other chapters in this book, blockchain enables multiple entities and actors in a complex value chain to share and validate tasks and activity, delivery and payment data in a way that is transparent, immutable and standardised.

Blockchains are already in use in some trade finance solutions as they are perceived to fix existing problems and reduce risk. Using blockchain technology in trade finance also reduces stack size and means that indirect benefits, such as cash flow optimisation and faster invoice payments, may be realised.

What Is Trade Finance?

Enterprises, i.e. private-sector businesses, governments and organisations large or small, procure billions of dollars' worth of goods and materials from each other and third-party suppliers all the time and have done since the earliest days of commerce.

Today, as a result of decades of management science, process optimisation and software development, enterprise-level procurement is carried out within a structured software system and as part of a defined operating model that is subject to an organisation's procurement and other policies. This is true for larger organisations, but also applies to governments and the public sector, for example.

The managed, end-to-end process of enterprise-level procurement now goes by the shorthand business label 'trade finance' (or procure to pay, P2P), which describes the whole cycle of procurement from start to finish.

Figure 7.1   A sample trade finance (or 'procure to pay') lifecycle diagram.

Source: Ramco Systems Ltd. www.ramco.com/resources/business-processes/procure-to-pay.aspx

Figure 7.1 shows the main, high-level stages of a typical trade finance process.

Request

In the example of Figure 7.1 the trade finance process begins with a request made within an organisation for materials or goods to be bought, either for use within the business and/or as part of a larger project or programme, for example, construction or civil engineering work.

Request for Quotation

The next step is for the organisation to process the internal request and publish it as an external-facing 'Request for Quotation', RFQ. Note: in some cases this artefact is also referred to as a 'Request for Proposal' (RFP) or 'Request for Information' (RFI).

The RFQ is usually in the form of a detailed written statement in template form. The purpose of the RFQ is to crystallise the procurement request itself into a standardised format so that the potential supplier responses may be measured against one another by the organisation – comparing apples with apples. Standard categories for quotation by suppliers in a typical RFQ are price, delivery dates, quality, volume, delivery location etc.

Quotation

After the RFQ has been published, one or many supplier quotations will be received back by the organisation on or before a deadline date. Following further internal processes, and subject to potentially complex rules within the organisation concerning price, quality and other attributes of each individual supplier's offer, the winning supplier quotation will be selected by the organisation.

PO

Organisations usually procure through the mechanism of a legal instrument known as a purchase order (PO). A PO sets out the details of the organisation's confirmed procurement plus price, delivery dates and other information. Often a PO will incorporate specific contractual terms and conditions. Acceptance of a PO by the parties constitutes a legally binding agreement between them. The PO requires the supplier to supply the required goods and materials to the organisation and provides for the matching right of the supplier to issue, present and receive consideration (payment) of its invoice from the organisation post-delivery.

Goods Receipt

Once the PO has been agreed and executed (i.e. signed), the supplier will – at the specified time and location – deliver the requested goods and materials to the organisation.

This is a critical stage in the trade finance cycle: the delivered goods and materials must be inspected and accepted by the organisation to their satisfaction and then both the supplier and receiver of the goods and materials, who may themselves both be third parties, approve in writing in the form of a delivery note (DN) or receipt and then advise the organisation and bank or finance provider accordingly.

Supplier Invoice

Immediately after delivery/receipt the supplier will issue its invoice and present it for payment by the organisation, as is its right.

Release Payment

So, following a process of checking and validation of the invoice vs. delivery (and reconciling the delivery against its own internal checks), the organisation, either acting alone or via a bank or finance provider, makes cash payment of the invoice to the supplier.

CN/DN Adjustment

There is then a final stage, if necessary, of credit note (CN) and/or delivery note (DN, related to the receipt) adjustment by the organisation and potentially the supplier where there may be final changes made following reconciliation etc. of the actual delivery vs. PO. At this point the standard trade finance process ends.

Trade finance is a journey, a life cycle, moving in stages and through specific transactions, and between legal entities, currencies and across national/customs borders. Trade finance has a direct correlation with payment and cash transactions. 'Follow the money' is as relevant in understanding trade finance as ever.

Key Trade Finance Concepts

This is a good place to pause and explore the entities and actors involved in the trade finance stack. By 'stack' we mean here the hierarchical and individual nature of the principal legal and technology entities and actors in the systems and operating models of trade finance.

This section will set out the main enterprise-level trade finance stack entities, actors, types, models and some of the benefits and challenges to organisations.

Legal Entities

There are several key principal legal entities involved in trade finance as follows:

Buyer

The buyer is the legal entity of the organisation, usually a private or public company or a public organisation. The trade finance domain excludes 'natural persons', e.g. consumers or retail customers. A buyer, in the context of trade finance, must have full legal status in its country of domicile and will be a principal to any supply agreements and purchase orders. In trade finance a buyer should be able to demonstrate the financial means to pay its liabilities as and when they fall due, i.e. it should be solvent and able to trade.

Supplier

A supplier is a legal entity, often (but not always) 'external' to the buyer. For example, in the context of large multinational businesses, one division of the company may 'procure' from another internal unit. More often, however, the supplier is a third party whom the buyer has sourced from previously and may already be an established procurement counterparty. Suppliers must be solvent and have the capacity to execute the buyer's purchase orders. Suppliers may have their own trade finance systems and operating models in place.

Bank or Finance Provider

'Bank' means any qualifying deposit-taking, payment processing, credit broking or finance provider in a trade finance value chain. The bank operates on behalf of the buyer and has a legal and financial interest in the goods and materials ordered by the buyer and delivered by the supplier. Sometimes a bank will be the legal owner of the goods and materials even after delivery to the buyer as, in some cases, the same may be resold or only legally transferred to the buyer on a 'just in time' delivery basis.

Receiver

A receiver is the legal entity responsible for overseeing the movement of goods and materials in the trade finance value chain. A receiver may be neither a buyer nor a supplier (nor even a bank); the role of receiver is often that of project manager, for example, who is on site when goods and materials are delivered and who has capacity and experience enough to test for quality and delivery conditions.

Actors in Trade Finance Stack

In addition to the legal entities, trade finance also engages with actors within the trade finance system and operating model as follows:

Project Manager

This function is not a discrete legal entity (although it may be; see 'Receiver', above). Rather, a project manager is a professional actor in the trade finance value chain with responsibility for ensuring the smooth day-to-day running of the ordering, delivery and receipt of goods and materials.

Auditor

After the facts of delivery and payment, an auditor will act on behalf of both or either of the buyer and supplier, ensuring that the supplier supplied the correct goods and materials and that payment, reconciliation and accounts have been maintained to the required standards. An auditor may also be deployed in enterprise trade finance solutions by a bank, for example.

Bookkeeper

Keeping accurate records of all aspects of trade finance, especially records of POs, deliveries and payments, is key to the smooth running of any trade finance operating model. Bookkeepers may be both human employees and enterprise-level software systems and databases; and it is in this area where – for example – blockchain-related solutions are often found.

Types

The following are all types of enterprise trade finance that are found in organisations:

Payment on Delivery (also known as 'Payment versus Delivery')

In this type of trade finance, the buyer will settle, via cash, a supplier's invoice immediately following delivery to the buyer or the receiver.

Payment of cash may actually be executed by the bank on behalf of the buyer or by the buyer itself.

Payment by Rolling Line of Credit

This type of trade finance relies on the bank to settle all the buyer's liabilities to suppliers (based on POs) on behalf of the buyer. Later on in the manufacturing or delivery cycle, the buyer will settle its line of credit with the bank. The reader might most easily think of this as being similar in status and functionality to an organisation's 'credit card'.

Payment on Account

This type of trade finance involves a revolving credit account between buyer and supplier – for example, a buyer may receive several deliveries of goods and materials from a supplier but only settle these, perhaps by offsetting for other goods and materials delivered in reverse between the parties, at the end of an accounting period. In this arrangement one would typically find a close or long-standing relationship between the parties, perhaps through common ownership.

Models

Not all trade finance models are the same and we explore the differences here in more detail and set out the economic rationales for each.

Internal Trade Finance

This model is where an organisation establishes, sets up and manages its own trade finance process, software system and operating model. Enterprise-level trade finance is usually in-house, given the sensitivity of the procurement itself, including for data controlling purposes as well as in relation to price, delivery and reputational risk management.

Externally Outsourced Trade Finance

This model reflects the desire of some buyers to outsource their procurement. There are different economic rationales for this, for example, some buyers may be looking to save on the total cost of ownership of their trade finance; others may be looking to 'pool' their buying power with other organisations (and thereby mitigate risks); yet more may simply want to delegate responsibility for complex buying decisions to professionals and take the risk out of their own organisations.

Ad Hoc or Project-related Trade Finance

As it implies, this model looks at trade finance solutions as project driven. Even larger organisations use this approach where there is a requirement to segregate projects, for example for regulatory reasons, or where the viability of one project threatens another and therefore a different procurement approach is deemed relevant on a project-risk measurement basis.

End-User Computing Trade Finance

Small organisations, local public organisations and traders will deploy an 'end-user computing' (or EUC) model. This is an area of trade finance, although not covered in this book, which is focused on the enterprise. EUC trade finance is a functioning solution for millions of (usually private) organisations, and, although it is not without its own challenges, it is a viable, effective and low-cost operating model.

Stresses in Trade Finance

The following stresses are among the known issues within typical trade finance models:

Credit Note/Delivery Note

Reconciliation post-delivery, meaning the adjustment of the purchase, delivery and payment records, is a common activity in trade finance. More down to 'reality' than fraud (although see below), the management and administration of trade finance credit and delivery note reconciliation is an area full of additional cost, effort, risk and complexity.

Fraud in Delivery and Payment

Conspiring entities and actors in parts of the trade finance value chain may, for criminal reasons, seek to fraudulently validate and process orders, deliveries and payments. This is not common but, nevertheless, it's a stress both actual and virtual in the trade finance industry and one that must be considered in both the design and deployment of trade finance operating models and software systems, including blockchain.

Change of Supplier/Third Party

Suppliers and third parties are a stress on buyers and especially banks. This is down to a lack of general supplier information (for example, solvency); a lack of clear data governance boundaries between procurer, supplier and other third parties (whose data is it and how is it managed, especially in multinational situations and with the impact of cloud computing?); and in issues with supplier onboarding and administering suppliers and third parties by buyers and banks generally.

Challenges More Generally

There are non-trivial challenges with trade finance that, although not specific stresses, nevertheless have an impact on running a trade finance system and model well, for example:

Cross-currency and Cross-border

Global trade increases year on year. Currencies reflect variance in trade values and this is exacerbated by swings in international trade movements and tariff disputes. All trade finance operating models, entities, actors and software systems must be configured to cope with the complexity and rules-based processes that multinational trade finance demands.

Government Procurement Rules

The example given here is in government-defined building regulations. While such regulations are nominally the responsibility of the buyer (in value chain terms) we have witnessed the tragic real-life consequences of breach (for example, the quality of fire-retardant tower block cladding or the purity of concrete for bridge building).

Trade finance touches on this because, in construction for example, building regulations must be adhered to strictly. The day-to-day effect of this is that government procurement rules create an extra layer of complexity and rules that many trade finance operating models and systems have to incorporate. In the case of regulations, it is also a requirement to constantly update and validate the regulatory rules and boundaries – and whose responsibility is that, and how can government police breaches of regulations in a fractured trade finance value chain?

Changes of Ownership

The example of Carillion, in the UK, is pertinent. Carillion, a major construction and services private-sector enterprise, faced formal insolvency proceedings when it became unable to pay its liabilities as and when they fell due, and this was especially relevant in the context of Carillion's complex and opaque trade finance and supplier value chain.

In administration, and rendered effectively a ward of court, Carillion was unable to pay its trade finance suppliers. Because of Carillion's status, suppliers were unable to enforce payment against it. The UK government then switched ownership of some of the liabilities of Carillion to itself, enabling certain suppliers and third parties to be paid; but this haphazard and case-by-case approach was discretionary and a one-time outcome only. It only served to highlight the need for better transparency in trade finance at the enterprise level.

Summary and Opinion

Table 7.1 sets out an 'at-a-glance' matrix view of the roles and responsibilities of both the legal entities ([E]) and actors ([A]) in a typical trade finance system. Table 7.2 is a matrix of the data, security and access aspects of the various legal entities and actors in the trade finance value chain.

How Trade Finance Uses Ledgers Currently

Trade finance operates on a distributed range of systems, between currencies, in separate legal agreements/codes and frequently in different countries. It is likely that most international trade finance is conducted in the English language, although this is potentially only at the top level of documents. Local paperwork (such as delivery notes etc.) most often remain in the local language.

There are two key reasons why trade finance has been promoted as a prime, early candidate for migration to blockchain: risk and money. There

Table 7.1 The data actors and entities

Entity [E] or Actor [A]	Responsible for...	Status	Comment
[E] Buyer	RFQ, PO and payment	Owner	Principal legal entity in trade finance process
[E] Supplier	PO and delivery	Participant	Counterparty legal entity in trade finance
[E] Bank	Payment	Stakeholder	Active risk in fraud and credit
[E] Receiver	Delivery	Quality checks	Critical legal function in approving payments
[A] Project Manger	Planning	Participant	Day-to-day management of site and deliveries
[A] Auditor	Auditing	Participant	Post-delivery audit for all legal entities
[A] Bookkeeper	Record-keeping	Participant	Day-to-day reconciliation and records

is risk for all parties in trade finance: risk of non-payment for the supplier; risk of unaudited fraud for the bank; risk of supply chain breakdown and delayed delivery for the project manager; and risk of the withdrawal of credit facilities for the procurer. Money remains a key use case for blockchain; the function of currency was identified as the foundation role for blockchain tokens, with bitcoin as the prime example.

How Trade Finance Would be Different Using Blockchains

Trade finance is already being reshaped by blockchains.

There are three standard tests for the usefulness or relevance of blockchains in a specific industry, for example:

■ What's the asset to be tokenised? In trade finance, it's the lines of credit versus supply. The 'asset' is real money that is due to be paid against delivery.

Table 7.2 The data, security and access actors and entities

Entity [E] or Actor [A]	Data	Security	Access
[E] Buyer	Controls own data processes on suppliers	No specific security requirement	Access to published RFQs, POs for suppliers, banks and receivers
[E] Supplier	Controls own data processes on third parties	No specific security requirement	Access to invoices/CNs to bank and buyers; DNs to receivers
[E] Bank	Processes data on buyers and suppliers	Bank-level security mandatory	No access
[E] Receiver	Processes data on buyers and suppliers	High security required	Access to DNs
[A] Project Manger	Processes data on buyers and suppliers	No specific security requirement	Access to POs
[A] Auditor	Processes data on buyers, suppliers and banks etc.	No specific security requirement	Access to all documents
[A] Bookkeeper	Processes data on buyers, suppliers and banks etc.	No specific security requirement	Access to all documents

- Is there a requirement for a proxy for trust? Yes. In trade finance, the counterparties need to trust one another: the bank needs to trust that delivery has been physically made to the correct quality; and the supplier needs to trust that the buyer will pay. These two main parties are sometimes untrusting of one another.
- Will there be equitable access? Yes. 'Equitable access', in the case of trade finance, is the ability of all parties (see the section on Actors in this chapter) to view and verify all the stages of the trade finance journey, from RFQ to payment.

Blockchains offer transparency, immutability, security and equal access to the data to all parties. Increasingly, as smart contracts grow in capability and complexity, there will be a growing level of process automation in the various stages of trade finance. In relation to the conditions quoted above, the business rules of quality acceptance, dates for payment or 'cooling off' periods and the gate criteria for enforcement, for example, might all be a function of an underlying trade finance blockchain.

Finance System Comparison

This section of the chapter will focus on a current-state trade finance model stack, meaning not just the technology deployed but also the functional or legal components of trade finance and also how these interrelate to each other in the current state (i.e. using non-DLT technology). This chapter will then compare and contrast this with a proposed future-state stack that may be potentially powered by blockchain (DLT) technology.

We will begin with the non-blockchain systems and models. Figure 7.2 shows, as a logical diagram, how the various enterprise systems and principal legal entities interact in a typical trade finance life cycle using non-blockchain (current state) technology and infrastructure.

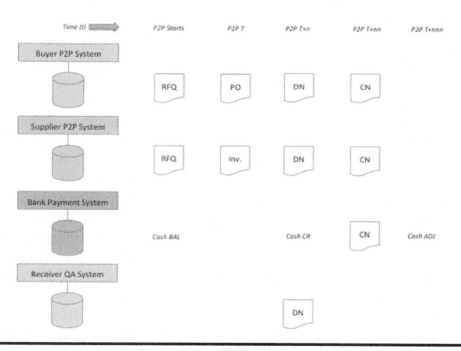

Figure 7.2   An approximate logical diagram between various trade finance legal entities and artefacts such as POs, RFQs etc.

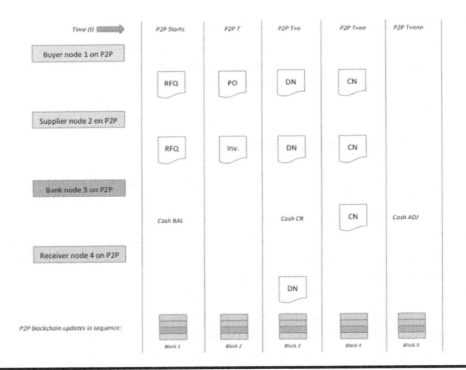

Figure 7.3 A logical diagram showing the probable sequence of blockchain updates with four nodes represented.

Note that in Figure 7.2 there are a mixture of legal entities, actors, artefacts such as POs, RFQs, invoices, delivery notes (DNs) and credit notes (CNs) as well as cash events such as opening balances (Cash BAL), payments to suppliers (Cash CRs) and post-delivery cash adjustments, here labelled 'Cash ADJ'. These components all interact with each other over time. The diagram reads left to right with the passage of time implied, e.g. T+n, T+nn (more, albeit unspecified, time) and T+nnn.

In addition, each principal legal entity has both a software system and an underlying silo of data that must be added to, edited and archived as well as made safe and secure, kept accurate, and potentially reconciled with all of the other entities' systems and their data too. It is not the intention of this chapter to delve inside each of the principal legal entities' specific 'black box' software systems and databases; rather we are going to compare the multilayered ecosystem of current-state trade finance in Figure 7.2 versus Figure 7.3, which is a diagram showing how the same trade finance environment might look in a future state if distributed ledger technology

(DLT, also known as blockchain) were used by the buyer organisation at an enterprise level, for example.

Note how the blockchain is updated with all stages/statuses for all parties automatically, meaning the information about the whole trade finance cycle is transparent, synchronous, immutable and fully reconciled.

Trade Finance Demonstration Problems and Use Case

The use case here is civil engineering. In this fictional use case, Highways England (a centralised, government-funded roads management agency) and Kent County Council (a UK local authority) have jointly commissioned a new road bridge for construction and delivery by a consortium of suppliers led by a major building firm. Although ultimately paid for by the UK government, the bridge's finance is delegated to banks and finance firms for settlement out of the project budget that will be reconciled at the end of the project.

Caselet 1: 'Some of our Concrete is Missing'

Current state: How it can be difficult to quality-check (and pay for) a delivery of a truck-load of concrete to a civil engineering site in the current state (non-blockchain) model.

Against an agreed PO a supplier's concrete transportation vehicle arrives at a major civil engineering site for a new road bridge in Kent, England to deliver 20 tonnes of liquid concrete. On arrival at the site the truck is marshalled to the correct delivery zone by the receiver's staff and commences delivery by unloading liquid concrete. The truck driver provides the project manager at the delivery point with a paper document and matching barcode stating the date, time and weight of the concrete delivered.

Following weighing and quality assurance checks (and as the liquid concrete is poured) the project manager scans the delivery note barcode, which is immediately updated in the buyer's trade finance system. The project manager signs and approves the paper delivery note, keeps a copy and returns the completed delivery document to the truck driver. Once delivery has been physically completed when all the concrete is poured, the truck driver departs the site and returns to the supplier's base.

The buyer and supplier process their copies of delivery notes in their respective trade finance systems. The buyer and supplier reconcile their trade finance system records and check and reconcile the same with the receiver's physical records and system. If there are any discrepancies or exceptions, then all the parties' trade finance systems must be updated accordingly once agreement has been reached. Once the legal entities have reconciled their systems the buyer instructs the bank to make payment ('payment versus delivery' model). The bank pays the supplier on the basis of instructions from its arrangement with the buyer.

Future state (using blockchains): How it would be more efficient, accurate and transparent to process the same trade finance delivery where blockchain is deployed.

The trade finance blockchain is updated with a PO requesting a delivery of 20 tonnes of concrete from the supplier to the buyer's road bridge construction site in Kent, England. On arrival at the site, the supplier's truck is marshalled to the correct delivery zone by the receiver's staff and starts delivery by unloading liquid concrete. The truck driver provides the project manager at the delivery point with a barcode for the delivery.

Following weighing and quality assurance checks and as the liquid concrete is poured, the trade finance blockchain is updated for all parties (buyer, supplier, bank and receiver) with delivery status completed. All parties ('nodes' on the blockchain) receive an updated block and payment is made immediately to the supplier by the bank on behalf of the buyer.

There is no reconciliation or exception process required.

Caselet 2: 'Improved Credit Management, Lower Risks and Costs'

Current state: How credit is assessed, calculated and repaid using non-blockchain data and systems.

Buyer issues an RFQ for the next major phase in the Kent bridge building/civil engineering project to several suppliers with whom it has worked successfully previously. RFQ responses from suppliers are received and validated; one winning quotation is selected by the buyer. Buyer and bank agree a line of credit to cover all the expected POs for the RFQ and deliveries, including a tolerance of x% for contingency.

The bank sets aside the required liquidity and awaits the flow of delivery notes etc. from supplier and receiver. Each delivery note, once approved, is paid by the bank on behalf of the buyer and, at the end of the process and following reconciliation, the whole credit facility is repaid to the bank by the buyer.

Future state: How the same would work in a blockchain environment.

Buyer issues an RFQ for the next major phase in the Kent bridge/ civil engineering project to several suppliers with whom it has worked successfully previously. RFQ responses are received and validated; one winning quotation is selected by the buyer.

Because the bank is a node on the blockchain along with the buyer, each delivery note is paid on a case-by-case basis and settled by the buyer at the same time, lowering the size of the credit facility, cutting the total cost of the credit, accelerating the speed of payment for the supplier and reducing the total liabilities and risk for the bank.

The caselets give a specific, practical example of the benefits of enterprise-level blockchain in civil engineering. In addition, there are other benefits that pertain to the future-state (blockchain-powered) trade finance solution as follows:

- **Bank benefits**: Blockchains assist with a reduction in potential occurrences of financial fraud, speed up settlement and help make more efficient financial projection/cash flow for credit arrangements. With a more streamlined ledger offering immutability and transparency, banks benefit from blockchains in trade finance.
- **Buyer benefits**: Blockchains, at the enterprise level, simplify trade finance complexity, reduce delivery risk and make quality control transparent. Solutions on DLT in general (compared to current-state stacks) offer buyers greater control and transparency over the whole procurement cycle with less likelihood of a 'Carillion' type corporate failure.
- **Supplier benefits**: Blockchains provide a trade finance enterprise-level solution for recurrent supplier problems with payment delays, paperwork and bureaucracy, reconciliation issues and invoice complexity. DLT trade finance offers the prospect of faster invoice payments, quality assurance, managing the supplier's own supply chain and workforce, and better relationships for good suppliers with their customers.
- **Project management benefits**: Blockchains provide potential trade finance benefits in respect of the risks facing project managers in delivery, potential errors in reconciliation and the task of reporting

Table 7.3 Problem statements in current and future states

Trade Finance Problem Statement	Current Trade Finance State (Non-blockchain) Solution	Future Trade Finance State (Blockchain) Solution	Comments
Trade finance cash flow delays and reconciliation breaks cause stress in the value chain	Disparate systems slow down reconciliation and payments	Synchronous updates to all nodes to all blockchain	Blockchain provides immediate updates and payment without further reconciliations
Cost of trade finance credit to buyers and risks of credit to banks	Non-linear POs, invoice and delivery notes	Synchronous PO, invoice delivery and payment	Transparent process means shortened lines of credit
Inaccurate multiple sources of data and information	Trade finance data is in different states in different trade finance systems	There's a single reconciled and distributed ledger	One of the key benefits of blockchain in trade finance is a 'single source of the truth'

back to both buyer and supplier. DLT offers potential solutions with accuracy, transparency, immutability and portability.

Table 7.3 shows a comparison of example trade finance problem statements and the benefits provided by future-state blockchains versus current-state technology.

Summary and Conclusion

Trade finance is a vertical industry full of duplication of effort, data, process and cost. What this also means on a practical level is that there are multiple places for error, potential criminal activity (or at the very least, incompetence) and poor practice to hide. Decentralising the stages and steps of trade finance, and deploying, via blockchain, better accuracy, security, speed and access to information means a better overall trade finance system and fewer issues both micro and macro.

It is no accident that trade finance has been seen as an early adopter of distributed ledger technology. Given its challenges, trade finance is sorely in need of the solutions that blockchains can offer.

Before You Go On

- Consider the relevance of the benefits provided by blockchain in the trade finance value chain at the enterprise level. These are more than just administrative advantages – there are potential savings in trade finance costs, time and effort compared to non-blockchain models.
- Reflect on the possible barriers to adoption for blockchain in the enterprise, for example, the costs and risks in changing systems from non-blockchain to DLT and the requirements to retrain and reskill key staff.
- Remember that not all trade finance value chains and models are suitable for blockchain deployments; for example, small firms or ad hoc projects that may just as easily be administered by expert users and EUC.

Note

1 *Money, Money* lyrics © Trio Music Company, Alley Music Corp., Times Square Music Publications Company, UNICHAPPELL MUSIC, INC., TRIO MUSIC COMPANY, INC., TRIO MUSIC CO., INC.

Further Reading

www.marcopolo.finance/evolution-of-trade-finance-blockchain/
www2.deloitte.com/content/dam/Deloitte/global/Documents/grid/trade-finance-placemat.pdf
www.capco.com/-/media/CapcoMedia/PDFs/blockchain-trade-finance.ashx
www.ft.com/content/04a4fcde-dfb5-11e9-b8e0-026e07cbe5b4 (note: behind paywall)

Chapter 8

Healthcare Software and Data Use Case

It is more important to know what sort of person has a disease than to know what sort of disease a person has.

Hippocrates

"According to the computer, I need to back up your kidneys, defragment your liver and reboot your heart."

© Randy Glasbergen / glasbergen.com

DOI: 10.4324/9781003132592-8

Summary

This entire chapter is a use case, a case study. At the end of this chapter you'll be able to

- Understand an overview of healthcare software, data and blockchains;
- Know which applications within healthcare may use a blockchain type of approach;
- Define the key healthcare legal entities and actors;
- Know about the different types of healthcare software and data deployments;
- Compare blockchains in healthcare software data to current solutions;
- Get an understanding of a specific healthcare use case (a case history);
- Understand the positives and potential negatives in the healthcare use case;
- Understand the likely future direction of healthcare.

Chapter Overview

Healthcare – the provision of scarce personal medical services and support to people and communities – is a vital, worldwide global industry: 'Global health care expenditures are expected to continue to rise as spending is projected to increase at an annual rate of 5.4 percent between 2017–2022, from USD $7.724 trillion to USD $10.059 trillion'.[1]

Healthcare is primarily a human-to-human service, although some process automation is slowly being introduced, for example, artificial intelligence in ophthalmology to verify disease diagnoses, read scans and images, and augment surgical work. Alongside personal healthcare is specialist machinery such as highly advanced medical software and hardware, medical and pharmaceutical supplies and large volumes of sensitive and private medical data.

Personal (patient) health records, clinician data and records (including qualifications), clinical research information, medicine development, and diagnosis, treatment and testing data are also vital parts of the healthcare system.

We've all imagined (or even seen) the spidery handwriting of a stereotypical physician: an apparently illegible scrawl that only other medical professionals can safely translate. Today, in reality, medicine is predominantly a systems-led activity, making extensive use of software, data and information. The result is that pharmaceutical companies, hospitals and clinics, online doctors, doctor's surgeries, appointments, clinical research, prescriptions, medical qualifications and (especially) personal patient data have all shifted to digital solutions rich in medical data.

Medical data is different to other data: it's strictly confidential, highly personal, varied and critical in the sense that getting medical data wrong – or worse, losing it – could constitute a potentially life-threatening outcome for vulnerable or very ill patients.

Understanding and managing healthcare data is central for the medical industry worldwide.

- In this chapter we will examine the healthcare use case and smaller 'caselets'.
- The chapter will explain the main features, challenges and benefits of healthcare software for managers and administrators.
- This chapter will cover typical healthcare software and data supply chain entities and actors such as doctors, patients, medical staff, pharmaceutical companies, hospitals/clinics, clinical research and online healthcare apps.
- The chapter will also include a detailed look at how blockchain provides a robust, efficient and cost-effective improvement to current healthcare software applications in medical services, and what this means for doctors, patients and the supply chain.

Healthcare Software and Data in More Detail

Healthcare, as a working definition, is a wide, elastic range of activities around primary care medicine (physicians/doctors, nurses and patients) and all the integrated supporting services and suppliers, ranging from hospitals and clinics, doctor's surgeries, pharmacies, care homes, hospices, dental surgeries and online health care providers too.

Physical healthcare (i.e. real-life doctors, nurses and patients) is a complex industry with high risks, high costs and – for the successful – high margins. It's an electronic/digital industry too, with software and data on demand a key part of physical medicine's diagnosis and treatment protocols.

Healthcare is online. This is an exponential growth factor for healthcare software. Self-diagnosis is not for the faint-hearted (and most medical professionals always recommend seeing a qualified healthcare professional), but the engagement of the public with 'Dr Google' is a phenomenon that is not going to go away any time soon. The SARS-Cov-2 pandemic has only served to put even greater emphasis on the need for digital medicine in all types of society and economies.

Overall, the core elements of healthcare software and data encompass the following (non-exhaustive) list:

- Clinical datasets
- Other data sources for patient safety information
- Medical histories
- Allergies
- Immunisations
- Social histories
- Vital signs
- Physical examination records
- Physicians' notes
- Nurses' notes
- Laboratory tests
- Diagnostic tests
- Radiology tests
- Diagnoses
- Medications
- Procedures
- Clinical documentation
- Clinical measures for specific clinical conditions
- Patient instructions
- Dispositions
- Health maintenance schedules
- Policies and procedures
- Human resources records
- Materials management systems
- Time and attendance records
- Census records
- Decision support alert logs
- Coroners' datasets
- Claims attachments

- Admissions data
- Disease registries
- Discharge data
- Malpractice data
- Patient complaints and reports of adverse events
- Reports to professional boards
- Trigger datasets (e.g., antidote drugs for adverse drug events)
- Computerised physician order entry systems
- Bar-code medication administration systems
- Clinical trial data

Healthcare Software

Healthcare software supports the vast healthcare sector and is, itself, a multi-billion-dollar worldwide industry in the medical, pharmaceutical and clinical sectors.

From vintage pre-relational 'green screen' hospital appointment booking systems such as MUMPS (the Massachusetts General Hospital Utility Multi-Programming System), a screenshot of which is seen in Figure 8.1, to the latest laser-powered scanning equipment, 'healthcare software' incorporates a huge range of software and infrastructure.

Healthcare software is rarely developed (as software) by doctors/physicians, hospitals/clinics and doctor's surgeries. Most healthcare software

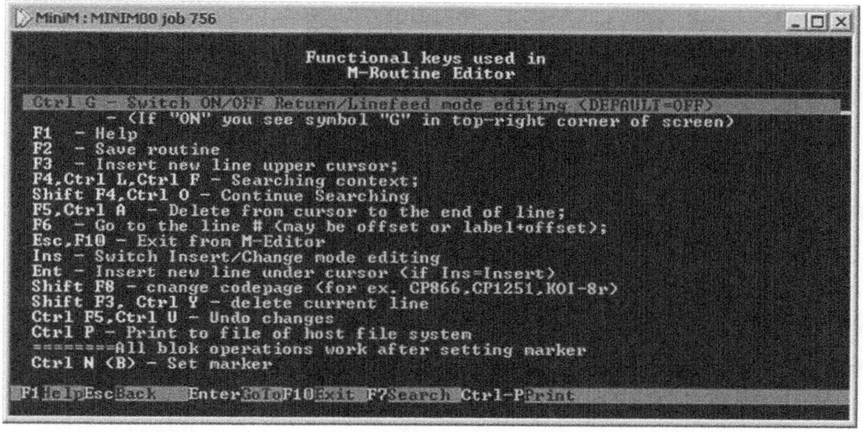

Figure 8.1   A screenshot of MUMPS (the Massachusetts General Hospital Utility Multi-Programming System).

is designed and developed by a third-party software company and, as in the example of MUMPS, may often start out life as a database or software designed for an entirely different purpose.

This healthcare use case chapter is not focused on medical 'hardware', for example, scanners or surgical equipment, except where that hardware has a notable software element to it. We're going to look in detail at how healthcare software generally operates and what the past and recent developments in that area are and how healthcare policy and reality collide – and the effect that has on the software design and usage.

This is not intended to be a detailed analysis of low-level software code. The chapter focuses on the real-life application of blockchain in healthcare scenarios, and outlines the implications of that.

Healthcare Software and Data Policy, Past and Present

There are common threads to healthcare policy (specifically, in relation to data and technology). Security, access, control of data and the recognition of the inherent sensitive value of medical data is obliging healthcare industry stakeholders, including government and regulators, to continually consider and develop entirely new policy standards.

Policy towards healthcare software has a chequered history. In the paper era – and even now paper documents and files play a significant role in healthcare globally – the provision and keeping of healthcare records was cumbersome and time (and space) consuming. If a patient moved residence, for example, the paper records would ultimately need to follow them. Even in the digital/modern era, legacy paper medical records are often required to be scanned and digitised creating a burden or barrier to adoption of a digital-only solution.

The way the industry is now in respect of healthcare software and data policy is a state of 'guarded welcome'. The absolute benefits of digitalisation of healthcare software and data are obvious: its significant advantages of efficiency, access and analysis over paper is easy to state. But, ironically, those very same attributes create new risks – for example, what happens if my newly digitised personal medical data is hacked into by a malicious actor – or even by accident?

Blockchain brings key benefits to healthcare data, adding the attributes of trust, equitable access and immutability to the data already deployed as medical and research records.

Healthcare Software and Data in the Real World

There are real-world impacts for healthcare software and data suppliers and users, both as benefits and constraints. Getting healthcare software and data right is expensive and a long-term undertaking for both the supplier and the user – imagine the consequences of mixing up medical records between two patients.

Real-world healthcare software and data consequences, both beneficial and negative, include, for example:

■ Inaccurate healthcare test data for clinical research and drug development;
■ Insecure personal patient data;
■ Inability to scan and tag paper medical records accurately;
■ Multi-channel access to medical data, e.g. by patient, doctor, hospital and pharmacy; and
■ Emergency room access to data for a specific patient.

The Role of Physicians and Nurses in Healthcare Software

Physicians and nurses are front-line staff in healthcare. So much is obvious. But they are also arguably the most important constituency of healthcare software users, even, perhaps, more so than patients.

Understanding the requirements of physicians and nurses as healthcare software and data users is key to designing and developing the right healthcare software and data for them and, by extension, a large section of the medical industry itself. What is the day-to-day healthcare or medical activity that's being automated at a process level, for example? What new risks will digitalisation bring, as well as mitigations to existing risks?

Physicians and nurses are responsible for the outcomes of their patients, and healthcare software and data have a primary objective in augmenting this life-and-death responsibility. There is no smart contract for the Hippocratic Oath – yet.

The Role of Patients in Healthcare Software

Patients are the principal subjects and objects of healthcare software and data. This is a data definition categorisation and not related to the individual characteristics of each patient, for example, diagnosis, treatment or patient needs.

Patients engage with healthcare software and data as users who are also recipients of care; who may be testbeds for treatment and drug analysis and as both in-patients and out-patients. Patients may be both active and inactive subjects – for example, in emergency medicine. Patients have this dual state (being both subject and object of the healthcare software and data), but are also, surprisingly, not considered the software's primary user, a role which naturally reverts back to the carers, the physicians and nurses.

The Role of Hospitals and Surgeries in Healthcare Software

Hospitals, clinics and doctor's general practice/surgeries are also users of healthcare software. Not just as buildings, but also as nodes of care provision, stores of drugs, resources, centres of excellence and so on.

A hospital, for example, is not just a centralised location for the delivery of healthcare. In- and out-patients, maternity and emergency medicine units, dental and eye surgery, and children and old people are also satellite users of hospitals and clinics. For healthcare software and data, the hospital is a node of users, records and integrations: does the MRI scan database connect, for example, with all local doctor's surgeries?

The relevance of this interconnectedness will be described later in this chapter.

The Role of Pharmaceutical, Diagnosis and Testing and Records in Healthcare Software

A final major group (there are multiple minor actors not referred to here) in healthcare software are the entities of clinical research, diagnosis, testing and results. The role played by this group is that of non-primary care and engagement: making sure that the data and outcomes for patients, as managed by physicians and nurses, is progressed, audited and accessed in the right way at the right time and can be used for clinical research to design and develop new and better drugs, for example.

Getting solutions to the requirements of this group right is a complex but key (and perhaps, sometimes overlooked) part of the way healthcare software works.

Blockchains in Healthcare Software

'Healthtech' is roughly defined as the forward-looking group of software applications and services designed and built for specific use by physicians/doctors, nurses, patients, hospitals, surgeries and pharmaceutical, diagnosis, testing and record-keeping companies, as set out in the above sections.

Blockchains are already in use in healthtech, for example in the areas of clinical research, auditing and maintaining medical qualifications for physicians, record-keeping and treatment notes, and so on. This is clearly not an exhaustive list. But the key conditions for use of blockchain (i.e. its noted, direct attributes of trust, immutability, security, access etc.) and blockchain's distributed, decentralised nature mean that it isn't simply considered a database replacement.

Blockchain's value lies in the efficiency it can offer certain specialised healthcare functions and these will be discussed in more detail in this chapter.

A Day in the Life of Healthcare Software

In order to best understand the 'real-life' requirements placed on healthcare software, and to see where a blockchain approach would fit that, we're going to first step through 'a day in the life' of a potential deployment of healthcare software and data.

This isn't the use case under review and no mention is made – deliberately – of what kind of software or blockchain is in use. The object of this exercise is to go through the step-by-step stages of a typical healthcare user journey.

An example of the main, high-level stages of healthcare software processes is shown in Figure 8.2.

The Patient

P is female, a mother of two children under five, in her late thirties, lives in Bristol, United Kingdom, and works in the aerospace industry as an electronics engineer. A non-smoker and of good general health, P has access to the UK's national health services (NHS), which provides 'free at the point of use' healthcare. P also has access to private health insurance as provided by her employer of 12 years.

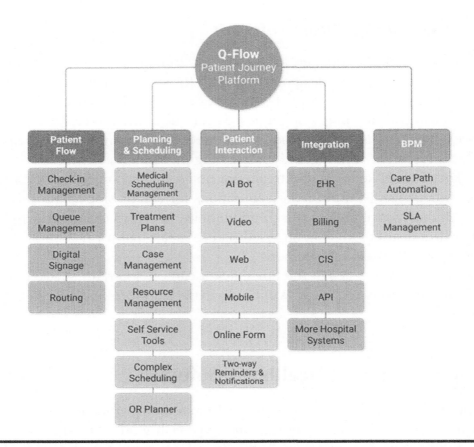

Figure 8.2 The main, high-level stages of a typical healthcare software process.

P becomes aware of a range of persistent issues relating to her general health but specifically a sharp, stabbing pain in the upper thigh area. The pain has arisen following P's reaching down to pick up her three-year-old daughter who was wriggling.

P suspects she may have slipped a disc in her lower back and there is a dull, throbbing pain.

The Appointment

On day five of the pain, P decides to make an appointment with her local general practitioner (GP) in Bristol. She goes online to the GP clinic (in the UK, known as a 'doctor's surgery') and makes an appointment for two days' time.

The appointment system books P in and P is obliged to answer some general questions in advance of the appointment.

On the day of the appointment P arrives at the doctor's surgery and, using the reception-area iPad screen, registers her arrival for the appointment. P is duly called to see the doctor – only five minutes late versus her original appointment time.

Doctor

The doctor, a general practitioner (GP) of 30 years' qualification and a family doctor specialist for most of that time, asks P to sit down and begins the appointment, which is scheduled to last around 10 or 15 minutes.

P explains her pain and describes what she believes are the reasons for her discomfort while the GP takes her blood pressure as a matter of routine, entering the results into the surgery's own database as he talks to P.

The GP makes further enquiries as to P's general health, her life circumstances and work and then proceeds to make his diagnosis.

The Diagnosis

The GP explains that he believes, from what P has said and from his interaction with her, that she may have a slipped disc or bruised spinal nerve in her lower back and recommends that P have a more detailed MRI scan and X-ray appointment at the local hospital.

When the results of these tests are available, the GP will invite P back for a further appointment where they will discuss the findings of the scan and treatment options. In the meantime, and to keep P from pain, the GP prescribes P a course of stronger-than-average painkillers, making a careful note of the prescription in the surgery's patient database.

The GP emails the prescription to P who confirms it has arrived via her mobile phone.

The Nurse

At this appointment, there is no requirement for a nurse practitioner to be involved. However, should P require after-care, a more detailed medical examination or other therapies, then the GP surgery has a small team of professional, specialist nurses available for appointments to do just that.

The Hospital

P is referred to the local hospital, where there are MRI and X-ray facilities, and her next appointment back at the GP surgery is also automatically processed by the local healthcare software. P receives email notifications for both and she selects to save these into her Google Calendar app on her phone.

P attends the hospital at the set time and date and the scan goes ahead. P is discharged immediately and awaits the follow-on appointment with the GP.

The Medicine

P continues to take the prescribed medicine throughout the period between appointments as she continues to be in significant pain. The painkiller enables P to carry out her work.

P's employer also notifies P, following receipt by the employer of a forwarded email from P herself about the hospital appointment, that P is entitled to various privately provided specialists and consultant doctors (as well as therapies for recovery) should P decide to use them.

P acknowledges the information from her employer and decides to make up her mind about her treatment options after she has had her follow-on appointment with her local GP, the doctor who saw her initially and who knows her case.

The Follow-on Appointment and the Results

P attends the local GP surgery at the allotted time and date. The same GP who saw her the first time now sees her again. It is a slightly longer appointment this time, with 20 minutes set aside to look at the specific images and reports from the hospital referral.

P's GP explains that her disc has not slipped but has protruded slightly and is bruising her spinal cord, which is causing P significant discomfort. The GP explains that the treatment options are limited, but suggests, before exploratory surgery on P's back is carried out, that P try a range of other therapies, such as Pilates, to see if the pain eases.

If P agrees to this approach, the GP makes a further hospital appointment for scanning in six months' time. P agrees to the non-invasive approach (for now) and the GP writes out a prescription for more painkillers, but explains that these are potentially addictive and suggests to P that once the Pilates begins, the prescription will naturally expire of itself and that P would have to come and see the GP again for a repeat prescription as a way of keeping both P and the GP aware of the progress of the injury.

P agrees and the appointment ends with the GP updating all of the above to P's online surgery portal account.

The Long-Term Recovery

P does attend the Pilates classes, in a classical Pilates studio, and over a period of three months notices a significant improvement to her pain (less) and mobility (higher) levels. The Pilates sessions are paid for via her employer-provided private health care, as in this way P gets more individual, one-on-one attention from the Pilates teacher.

P has two more follow-on appointments with her GP, each time reducing the prescription of painkiller until finally, after another MRI scan six months later, her GP tells P that the spine has managed to settle itself and there is no longer any pressure on the spinal cord from the injury.

The long-term prognosis is therefore that with continual therapy and exercise (such as Pilates), P should not see a recurrence of the pain.

Key Healthcare Software and Data Concepts

To give the healthcare software and data use case more relevance and context, this section defines clearly and uses real-world examples of the key concepts used in healthcare software and data.

Healthcare Software

Healthcare software is no different from the software languages and operating systems found anywhere else. But its applications are unique and specific.

Software Used

Healthcare software doesn't have a type or standard; as with other industries, each individual healthcare software design and deployment is considered on a case-by-case basis.

Applications

Even in a highly centralised healthcare market such as the United Kingdom there is no requirement for a single application standard or protocol. Applications (not phone apps) are service and functional layers in the healthcare stack and are deployed on a case-by-case basis.

Operating Systems

A single operating system would create a common platform for support and enterprise cost control but, equally, a single point of failure from a commercial, security and control risk standpoint. Healthcare software is potentially better served with a range of different, but complementary, operating systems.

Healthcare Data

Healthcare data isn't only medical records. There is a huge range of static, dynamic and transactional data that is exchanged between parties, data for archive and data for clinical analysis.

Privacy

Privacy of data is often cited (by patients) as the most important requirement of any healthcare system. Patients understand the need for physicians/doctors, nurses and other primary care staff to have access to patient data but want reassurance that this is restricted and controlled as strictly as possible.

Security

Security of data, alongside the issue of privacy, is a key requirement of all primary care users regarding healthcare data. Losing control of medical data, granting control of data to an unauthorised third party and the reputational damage incurred could be a catastrophic event for a healthcare provider.

Trust

The question of trust is connected to security and privacy. If these two attributes are present, it is likely that trust in the healthcare system will be earned by the software provider and granted 'on licence' from the users.

Access

Equitable access to data is a cornerstone of user satisfaction. Most legacy systems include a user access matrix, where administrators can configure which users can carry out the relevant system functions.

Healthcare Software and Data Transactions

Healthcare is not, at face value, a transactional industry. But in software and data terms it is, because every time an action or activity occurs within a system the data moves between actors and parties and is updated as a 'transaction' accordingly. And by transactional rules there are related reconciliations, possible reconciliation breaks, audit requirements and so on.

Physician Updates

Physicians/doctors are daily users of healthcare systems. Writing notes of appointments, diagnoses, prescriptions, further appointments and sourcing consultant reviews of patients are typical examples of physician transactions in the system.

Prescriptions

Each diagnosis, if required, has a prescription that is written for the patient. And each prescription must be processed by the pharmacist and – potentially – renewed following authorisation by the physician, sometimes without the patient needing to be seen.

Treatments

Healthcare treatments range from physiotherapy, a course of drugs, in- or out-patient care, and cover a plethora of complex, customisable and flexible requirements. Treatments must be in the context of the diagnosis and prescriptions and are a care-giving transaction in the healthcare system.

Healthcare Software and Data Outcomes

After patients get ill they also get better. Understanding and tracking that journey and the outcomes it creates is a critical role played by healthcare software and data. Long after the physician/doctor, nurse (and even the patient) has gone home or back to their non-medical life, the various healthcare software and data remain up to date (and is an invaluable trove of data for clinical research, for example).

Hospital Discharge

Leaving hospital (moving from being an in-patient to out-patient) is a physical change for the patient and also a healthcare software and data outcome. Records are changed in the relevant medical systems and information on the patient's treatment in the hospital is updated.

Long-term Health

'Value for money' for healthcare providers, especially in a world of scarce (i.e. expensive) medical resources, requires a careful balance of investment in qualified staff and facilities, good returns on investment, and a focus on the long-term health of patients. Healthcare software has to address the same factors too or risk being superseded by more efficient, decentralised (for example) replacements.

Clinical Research

A secondary outcome of primary care is the availability of data on patient illness and disease, diagnoses, treatment and long-term health outcomes. Taken together, this information is exactly what's required by the clinical research professionals in pharmaceutical companies. Providing there are clearly defined boundaries, clinical research and primary care can sit alongside one another in a non-conflicting, mutually beneficial way and not interrupt good patient outcomes.

Specialisations

Healthcare software and data are commonly encountered at the general practice and/or emergency room 'point of delivery'. However, much healthcare software and data is clustered around medical specialisations as follows:

Surgical

Surgical software is on the rise. Robotic keyhole surgery, virtual reality simulations, remote surgery and 'augmented' surgery are specialist software- and data-powered solutions.

Paediatrics

Our children will enter their adult lives (as patients) having been 'born digital'. This means that, from early childhood, their medical records, possibly even their personal diet and exercise regime, will be system-based. The direct consequences of this are not yet clear but, in a world of the internet of things, a connected patient base will only drive healthcare software and data forward further and faster.

Gerontics

The 'Baby Boomer' generation (those born between 1944 and 1964) are the largest and wealthiest cohort that the human race has ever witnessed. Ironically, these two characteristics (size of cohort and wealth) also ensure that 'Boomers' are the best-catered-for healthcare generation ever too. Healthcare software and data have a natural and compelling use case for gerontic applications.

Breaks in the Healthcare Software and Data Model

It is assumed, rightly or wrongly, that healthcare software and data are infallible; that outcomes, as mediated by human healthcare professionals, can always be quality-assessed; that poor outcomes may be avoided; and that the related software and data will ultimately make things better. But this is not always the case.

Wrong Diagnosis

It is rare, but serious misdiagnosis is potentially a significant error in primary care environments. Second opinions are vital. Their use is manifestly obvious and in this regard healthcare software and data are ready (and non-judgmental) allies in the cause.

Lost Data

'Lost' data is a seemingly innocuous phrase that can, in healthcare terms, have serious consequences for patients and sometimes for primary caregivers too. Having made a diagnosis and prescription, for example, a physician needs continuing access to that information in order to help the patient reach their good outcome. Lost data inhibits this. A well-secured healthcare software and data resource is a prerequisite to good medicine.

Wrong Prescription

It's hard to measure the impact of a wrong or inaccurate prescription on patients: much depends on the severity or otherwise of their disease.

Healthcare Software and Data Challenges More Generally

Healthcare software and data do not stand alone or in isolation from the real world in which they are deployed. There are extensive 'non-functional' requirements that affect their design and use, not all positive.

Litigation

The law has a major role to play in healthcare. But what does it mean for healthcare software and data? By adopting and using healthcare software and data, the medical industry is creating the means and mechanisms for litigation to potentially proliferate. After all, with computer records and information to hand, then the actions and outcomes of specific physicians, hospitals and medical suppliers can be tested in court as evidence.

Transparency

Transparency is a key battleground for medical benefits and costs. And as the old saying goes, 'sunlight is the best disinfectant'. Clarity over who has done what and when – and to whom – means that all actors in the healthcare industry can see and validate activities and their outcomes continuously. Transparency also provides quality reassurance and the means by which independent adjudicators can reach a decision if required.

Portability

Good healthcare software and data can't simply lock physicians/doctors, nurses and patients inside. What are the options for taking my patient data (in particular) with me when I move on? What happens if the healthcare software and data provider I use, as a doctor or patient, becomes formally insolvent and a migration to a new solution or system is required? The best healthcare software and data are designed with this in mind and are therefore critical components in a well-functioning industry.

How Healthcare Software and Data are Used Today

The current healthcare industry uses software and data on what might be politely termed a 'distributed' model. In other words, healthcare providers will use a patchwork of systems, solutions, applications and databases depending on their specific needs.

Some more integrated healthcare providers, such as the United Kingdom's National Health Service (NHS), have some core policies and even shared infrastructure for its participants, and the resulting economies of scale, common access points and data standards and the ease of data and entity transfers are of benefit. The issues arise when a specialist use case is required or when divergence happens (deliberate or not).

The 'one size fits all' approach is not the answer for healthcare software and data, but equally, an unregulated market is not necessarily efficient either. Finding a happy medium is a viable ambition; making sure costs, security, access and trust are maintained too is perhaps even more key for a successful healthcare platform.

Enter the blockchain.

How Healthcare Software would be Different Using Blockchains

How do blockchains fit in healthcare, if at all? Typically, there are three standard or commonly used tests for the usefulness or relevance of blockchains in a specific industry, for example:

■ What's the asset to be tokenised?
■ Is there a requirement for a proxy for trust?
■ Will there be equitable access?

In addition, the known benefits of blockchain, for example transparency, immutability, access and decentralisation, create the conditions for great efficiency, an improving back office and a reduced error rate.

The key question in realising these apparent benefits is the approach taken to design, configuration and deployment. Take, for example, the role of smart contracts: although viable, the transfer of business rules from legacy software and data into a new smart contract-oriented system is a transformation as well as a migration.

The rules will not necessarily need to be the same in the blockchain as they were previously, but who decides on the variance, the quality required, the testing and whether the outcomes produced by a blockchain/ smart contract replacement are better or worse than (or just different to) the system being replaced?

Healthcare System Comparison

This section of the chapter will focus on a current-state healthcare software model stack, meaning not just the technology deployed but also the functional or legal components of healthcare and also how these interrelate to each other in the current state (i.e. using non-DLT technology). This chapter will then compare and contrast this with a proposed future-state stack that may be potentially powered by blockchain (DLT) technology.

We will begin with the non-blockchain systems and models. Figure 8.3 shows, as a logical diagram, how the various enterprise systems and principal legal entities interact in a typical healthcare software and data lifecycle using non-blockchain ('current state') technology and infrastructure.

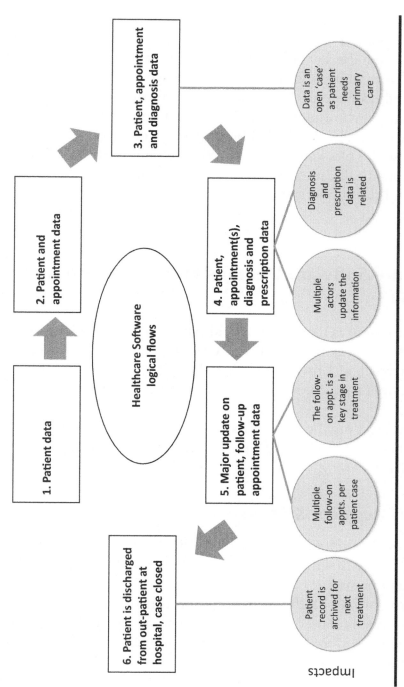

Figure 8.3 An approximate logical diagram between various healthcare software and data entities.

In addition, each principal legal entity has both a software system and an underlying silo of data that must be added to, edited and archived as well as made safe and secure, kept accurate and potentially reconciled with all of the other entities' systems and their data too. It is not the intention of this chapter to delve inside each of the principal legal entities' specific 'black box' software systems and databases; rather we are going to compare the multi-layered ecosystem of current-state healthcare software and data with how the same environment might look in a future state if distributed ledger technology (DLT, also known as blockchain) were used.

Note how the blockchain is updated with all stages/statuses for all parties automatically, meaning the information about the whole healthcare software and data cycle is transparent, synchronous, immutable and fully reconciled.

Healthcare Software Demonstration Problems and Use Case

The use case here is that of a fictional patient, taken ill with a suspected heart attack in London (UK), driven via emergency ambulance to the emergency room at University College Hospital, London, and treated there as an in-patient for a period of 36 hours before being released home as an out-patient.

We note the simplification of the use case in which the UK operates a 'free at the point of delivery' healthcare system, the National Health Service (NHS).

Caselet 1: 'Accident & Emergency'

Current state: Distributed software and data solutions make effective and rapid emergency treatment more costly, slower and error-prone than the potential alternatives.

At approximately 21.20 a patient, Harry, is taken ill at a restaurant in Shaftesbury Avenue in London, UK. The emergency ambulance arrives at the restaurant after one of the restaurant staff calls the emergency services hotline (999 or 112). Harry is treated at the scene by the emergency ambulance paramedics. Harry is asked for his name and provides his National Health Service number (which he keeps in the ICE contact in his mobile phone).

The paramedics rush Harry to University College Hospital (UCH), London, which has one of the capital's most advanced emergency rooms (known in the UK as Accident and Emergency (A&E)). The paramedics hand Harry over to the A&E staff with a verbal update followed by a detailed paper report written up after the incident. The ambulance paramedics revert back to their duties in the ambulance and, after writing up their case notes for Harry, are called to another emergency.

The A&E staff try to talk to Harry who is drifting in and out of consciousness; using the NHS number already provided via Harry's ICE contact, the team track down some of his partially digitised personal medical records. Harry's doctor is not working and the doctor's surgery is closed. The A&E team are left to make their own field decisions and decide to diagnose Harry with a cardiac arrest and to treat him urgently accordingly.

Harry responds well to treatment under the supervision of the expert staff at UCH A&E and eventually he is moved to the recovery ward, where he is kept under close medical supervision.

Harry's family arrive several hours later (from out of London) and are reassured by the A&E primary care staff (physicians/doctors and nurses) that Harry has suffered a cardiac arrest but, given his treatment and the speed with which he was brought to A&E, he has a fair chance of recovery.

Harry is discharged two days later with his family in attendance. The hospital types, prints and emails two letters: one to Harry's GP and another to the hospital's out-patient facilities ensuring Harry's treatment continues seamlessly.

Future state (using blockchains): A decentralised blockchain means better access to data and a rapid sharing for key information, especially in an emergency situation.

At approximately 21.20 a patient, Holly, is taken ill at a theatre in the Covent Garden area of London, UK. The emergency ambulance arrives at the theatre after one of the theatre staff calls the emergency services hotline (999 or 112). Holly is treated at the scene by the emergency ambulance paramedics. Holly is asked for her name and it matches the suggested National Health Service number which she keeps in her new NHS app on her mobile phone and which was linked to the paramedics' own super-user NHS app as they arrived at the theatre to treat Holly (with Holly's permission; she is conscious at this stage). The two paramedics' NHS app serves up Holly's personal medical records and they can immediately see her previous diagnoses, bloods, exercise regime, drinking and smoking etc. Holy has also had a heart attack before and this is shown in her records.

Based on this information, the paramedics forward all of Holly's data to the University College Hospital (UCH), London, A&E team plus their current GPS location. Knowing the time of arrival of the casualty Holly (and her precise medical history), the A&E team open a heart attack bed and are waiting for her arrival.

There is no requirement for a handover between paramedics and A&E as the data has already been shared. There is no requirement for a further case write-up as the paramedics' diagnosis and treatment of Holly while driving her to hospital are already saved on all participating users' NHS app, so the paramedics are free to race to their new callout.

Because of Holly's history, her family (who also live outside London) are advised on their NHS app of the incident and provided with an edited status report on her condition by the A&E team. Knowing exactly where Holly is and what her progress is means the family can make an informed choice about getting to see their relative.

Holly is treated and – when she feels better – has her case history shared to her GP's surgery and the out-patient clinic nodes on the blockchain, following which her long-term recovery will be managed. There is no change to the distributed, specialist systems used in the ambulance or hospital by the physicians/doctors and nurses. But the decentralised medical records and case management system embedded within the patient's NHS app (and the 'super user' versions of the app used by paramedics and hospital staff that integrate data for that) mean that not only does Holly get faster, more personalised and accurate treatment on arrival at the hospital but also her family, GP and long-term recovery support team are also fully updated and more efficient in their primary and secondary care roles.

Caselet 2: 'Exercise Saves Lives?'

Current state: Patients get the best outcomes when their lifestyles are improved 'pre-medicine'. But how to keep track of that?

A busy doctor's surgery is running a campaign of better preventative health with patients. A local, 'Live Better' healthcare maildrop is delivered to patients' homes.

Over the next year, the GPs and primary care staff track the incidence of long-term healthcare issues and prescriptions etc. among patients using a paper and spreadsheet-based recording system. A pattern of long-term healthcare improvement (compared to the previous year) is detected within the first six months of the campaign, but then tails off. However, this is within the statistical margin of error.

The surgery plans another, more direct campaign the following year and will keep and contrast the data. It is assumed that a multi-year statistical analysis will provide sufficient data points to assess the effectiveness of the lifestyle improvements.

Future state: How the same would work in a blockchain environment.

A busy doctor's surgery is running a campaign of better preventative health with patients. A cohort of local patients are signed up to join the new campaign and are asked to download a new NHS-provided app and to take home a small, electronic blood pressure monitor. Over a period of time, the local patients participating use the app daily to record their diet, exercise, heart rate and blood pressure on a blockchain. The app reminds them daily and the general participation rate is good. The surgery, a node on the blockchain, gets live data feedback in the trial. This provides an opportunity to modify and fine-tune or adapt the individual reporting.

Individual patient parameters, such as prescriptions, diagnoses etc. are factored into the results and – on a comparative basis – the app offers patients their own transparent, secure and private health plan suggestions, for example, when to exercise and for how long, which food to eat or avoid, and units of alcohol consumed.

The campaign becomes a rolling health feature and more patients are encouraged to use the app.

The caselets give a specific, practical example of the benefits of enterprise-level blockchain in medicine and healthcare software and data:

- **Physician/doctor benefits**: Blockchains assist with trust, meaning that the doctor–patient relationship, based on trust, is enhanced.
- **Patient benefits**: Blockchains provide a decentralised store of immutable, trustworthy and transparent data for better outcomes
- **Supplier benefits**: Blockchains provide hospitals, clinics, pharmaceutical companies, clinical researchers and suppliers with reliable, decentralised data that can be used equitably for better non-primary care outcomes.
- **Healthcare industry benefits**: Blockchains provide planning accuracy, transparency and security of data.

Table 8.1 Problem statements in current and future states of healthcare software

HC Problem Statement	Current HC State (Non-Blockchain) Solution	Future HC State (Blockchain) Solution	Comments
Distributed software and data create breaks or gaps in the delivery of primary care	Requires manual intervention to resolve	Decentralised solution enables business rules and data to interact better	Blockchains are not a stand-alone solution but can provide a trusted, decentralised route to better patient outcomes
Clinical research data is centralised and non-synchronous	Requires manual intervention and integration to be exploitable	Decentralised solution enables business rules and data to interact better, plus security, equitable access and trust	Better clinical research, using better data, is more trustworthy and provides speedier results in a confirmed dataset

Table 8.1 shows a comparison of example healthcare software and data problem statements and the benefits provided by future-state blockchains versus current-state technology.

Summary and Conclusion

Software and data for healthcare is vital for our wellbeing but also prone to creating an artificial and unwanted barrier between primary carer(s) and patients. It has also become, in some cases, monolithic and difficult to innovate in healthcare technology.

Distributed ledger technology, or blockchains, offers a less intensive route to cutting the size and scale of healthcare technology, software and data without 'throwing the baby out with the bathwater', i.e. allowing us to keep the benefits.

Careful assessment of current healthcare software and data will mean that gradual change can take place, avoiding putting at risk those who most need good healthcare: us.

Before You Go On

■ Consider how current healthcare software and data, built as a patchwork even within integrated systems like the UK's NHS, are difficult to manage as a collective infrastructure.

■ Reflect on the role that primary carers – and their often rapid and sometimes life-changing decisions – have and their requirements for trustworthy, secure and easily (and equitably) accessible data.

■ Remember that blockchain is not a magic-wand solution. It has a limited (but effective) role in helping primary and secondary carers to receive trusted and secure updates on the progress of a patient through, for example, an emergency case.

Note

1 Deloitte, 2020 Global Health Care Outlook. www2.deloitte.com/content/dam/ Deloitte/cz/Documents/life-sciences-health-care/2020-global-health-care-outlook.pdf.

Further Reading

https://pdfs.semanticscholar.org/7e8e/cdfebdd8122094bad7993b9710c7f1df 04d1.pdf

www.mdpi.com/2227-9032/7/2/56/pdf

www.capgemini.com/wp-content/uploads/2017/07/blockchain-a_ healthcare_industry_view_2017_web.pdf

www.ehidc.org/sites/default/files/resources/files/blockchain.pdf

Chapter 9

Retail Investments Use Case

The four most dangerous words in investing are: 'this time it's different'.
Sir John Templeton[1]

Economist cartoon

DOI: 10.4324/9781003132592-9

Summary

This entire chapter is a use case, a case study. At the end of this chapter you'll be able to

- Understand an overview of retail investments and blockchains;
- Know which applications within retail investments use a blockchain type of approach;
- Define the retail investments key legal entities and actors;
- Know about the different types of retail investments deployments;
- Compare blockchains in retail investments to current solutions;
- Get an understanding of a specific retail investments use case (a case history);
- Understand the positives and potential negatives in the retail investments blockchain use case;
- Understand the likely future direction of retail investments.

Chapter Overview

Retail investments ('retail' is a specific word in this context because these are investments made by consumers and we differentiate 'retail' from 'wholesale' or 'corporate' or institutional investing) is the activity of buying and selling financial instruments, for example, mutual funds, equities/shares and fixed income bonds. Investments are usually held in an electronic portfolio and the investor usually has access to advice and an ongoing portfolio management service.

Retail investments is a global industry, sometimes also referred to as 'wealth management', 'portfolio management' or financial advice. Figure 9.1 shows the distribution of funds under management by the largest fund managers worldwide.

Mutual funds are the primary instrument bought and sold as part of the process of retail investing. Note: although this chapter makes frequent reference to funds as the core part of retail investing, this is not the exclusive interest of the chapter. Retail investing involves a portfolio of instruments, albeit with funds usually predominating. There is a further section in this book focusing on fund management and the effect of blockchains on that.

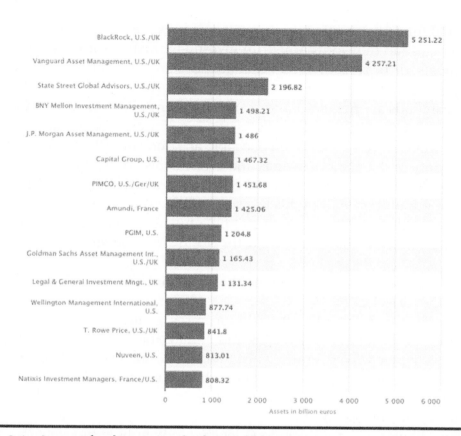

Figure 9.1 Largest fund managers in the world by assets.

Source: Statista Inc. www.statista.com/statistics/322452/largest-asset-managers-worldwide-by-value-of-assets/

   Mutual funds (and for the purposes of this chapter, also referred to as just 'funds') are legally established and regulated retail investments entities or vehicles. Mutual funds are created with the sole purpose of buying, selling and administering, in a portfolio, an underlying made up of third-party investments. Funds buy and sell their underlying based on a published prospectus and subject to specific rules around good portfolio management, so (for example) collectively and transparently. Mutual funds vary in style and may be closed-ended, open-ended and also 'exchange traded' funds (ETF). Mutual funds may be passive (i.e. the fund is set up to track an equity or interest rate market index blindly, up or down, by buying and selling financial instruments accordingly) or active (i.e. the fund is managed by an expert fund manager with or without the help of algorithmic tools).

Mutual funds have different objectives – for example, some funds will specialise in the North American investment market, or in cleantech investments, or be a risk-rated fund that is designed to suit 'cautious' or 'adventurous' investors best etc.

Mutual funds are not the only way that consumers may engage with retail investments. Other investment assets exist, for example gold, cryptocurrencies, real estate and collectible art. And since Roman times the vast majority of the planet's savings and investments are held in fiat cash – these days major currencies such as US dollars, euros, pounds sterling, Japanese yen and so on. But this use case will focus entirely on mutual funds.

Understanding and managing retail investments is central to gaining knowledge on how the wealth industry worldwide operates.

- In this chapter we will examine the retail investments use case and smaller 'caselets'.
- The chapter will explain the main features, challenges and benefits of retail investments for managers and administrators.
- This chapter will cover the typical retail investments supply chain and stack and entities and actors such as financial advisers, brokers, administrators, portfolio managers, nominees, custodians, cash managers and so on.
- The chapter will also include a detailed look at how blockchain provides a robust, efficient and cost-effective improvement to current retail savings and investment software applications and what this means for advisers, investors and the supply chain.

Retail Investments in More Detail

Retail investments is a wide industry with a long history. Most developed world economies have a retail investments sector. Retail investments is a regulated industry with strict rules of governance, price controls, entry and exit criteria, and is subject to extra checks and obligations such as 'know your client' (KYC) and anti-money laundering (AML) rules and procedures.

The retail investments industry regulator and government expect participants to assess retail investors' attitudes to risk, their inherent and explicit vulnerabilities (whether visible or not) and to report constantly on the state of the mutual funds and market conditions generally.

In return, mutual funds are allowed to charge consumers an annual management fee (and other fees, for example for the administration of life events such as the estates of deceased fund holders, splitting fund holdings on divorce, processing withdrawals and transfers etc.). Other actors in the mutual fund management stack may also charge fees for custody, dealing (or arranging dealing in) the fund's units or shares, holding the units in a nominee structure and for the provision of a software and services platform. There may also be financial advice fees, an additional investment management or portfolio fee and a fee based on a cash interest rate (although this latter fee is less common in the era of ultra-low interest rates).

It all adds up. One recent study assessed the effect of cumulative fees on a pension fund, a very long-term mutual fund structure in which investments may be held and contributed to for decades, and Figure 9.2 sets out the results: the overall impact of the high fees (in this case, 1.5% or 150 basis points) was to reduce the overall size of the pension fund by a significant percentage at the end of the period invested.

Overall, the core elements and classical technology stack of retail investments (sometimes referred to as a 'platform') are as follows:

■ The 'front end' or user experience layer. This is usually both an app and a browser-based website. Both app and site have a secure logon and allow consumers to view and interact with their portfolio(s), messages and performance statistics.

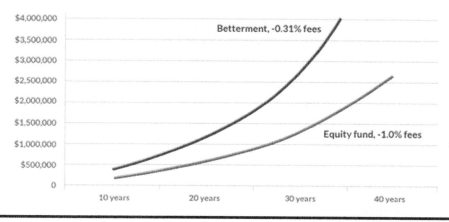

Figure 9.2   Effect of fees over time.

Source: Editorial Staff, Betterment Resource Center. Published May 12, 2014. www.betterment.com/resources/five-secrets-to-help-you-build-wealth-by-investing/

- The portfolio and cash administration layer. This layer enables the retail investments staff to administer the instruments (buying and selling), to look after the cash (held as a client money account and looked after via general ledger software), and to update and make changes, whether automated or manual, to the portfolios of individuals and groups of investors.
- The nominee, depository and custody layer, where the legal and administrative entities are reflected in specific records as (variously) the owners, nominee and custodian(s) etc. of each of the investments within the portfolios.
- Finally, there's the brokerage, trading, market and counterparty infrastructure that a typical fund manager interacts with.

Retail Investments Software

Retail investments software has been around since the early days of the spreadsheet and the internet, but the fund management industry could never be categorised as a modern or technologically advanced industry.

Early retail investments systems were attempts to partially automate and streamline the work carried out manually by fund and portfolio managers. For example, each fund (a type of retail investment) has a 'box' (originally, a wooden box) containing the physical paper certificates and statements for each fund unit or shareholder. As unit/shareholders buy and sell their certificates in the fund, the box would be updated with a new set of papers relating to that day's transactions. The share certificates and ledgers for cash management would also be catalogued by the box and the overall effect was to maintain the fund and all its holdings, whether in cash or instruments, on a daily basis. At the middle of each day, the fund's overall holdings (including cash) and the securities within it would be valued and a daily 'net asset value' (or NAV) of the fund would be published as a unit or share price.

A General View of Retail Savings and Investment Policy, Past and Present

Partial process automation drove the design and development of the earliest retail investments computer systems. At face value, these systems were evolutionary: they were explicitly designed to replicate and improve upon the manual operations processes they were to replace. As automation entered the retail investments industry, additional features (such as automated trading, price feeds, currency feeds, a wider investment/fund marketplace etc.) also began to be deployed that would enhance the performance and competitive edge of the retail investments or portfolio itself.

Throughout the 1970s onwards, however, there were limited attempts to re-engineer or otherwise evolve by deviation from established and ingrained fund management practices. For example, why has the retail investments industry, even with automation, continued with a daily NAV when computer power made it immediately obvious that a per-second NAV was also possible?

The partial answer to this is that the retail investments industry is a slow-moving, conservative and well-paid sector. Drivers for change are limited when incumbency is ingrained, fees and commissions are often layered with different participants (such as broker, nominee, adviser etc.) and there is also the practical challenge of coping with investments at either end of the technology spectrum – e.g. some retail investments, principally funds, were available on a computer system early; others are still using paper, fax and spreadsheets.

The future of retail investments technology is very different. As tokenisation creates a revolution in the way both retail and institutional investments are issued and managed, so retail investments will also be brought directly into the very modern era. Blockchains are an almost perfect use case for retail investments. A distributed ledger that is full of tokenised instruments, tokenised cash, and requires immutability, trust and equitable access is ideal. Add in the need for reducing the stack of incumbents such as portfolio administrators, nominees, brokers, depositories and more and the case becomes obvious.

On top of all that is the revolution of automated (or augmented) advice where artificial intelligence (AI) and predictive statistical forecasting, along with behavioural economics for correcting consumers' inherent biases and assessing their appetites for risk, optimises each individual portfolio construction and maintenance.

How Retail Investments Work in the Real World

Retail investments, in the real world, operates in a mixture of mechanical and human processes. Advice and professional support for investors, for example, are usually carried out by expert and qualified staff. Known as wealth managers, portfolio managers or independent financial advisers (IFAs, in the UK), these professionals charge an annual fee to investors in return for which the administration of the investors' assets, the client money, performance reporting and any income requirements are looked after.

The following activities are typical (but not exhaustive) of a professional retail investments service:

- Investor onboarding, including
  - 'Know your client' or KYC;
  - Anti-money laundering checks (AML); and
  - The testing of each individual investor for their attitude to risk or ATR which includes their biases, capacity for loss, and overall views of poor and good performance.
- Portfolio construction, including
  - Setting up the portfolio;
  - Buying and selling the instruments;
  - Client money (cash) management;
  - Tax relief and reporting; and
  - Management and investor reporting.
- Portfolio maintenance, including
  - Administering the portfolio on a day-to-day basis;
  - Settlement and reconciliations;
  - Corporate actions; and
  - Closing or transferring away a portfolio.
- Investor maintenance, e.g.
  - 'Life events' such as when an investor passes away/estate management, divorce, change of name, address or status, old age and infirmity etc.;
  - Beneficiary maintenance; and
  - Wills and probate etc.

Many retail investments managers offer a 'delegated' service, for example, where an investor gives the retail investments manager a power of attorney over the underlying investments and cash. This means the day-to-day decisions about the portfolio, what's bought and sold within it and the pooling of all cash (for example) are not known by the individual investor except in hindsight via their annual portfolio review. In these cases, also known as 'discretionary portfolio management', 'wealth management' or 'family office', the adviser tends to charge a somewhat higher fee for the additional work and risk involved.

The following section sets out the high-level roles and responsibilities of the individual actors in the retail investments stack.

The Investor

The retail investor is at the centre of the service and is the direct (or indirect) owner of the underlying investments and cash. The investor is usually a natural person, sometimes a family trust (very rarely, a company) and has the ultimate responsibility for the investment decisions made on its behalf. The investor is expected to pay the fees for the retail investments services used.

The Adviser

The retail investments industry would not function without the role of the adviser. To date, this has been a professionally qualified human being, but recent developments in 'automated' and 'augmented' advice has seen the introduction of algorithms and process automation in support of human fact finding and decision making, for example.

The Portfolio Manager

The portfolio manager is a role related to that of adviser but is usually not client-facing and is often highly technical in nature, for example, that of the discretionary fund manager. Portfolio managers are also automated – many of the newer retail investments platforms include automated rebalancing modules complete with decision-trees, edge case reporting, automated instrument and cash reconciliation, and bulk aggregation and disaggregation of trades for individual and group portfolios.

The Investment Manager

The investment management role is similar to that of portfolio manager and adviser but even more specialised, and usually focused on the specific requirements and issues relating to the underlying investments, for example their legal status, corporate actions relating to the investments and the construction and distribution internally of the investments themselves (i.e. which geographical areas they cover, which industries, sectors and whether or not they have green, ethical or other attributes etc.).

Blockchains in Retail Investment

Retail investments is a tailor-made use case for blockchain as retail investments requires blockchain's core attributes of trust, access, security and immutability, and the deployment of blockchain in retail investments drives efficiency, fewer layers within the regulated operations and technology stacks, and has far fewer errors, reconciliation breaks and provides better transparency to investors, advisers and managers alike.

A Day in the Life of Retail Investments

Retail investments is a thriving industry with a long history (in developed economies), a detailed and complex operating model, standardised infrastructures/technology stacks and a stable regulatory environment, for example the Financial Conduct Authority (in the United Kingdom), the US Securities and Exchange Commission (SEC) and the European Securities and Markets Authority (in the European Economic Area, EEA).

There's no single approach for administering and managing retail investments – and no single rulebook as to how, when and where the underlying investments or individual investors are to be dealt with. Client money management is more prescriptive in nature, as the subject of cash is the focus of more regulatory governance generally.

The following sets out a fictional 'day in the life' of the retail investments process, as it is currently.

The Inheritance

Luckily for her, an investor, Ana, is awarded a sum of money via an inheritance from the estate of her late grandmother. The lawyers for the estate contact Ana by letter and agree with her to pay the inheritance, US$250,000, to Ana's bank account within six weeks.

Ana is a Colombian national but lives in Cardiff in the United Kingdom on assignment in her career with a multinational petrochemical conglomerate. As a UK taxpayer, Ana decides – for the time being – to domicile her new wealth in the UK and to take advantage of the specific UK tax reliefs available to her, which she has heard about from work colleagues.

The Adviser

Ana is informally introduced to an independent financial adviser (IFA) in Bristol by her employer's human resources department. It's not a recommendation, as the HR colleague is only able to share a list of IFA options with Ana and Ana is expected to make her own mind up about which IFA she chooses.

Ana makes an introductory appointment to meet her new IFA by phone and the IFA's assistant then emails Ana with a link through which Ana can set up an 'onboarding' account. After onboarding, Ana will then be able to meet the IFA and have a face-to-face interview.

The Onboarding

Ana creates her new account using the IFA website. As part of the onboarding process, Ana is required to complete sections on 'know your customer' (KYC), anti-money laundering (AML) checks and to answer some questions on whether or not Ana is (or is connected to) any 'politically exposed persons', PEPs.

In addition, Ana goes through the user experience of determining her 'attitude to risk' (ATR). An individual investor's ATR is assessed using an online, automated process that asks the potential investor questions on their capacity for loss; how they think about gains and losses; where and how their individual biases might be corrected (the typical example is hyperbolic discounting, i.e. the tendency by which human beings seem to prefer rewards taken now versus those that might accrue later in life); and what Ana's specific goals might be for her investment, for example, does Ana intend to use the investment for retirement, family purposes and so on.

As part of the onboarding Ana is also required to upload any relevant documentary evidence of her existing circumstances, for example, her current level of earnings, any existing savings and investments, her levels of protection and cover and so on. The IFA system allows Ana to do this on the basis of 'save for later' as she is required to scan and upload documents etc.

The Appointment and Portfolio

Once Ana has completed the onboarding process, she is able to make an appointment with her new IFA to discuss her circumstances, goals etc. and options for a new portfolio to be set up and managed on her behalf.

Ana and the IFA meet for an hour in a meeting room at Ana's workplace in Cardiff. The IFA brings with him a set of contractual documents for Ana's review and signature, if she's satisfied with them, and a pre-prepared 'needs and requirements' letter specific to Ana's individual situation that the IFA has drafted.

Ana reviews the documents and agrees to transfer the US$250,000 (which she has now received from the lawyers looking after her grandmother's estate) from her personal bank account to the client money bank account of the IFA's firm.

Once the cash transfer has taken place and the documents are signed, Ana's new IFA (who is a discretionary fund manager, i.e. on whom Ana has granted a full power of attorney over her investment decisions) opens a new investment portfolio for Ana on the IFA firm's system and begins the process, on Ana's behalf, of buying investments (securities such as exchange-traded funds (ETFs), publicly traded equities or stocks and highly rated fixed income instruments like blue-chip company bonds and government bonds) according to the investment distribution profile of the IFA's agreed portfolio.

After a short period of time, the IFA confirms to Ana in writing that the new portfolio has been successfully set up and now can be viewed by Ana, complete with a full history of transactions and cash balances and so on, using the IFA firm's online app and software.

The Portfolio Performance

Over time, the investment performance of Ana's portfolio may be viewed online and is measured against other indices, for example, the annualised performance of different stock markets and a range of other commercially available performance indices.

Charting portfolio performance is a key feature of the IFA firm's services, especially as they are the ones responsible for the investment choices made on Ana's behalf. The IFA firm provides both an app and a website account where Ana can view this.

Importantly, the IFA firm is obliged to also display to Ana the effect of their fees (and any fees related to the underlying investments, for example). This is done both historically and, if Ana requests it, as an illustration or projection of performance and fees for the future.

The Annual Meeting

Going forwards, Ana and her IFA are scheduled to have a meeting each year to discuss Ana's situation (with reference to whether anything has materially changed, for example) and to review portfolio performance.

Prior to the annual meeting, the IFA will email to Ana a copy of the retail investments portfolio statement including, for example, details on cash balances, any new money to be invested in the portfolio, transactions in investments, the distribution of the investments versus the portfolio template (and an explanation of any deviation), the performance against agreed benchmarks and an illustration/projection of the future expected performance.

The meeting may also be used to reassess Ana's attitude to risk, capacity for loss etc. and the IFA and Ana might take the opportunity to look again at which portfolio Ana is invested in and whether or not that's appropriate for Ana's circumstances.

At the end of the annual meeting, in the future, Ana and the IFA will agree on the actions needed (if any) in respect of the portfolio and how the IFA will go about addressing these.

The Supply Chain

The retail investments supply chain is complex, often manual (operationally) and can be subject to delay, for example in respect of transactions and cash processing.

In addition, there are significant complexities in respect of the various different technological requirements, legal entities and regulatory requirements that add additional layers to the overall retail investments stack.

What this means overall for retail investments is that IFAs, like Ana's in this example, are obliged to commit considerable time and resources simply to setting up and operating their own technology platforms. The platforms used are expensive, cumbersome and often create a bottleneck or restriction on the flexibility of IFAs to use the best or latest advice tools.

The Follow-on Appointment and the Results

As a one-off, and specifically following their initial appointment and the activity of setting up Ana's portfolio, Ana's IFA recommends their having a follow-on meeting to discuss a couple of specific issues that have arisen.

One of the issues relates to Ana's other financial provision – for example, the level of health and medical cover Ana currently has and the scope she might have for increasing this given her relatively young age and the ability Ana has of securing a competitive quote for cover via her relationship with the IFA firm.

There are also the results of the initial portfolio set-up to discuss with Ana and a requirement by the IFA to confirm that Ana is happy with his work so far. Ana agrees to the meeting, although she is confident that – so far at least – she now trusts the IFA to carry out her wishes in a competent and professional way.

The meeting takes place and there are no open issues to discuss at this stage. Ana agrees again to settle the IFA firm's fees by deduction from her new portfolio.

Key Retail Investments Concepts

In relation to blockchain, retail investments have some already existing key concepts that are vital to understand in terms of how these are deployed currently and what a future state – for example, in a blockchain-type solution – might look like with reference to the same concepts.

Retail Investments Software

Since the advent of the spreadsheet, the 'buy side' (retail investments market terminology for the general industry of fund managers) has used software to make and manage retail investments. What this means in practice is that all retail investments currently sit on, and are operated by, some form of software application and database.

Software Used

Most retail investments software is specialised for the setting up and maintenance of portfolios, including cash. These are often referred to as 'platforms' but also include either their own customisable 'user experience' layer and/or an API-style access point so that IFA firms and especially discretionary fund managers, for example, can gain access to the services offered by the platform.

Applications

There are no special requirements for retail investments software applications. Most run on standard, third-party or open-source applications and these are configured within each platform accordingly.

Operating Systems (OS)

Again, it is not a specific requirement of retail investments software to use a certain type of operating system. Interoperability is useful and there is a trend away from proprietary OS over time for commercial and practical reasons, especially given the increasing maturity of most OS.

Retail Investments Data

Retail investments data is both 'static' and 'individual' in nature. We're going to talk mostly about the 'individual' data here, but a brief and passing reference to the depth and importance of static data is also required.

Static investment data is critical in determining both historical performance and potential future illustrations. Without a deep and reliable (i.e. accurate) pool of data in this respect, no retail investments system or process would be viable.

Individual investment data relates to the specificity of the individual retail investors, for example their 'attitude to risk' score.

Privacy

Keeping investment data private (i.e. kept strictly within a firm and shared only to an individual investor, for example) is a fundamental principle of the industry, subject to regulatory and tax reporting and for which most investor data is anonymised, for example.

Standard consumer privacy rules and regulations also apply, for example, the GDPR regime in the EU and EEA.

Security

Although no IFA keeps any actual physical or digital retail investments such as securities, investments or cash within their systems (all of the above are kept in safe custody by regulated third parties such as deposit-taking banks or custodian banks, for example) there is an assumed requirement for 'bank level' security and encryption at all stages of the retail investments lifecycle.

Trust

No retail investments firm or system would work without trust. This is a contractual, ethical and practical concern, as without even a basic level of trust, all investors would simply withdraw their cash and investments immediately.

Trust can break down at any stage but in the sense of data, it also means trust in the accuracy, salience and timeliness of the data.

Access

Not all retail investors want or need access to their investments data at all times. For example, when a market crashes, investors typically want very frequent updates on their investment performance in order to make informed decisions. Without the right level of data access, therefore, a retail investments system that was absent this functionality would fail.

The Retail Investments Stack

It's worth considering here the relevance and functioning of the overall retail investments stack: 'In computer science, a stack is an abstract data type that serves as a collection of elements, with two principal operations: push, which adds an element to the collection, and pop, which removes the most recently added element that was not yet removed'.[2]

The UX Layer

A UX layer enables individual IFAs and investor actors to log on, 'onboard' and process their own interactions with the overall retail investments system. The rules of the UX layer are extensive, configurable by individual investment managers and IFA firms and closely defined, for example, an attitude to risk test or similar.

It's a truism, but in a world of increasing homogenisation, most IFAs and discretionary fund managers in the retail investments industry create value by being different, and it's usually in the UX layer that these differences are found.

The Individual Account and Advice Layer

Each investor is expected to have a segregated account (in both practical and legal terms) and this is usually the first layer of significant or material complexity in a standard retail investments system.

Managing and keeping in ledgers individual client cash, identifying fractional ownership of cash or instruments, processing personal updates such as death, divorce or incapacity, and personalised reporting for both performance and regulatory/tax purposes means that the 'individual account' layer is more than just a typical customer relationship management (CRM) function.

Add in the keeping of financial advice (and even product records) and this layer is expanded again. As for the UX layer, many IFAs will quote the individual account layer as a key differentiator for their business offering and show a great deal of interest in setting it up correctly.

The Portfolio Administration Layer

Although no physical cash, instruments or securities are kept in the portfolio administration layer (all are stored purely on a 'books and records' basis), this is the core piece of functionality in the retail investments stack.

The portfolio administration layer not only stores records of all historical transactions, balances, holdings, reconciliations and so on, but it is also used for bulk dealing, aggregation and disaggregation, portfolio income calculations, maintaining individual portfolios to the distributions set out on portfolio templates, and for performance measurement.

The Depository Layer

In retail investments terms, the depository layer is a technical layer that refers to where an individual instrument (usually an exchange-traded equity) has been sourced from. Sometimes this is referred to as a CREST record, for example.

The Nominee Layer

In some retail investments markets, individual investors own their investments by means of a legal nominee. This is a historical arrangement that was designed to make it easier for bulk trading; however, many retail investments agreements and contracts now specifically set out the role of the nominee too.

The Custody Layer

All retail investments, whether cash or instruments/securities, are required to be held in custody by a separately established and regulated custodian. For cash, such a custodian is usually a fully regulated deposit-taking bank. For exchange-traded instruments and securities, depending on the security, this is usually a fully regulated custodian bank. Some mutual funds themselves do not require a custodian, as they themselves provide only books and records of their own underlying; however, it remains the fact that all physical investments are ultimately in safe custody.

In the event of a portfolio administrator's insolvency, for example, it is the safe custody provider's role to return the client cash and investments to the investor.

The Cash Layer

Most retail investments cash (both the cash that is part of the portfolio distribution and balances of cash in general terms) is held by means of a pooled client money account with a fully regulated deposit-taking banking institution.

However, in order to account for that cash, portfolio administrators are obliged to maintain fully reconciled cash general ledger entries on all cash movements, reconciliations/breaks and balances.

Again, in the event of a portfolio administrator's insolvency, the pooled cash and general ledger records are used to calculate and return client money safely to investors.

The Transaction/Counterparty Layer

All retail investments (including any cash element) are bought and sold at some point. What this means is that there is a significant transaction/counterparty layer where the different entities related to buying and selling are processed, both manually and through automation.

Specialisations

Not all retail investments are standardised or automated in any case. On the other hand, some are *only* viable when totally automated. A handful of retail investments providers are looking to not only automate their standard processes but also to offer an advanced specialisation in order to attract new investors, for example AI or algorithmic trading. This chapter will look at some of these at a high level.

Algorithmic Trading

Algorithmic trading is commonplace in the 'sell side', usually corporate and investment banking. It means the process by which the trading of instruments and securities is managed by highly efficient computers that rely on nanoseconds of price information access to their advantage. For this reason, for example, many such algorithmic trading providers locate their servers right next door to the Chicago Mercantile Exchange in the US.

In the world of retail investments, such algorithmic trading is far less commonplace. It's not from a lack of awareness but more a function of the significant latency already existing in the typical legacy retail investments stack, as we have discussed earlier in this chapter. Reduce the stack and the case for algorithmic trading and its advantages becomes more relevant for retail investments too.

Predictive Analysis and AI

Given a significant data lake and the processing power to manage it, most retail investments providers would agree that there is a place for predictive analysis and AI in the industry.

However, with a complex and diverse legacy stack and the tendency for retail investments providers, as incumbents, not to seek to consolidate that, then not only does the 'science fiction' label of AI create obstacles to adoption but there is also a perception of 'greater complexity' to overcome.

Again, with a better technology base available (and we'll talk about blockchain in that regard shortly), the optionality for AI and prediction becomes attractive.

Automated Advice

In the US and UK there is a cohort of consumers who are deemed to be caught in an industry-wide 'advice gap'. What this means is that, given the costs of servicing a typical retail investor (based on the cumbersome legacy stacks of most providers), there is a minimum investable amount of capital required in order for most retail investors to be able to afford the fees of their adviser and portfolio manager. It's not a fixed rule but this is usually deemed to be a minimum of around US$250,000/GB£200,000.

For the majority of retail investors not in this bracket, therefore, there is assumed to be no provision available, as a professionally qualified financial adviser must charge a minimum fee that is simply unaffordable.

Enter the 'automated advice' solution. In an online world with enlightened consumers, the logic runs, there must be a safe, guardrail-directed self-service advice option. The data is not yet available to speak to the attractiveness or success of these automated advice propositions, but they are as likely to persist as their sister propositions in medical and other worlds suggest.

Breaks in the Retail Investments Model

Unlike the airbrushed marketing puffs of their proponents, it is an inconvenient fact that all retail investments systems and operating models include the inevitable 'breaks' (i.e. unreconciled outcomes) in their daily operations.

It is a measure of a well-designed retail investments model as to how well it can recover from a break. Below is a quick explanation of each type of break and its potential impacts.

Cash Break

A cash break occurs when the cash (client money) in a retail investments system no longer reconciles. Cash breaks are reportable incidents (to the regulator) and may incur a fine, inspection or both. Not just that, but a serious cash break will oblige a retail investments provider to implement improvements and offer redress to individual investors if there has been loss.

Stock Break

Like a cash break, a stock break is an unreconciled instrument or security position, usually as a result of a transaction (buying and selling a security or instrument from a counterparty), a corporate action or a transfer from one (external) portfolio to another. Like cash breaks, significant stock breaks are reportable and may require redress.

Reverse Transaction

The ability to reverse a transaction (for example, cancelling or adjusting a large aggregated instrument or security transaction) is not just a simple matter of reversal, as all of the affected portfolios will need to be re-assessed for their fractional and other positions, and if there is a material impact, offered proportional redress.

Reversing transactions is fairly common in a standard retail investments proposition and is a key requirement of any blockchain solution.

General Challenges

It is not only in the technology stack and day-to-day operations that retail investments encounter the majority of challenges. There are specific issues which we will outline here that are of relevance in any discussion with regard to blockchains.

Speed and Latency

Although, as we have discussed, retail investments are not especially fast at trading (there is, for example, little or no algorithmic trading taking place), there is a need for speed and latency not to adversely affect the general retail investments model.

What this means in practice is that if there were a retail investments solution that was faster, more timely etc., then this would not only deliver efficiency into the stack design but also encourage more direct benefits from fast trading etc. to be adopted.

Incumbency

To overcome the current retail investments legacy stack, and the incumbents who have settled firmly into place as a result of it, means any challenger solution such as blockchain, for example, must deal head-on with those same incumbents and be insurgent, new and revolutionary.

In the dusty world of retail investments this looks unlikely. However, what is more likely to make incumbency wilt is the potential process of the tokenisation of the underlying instruments and securities (such as quoted equities/stocks, ETFs and fixed-income instruments such as blue-chip/government bonds, for example).

Faced with a tokenised universe of instruments, most objections to a similar tokenisation of the retail investments stack would presumably also evaporate.

Portability

At the current time, it is expensive, cumbersome and slow for a typical retail investor to move their investments from one providers' stack/proposition to another. As a consequence, most don't. This is not a good consumer outcome.

The challenge is not only to improve the technology that would encourage portability, but also to optimise the process so that if this were also more secure, trustworthy, or equitable access etc. (all known attributes of blockchain), then portability of investments would be as common as changing a bank account or utility supplier, for example.

How Retail Investments Operates Today

As we have seen, and to recap, currently the retail investments industry operates in a multi-layered, complex, incumbent-driven and cumbersome stack of different legal, technological and operational entities where slow, expensive and non-portable functions occur.

Add in strict regulations, tax law, human habits and needs around trust, equitable access to information and data, and the delegation of responsibilities in consideration for fees, and we quickly realise that this is not only an industry in need of technological reform but also one crying out for disruption and innovation.

Enter the blockchain.

How Retail Investments Would be Different Using Blockchains

How do blockchains fit in retail investments, if at all? As we have discussed in earlier use cases, typically there are three standard or commonly used tests for the usefulness or relevance of blockchains in a specific industry, for example:

■ What's the asset to be tokenised?
■ Is there a requirement for a proxy for trust?
■ Will there be equitable access?

In addition, the known benefits of blockchain (for example transparency, immutability, access and decentralisation) create in themselves the conditions for greater efficiency, an improving back office and a reduced error rate.

The key question in realising these apparent benefits is the approach taken to design, configuration and deployment of blockchains in the retail investments industry.

Take, for example, the role of smart contracts: although viable, the transfer of business rules from legacy software and data into a new smart contract-oriented system is a transformation as well as a migration. The rules will not necessarily need to be the same in the blockchain as they were previously, but the question is: who decides on variance, the quality required, the testing and whether the outcomes produced by a blockchain/ smart contract replacement are better or worse than (or just different to) the system being replaced?

This is especially an issue in an industry such as retail investments, which is already weighed down by complex and entrenched constraints, with regulation-driven business rules, and with a somewhat disengaged consumer base who in any case believe that their investments are being managed just well enough on an expensive but 'delegated' basis by professionals. How would blockchains and smart contracts break this paradigm?

Retail Investments Comparison

This section of the chapter will focus on a current-state retail investments model stack, meaning not just the technology deployed but also the functional or legal components of retail investments and also how these interrelate to each other in the current state (i.e. using non-DLT technology). This chapter will then compare and contrast this with a proposed future-state stack that may be potentially powered by blockchain (DLT) technology.

We will begin with the non-blockchain systems and models. Figure 9.3 shows, as a logical diagram, how the various enterprise systems and principal legal entities interact in a typical retail investments life cycle using non-blockchain (current state) technology and infrastructure.
In addition, each principal legal entity has both a software system and an underlying silo of data that must be added to, edited and archived as well as made safe and secure, kept accurate and potentially reconciled with all of the other entities' systems and their data too.

The goal of this chapter, as a use case, is not simply to delve inside each of the principal legal entities' specific 'black box'; rather we are going to compare the multi-layered ecosystem of current-state retail investments with how the same environment might look in a future state if distributed ledger technology (DLT, also known as blockchain) were used.

Note how the blockchain is updated with all stages/statuses for all parties automatically, meaning the information about the whole retail investments cycle is transparent, synchronous, immutable and fully reconciled.

Retail Investments Problems and Use Case

As an aid to understanding the specifics of the retail investments industry, and the potential relevance of blockchain in multiple different levels that it

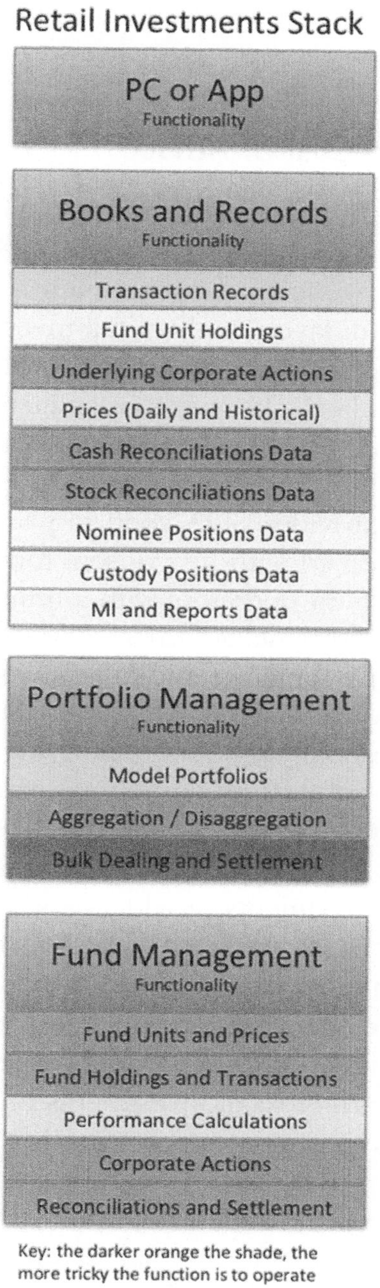

Retail Investments Stack

PC or App
Functionality

Books and Records
Functionality

Transaction Records

Fund Unit Holdings

Underlying Corporate Actions

Prices (Daily and Historical)

Cash Reconciliations Data

Stock Reconciliations Data

Nominee Positions Data

Custody Positions Data

MI and Reports Data

Portfolio Management
Functionality

Model Portfolios

Aggregation / Disaggregation

Bulk Dealing and Settlement

Fund Management
Functionality

Fund Units and Prices

Fund Holdings and Transactions

Performance Calculations

Corporate Actions

Reconciliations and Settlement

Key: the darker orange the shade, the
more tricky the function is to operate

Figure 9.3   An approximate logical diagram between various constituent elements of the retail investments stack.

Source: The authors

could potentially have an impact, we'll now give the 'real life' examples of two specific use cases by way of description.

Caselet 1: 'Cutting the Cost of Advice'

We previously discussed the existence of a potential 'advice gap' for those consumers seeking professional investment advice but lacking the minimum investable capital typically required by investment advisers.

Current state: Incumbent layers of the retail investments stack (in the UK) create unnecessary cost, complexity and inaccuracy.

Peter, a long-standing client of a wealth management firm known as St Paul's Investment Advisors (SPIA) in London, UK, decides to consolidate his various different retail investments accounts (two in the UK and one in Switzerland) to his SPIA provider. SPIA confirm with Peter that these are Peter's instructions and, armed with his consent form, SPIA approach his old retail investments account operators with a transfer request. Each of the three former retail investments advisers all process Peter's instructions differently, based on their own terms and conditions and subject to their different national regulators. All three of the individual retail investments providers hold Peter's variously different underlying instruments, securities and cash in segregated portfolios on entirely different platforms (systems) and have custody arrangements with different banks across multiple currencies.

One of the UK retail investments providers and the Swiss retail investments provider each contact Peter directly to confirm his instructions, which he does in written form. One by one, the three former retail investments providers arrange for the reconciled portfolios that Peter owns to be transferred to the new portfolio account service provided by SPIA.

As each of the three former retail investments provider's portfolios is received by SPIA, there is a new requirement for Peter's attitude to risk, the portfolio transaction and performance history etc., and all open transactions and balances to be accurately updated and settled into the new SPIA consolidated account on Peter's behalf. Eventually, Peter receives a communication from SPIA confirming that the transfer of all instruments/ securities, cash and data from the former portfolios to a new, consolidated portfolio has been completed. SPIA also advise Peter that there have been some significant cash and stock breaks, but that SPIA are working to resolve these and, if necessary, provide any redress. After a period of several weeks, Peter eventually can see, on his online SPIA account and app, the new portfolio content and transactions. Peter has been charged a significant fee for the transfer and consolidation based on all the work carried out on his behalf by SPIA and the former retail investments providers (all of whom have deducted, from his physical and cash holdings, their charges).

Future state (using blockchains): With blockchain, there is a reduced time and cost of advice.

Peter, a long-standing client of a wealth management firm known as St Paul's Investment Advisors (SPIA) in London, UK, decides to consolidate his various different retail investments accounts (two in the UK and one in Switzerland) to his SPIA provider. All of Peter's underlying investments (made up of instruments/securities and cash) are in tokenised form and each of the three former (and SPIA, the current) retail investments providers all use a similar blockchain database themselves to manage their investors' portfolios. SPIA's blockchain-powered portfolio database now, via smart contracts and in each case approved via his app by Peter, identifies the wallets holding Peter's non-SPIA tokens with the former providers. Peter can immediately see that all his non-SPIA tokens are visible in the SPIA app, and as there are no possible stock or cash breaks, he approves the new positions. The 'transfer' is in fact a re-registration of wallet information and is immediate, accurate, secure and does not cost Peter any additional fees. Over time, SPIA buy and sell Peter's tokens such that his overall holdings now align with the SPIA portfolio construction and thereby SPIA are entitled to charge Peter their ongoing fee for that.

Caselet 2: 'Augmented Advice'

Automated advice – where consumers self-select their options for advice in respect of investments – is an emerging area of retail investments. But what would the retail investments marketplace look like where human advisers, assisted by powerful analytics tools, used decentralised data to provide advice?

Current state: Current models of automated advice do not deliver the right outcomes for advisers or investors.

Using a silo of data, and with specific reference to investment performance and projections, an established bank in Spain sets up a new 'automated advice' service, via an app, and encourages its customers to use that for financial advice. Bank customers with large cash balances in their savings accounts are invited (on internet banking) via a marketing-led 'call to action' to click on a link to the new automated advice solution.

The new automated advice solution leads the customers through the attitude to risk, KYC, AML and 'life goals' segments, gathering data on them in an attempt to categorise their advice needs. Consumers may answer the self-service questions as they see fit and are not assessed for bias, for example, meaning that their vulnerabilities are effectively untested.

Over time, it becomes clear from reporting that the bank had made a category error with the configuration of the new automated advice system and has labelled a substantial (but wrong) cohort of customers as 'adventurous' in investment risk terms. The bank suspends the automated advice service, must report itself to the regulator and offer customers redress, even if (as in many cases) they have not yet experienced financial loss.

Future state: Augmented advice is a better option.

Using decentralised investment data, and with specific reference to investment performance and projections, an established bank in Spain sets up a new 'augmented advice' service, via an app, and encourages its customers to use that for financial advice. Each customer taking part in the new app must first complete an assessment stage and have their results mapped back to the decentralised database (a blockchain), and then will meet a human adviser to compare their own results with the adviser's opinions and to then agree to use the service on a hybrid, half-automated/half-advised basis.

As each consumer is compared to all others, as well as a centralised store of pre-existing investment performance data, there is a mitigation against systemic risk available. Also, as each consumer must first speak to the professional, qualified human investment adviser, there is also mitigation against consumer vulnerabilities escaping assessment – meaning the eventual investment offered is most suitable.

The bank's new solution is more expensive to set up but, as it is fully mediated (but reduces both risk and cost to serve), both the bank and the consumers are much less exposed to risk, redress or reputational damage.

The blockchain element of the new service is a critical factor in its functionality; because of the immutable, transparent and equitable access to the data, the bank is in a position to verify and validate its advice more efficiently.

The caselets give a specific, practical example of the benefits of enterprise-level blockchain in retail investments:

- **Saver/investor benefits**: Blockchains assist with trust, meaning that the adviser-investor relationship, based on delegated trust, is enhanced.
- **Cost benefits**: Blockchains provide a decentralised store of immutable, trustworthy and transparent data for better cost outcomes and less risk or redress.
- **Supplier benefits**: Blockchains provide supply chain outcomes in the sense that there are fewer component parts of the supply chain needed in total.
- **Overall industry benefits**: Blockchains provide planning accuracy, transparency and security of data.

Table 9.1 shows a comparison of example retail investments problem statements and the benefits provided by future-state blockchains versus current-state technology.

Summary and Conclusion

Retail investments are currently embedded in a world of arcane procedures and legal entities; antediluvian operations (the fax is still commonly used in retail investments) and fiercely guarded incumbents' stipends.

Table 9.1   Problem statements in current and future states

Retail Investments Problem Statement	Current State (Non-Blockchain) Solution	Future State (Blockchain) Solution	Comments
Financial advice for retail investments is expensive to deliver based on current costs and excludes those who need it	The current legacy stack is cumbersome, complex and expensive to run	Decentralised data means fewer stack layers are required for the same outcomes	Incumbency is a huge challenge, not only from a revenue disruption basis but also to change a cultural approach
Does technology alone provide an answer for an entire retail investments industry?	At the moment, most retail investments providers use technology that has arisen over decades, rather than been built specifically for their needs	Blockchain can offer a radically less complex technology solution, meaning that advisers can focus on service quality	Retail investments are ripe for a 'species jump' of technology. And by cutting away the dead wood of existing tech, free up people to offer and receive better quality advice and investment outcomes

All of the above adds up to more cost to both retail investments providers and consumers, which, in turn, restricts the availability of good financial advice, whether in-person or augmented, to the wealthy only.

By deploying sensible and limited (but effective) blockchain solutions, the whole retail investments industry could revolutionise its cost base and revert to what it does best: personal service.

- Consider how the current stack of technology, legal entities, operations and the segregation of advice from outcomes is affecting (negatively) both retail investments providers and consumers. How might this be addressed via blockchains?
- Reflect on the conditions that have led an entire industry (i.e. retail investments) to favour its incumbents over its consumers.
- Remember that technology itself is not a solution. What's needed is the deployment of better technology in specific circumstances, so that the things humans do well, like giving good advice, can shine through.

Before You Go On

- Retail investments are transactional (a transaction is any kind of programmable event; but in this industry the word specifically refers to the movement of cash and/or securities between counterparties). Do blockchains have any constraints in transactional terms that might impede performance?
- There are plenty of intermediaries in retail investments that can, in theory, be eliminated by a more streamlined DLT architecture. But is less always more – are there some third parties, such as custodians, who should remain in the stack?
- Reflect on the fungible nature of retail investments. How do blockchains affect that – and are there some securities, such as mutual funds which have no centralised exchange or liquidity, which are more complex and therefore more (or less) suitable for DLT?

Notes

1 https://kennonfinancial.com/2019/06/24/four-dangerous-words/.

2 Wikipedia, Stack (abstract data type) article. https://en.wikipedia.org/wiki/
Stack_(abstract_data_type).

Further Reading

www.hitachicapital.co.uk/media/2114/hitachi-capital-uk-plc-retail-
whitepaper-august-2018.pdf

www.pwc.com/gx/en/asset-management/asset-management-insights/assets/
awm-revolution-full-report-final.pdf

Chapter 10

Real Estate and Land Registry Use Case

He is not a full man who does not own a piece of land.

Hebrew Proverb

Homesandproperty.co.uk

Summary

This entire chapter is a use case, a case study. At the end of this chapter you'll be able to

DOI: 10.4324/9781003132592-10

- Understand and have an overview of real estate land registries (also known as cadastres) and blockchains;
- Know how real estate land registries work in real life;
- Define the land registry/cadastre key legal entities and actors;
- Know about the different types of land registry/cadastre deployments;
- Compare blockchains in land registries to current solutions;
- Get an understanding of a specific land registry use case (a case history);
- Understand the positives and potential negatives in the land registry use case; and
- Understand the likely future direction of land registries and cadastres.

Chapter Overview

The definition of land registration (the principal activity of a land registry) is as follows: 'Land registration generally describes systems by which matters concerning ownership, possession or other rights in land can be recorded (usually with a government agency or department) to provide evidence of title, facilitate transactions and to prevent unlawful disposal'.[1]

Land registry's sister word, cadastre, is defined as follows:

> A cadastre is normally a parcel based and up-to-date land information system containing a record of interests in land (e.g. rights, restrictions and responsibilities). It usually includes a geometric description of land parcels linked to other records describing the nature of the interests, the ownership or control of those interests, and often the value of the parcel and its improvements.[2]

Land registries and cadastres (we'll use these nouns interchangeably in this use case) perform very similar functions, i.e. they provide a secure and validated store of property and ownership data for use by buyers, sellers, lawyers, surveyors and governments in the administration and management of real estate.

To some extent, land registries are more typical in common law countries and cadastres usually appear in territories that have inherited or adopted Napoleonic codes of administration, after the French devised an efficient cadastre during Napoleon's reign that has become a template for others to adopt.

Understanding how land registries work is critical for all real estate professionals, lawyers, tax and local authorities and, albeit to a lesser extent, real estate buyers and sellers.

- In this chapter we will examine the land registry use case and smaller 'caselets'.
- The chapter will explain the main features, challenges and benefits of land registry for real estate professionals.
- This chapter will cover typical land registry entities and actors such as owners, sellers, agents, governments, banks, surveyors and lawyers.
- The chapter will also include a detailed look at how blockchain provides a robust, efficient and cost-effective solution for land registries and cadastres.

Land Registries in More Detail

A land registry is a dynamic (albeit slow-moving) public database of property and ownership data. A land registry is bound up with source and static information from geographical records, matters in the legal system and with taxation, policy and government.

Land Registry Software

There is no single or common standard for land registry/cadastre software and data. In fact, the legacy position of the land registries of the world is, by default, paper. Legal deeds, inheritance and estate documents, taxation records and so on are the predominant form of information on land and property transactions. These are almost entirely made up of paper files, certificates and court orders, some dating back decades or even centuries, and almost all of it privately held and therefore unlikely to be caught by public digitisation programmes.

However, many jurisdictions are fully aware of their need to update and modernise their land registries. As we'll discover in this use case chapter, making a direct leap, a 'species jump', from legacy paper to blockchain is both an upgrade to the registry itself and also makes it easy for third-party software and apps (for example, maps, financial calculators, tax systems etc.) to integrate seamlessly to a newly digitised register.

Land Registry Policy

Local authorities and governments, planning agencies, surveyors and real estate think tanks are all developing policy towards better (i.e. more secure and transparent) access to land registry information. This includes the digitisation of the records (through scanning and categorisation) and process automation of land registry activities such as search, download, edit etc.

Widening accuracy and access to land registry information is a policy bonus for the democratic institution responsible for its oversight and professionals who use land registries on a day-to-day basis such as agents, lawyers and surveyors.

Land registry policy in the developing world is an important case in point. Can democracy be enhanced when there is greater trust in and access to the underlying real estate, boundary and ownership information in the citizenry? Yes; add in some of the key ratios of developing economies (for example, 30% with bank accounts but 95% with smartphones) and their unique policy drivers (financial inclusion), then the digitisation of land registry, as a policy, feels more like a must-have.

Land Registries in the Real World

For such a crucial resource, land registries are often something of a backwater. 'Self sufficient' might be a good working definition of a typical land registry amidst a plethora of public institutions. Land registries, for example, are rarely profit making and often full of dusty paper information and cumbersome manual procedures. Figure 10.1 demonstrates the development of land registries by country, globally.

The Role of Banks in Land Registries

Banks and finance houses use land registries extensively to record real estate transactions, mortgages, charges or liens (collateralised debts secured on a property), tenancy information and other related data that specifically might be of relevance to other banks or financiers.

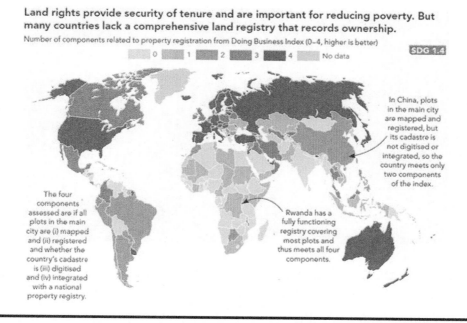

Land rights provide security of tenure and are important for reducing poverty. But many countries lack a comprehensive land registry that records ownership.

Number of components related to property registration from Doing Business Index (0–4, higher is better)

0   1   2   3   4   No data   SDG 1.4

In China, plots in the main city are mapped and registered, but its cadastre is not digitised or integrated, so the country meets only two components of the index.

The four components assessed are if all plots in the main city are (i) mapped and (ii) registered and whether the country's cadastre is (iii) digitised and (iv) integrated with a national property registry.

Rwanda has a fully functioning registry covering most plots and thus meets all four components.

Figure 10.1   Land rights and land registries by country, 17th September 2018.

Source: World Bank Data Tea. Published May 24, 2018 http://blogs.worldbank.org/opendata/2018-atlas-sustainable-development-goals-all-new-visual-guide-data-and-development?CID=DEC_TT_data_EN_EXT.

The integrity of the underlying land registry data is vital for banks and finance houses. Better land registry data and software mean banks can make faster, more accurate and less contentious decisions about real estate lending. And the potential for tokenisation of real estate means, in theory, a more liquid and accessible market for real estate finance.

Blockchains in Land Registries

Land rights (and land registries) are an obvious use case for blockchains.

However, as all land registries start from a different place (with paper records predominating), the case for adopting blockchain in a land registry varies according to the local government's capacity to invest in a new technology. Blockchain isn't simply an upgrade to tech; it requires a step change in the conventional use of the land registry itself.

Figure 10.2 displays the distribution of blockchain-based land registries around the world (correct at the time of writing). Unsurprisingly, the

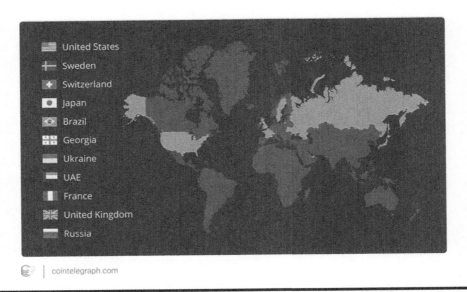

Figure 10.2   Blockchain-based registries available around the world.

Source: Cointelegraph Analytics

'developed' world predominates, but we note the potential for progress (via blockchain) for developing world economies in an expected 'second wave' of adoption.

What Is a Land Registry?

A land registry is a public institution that maintains, securely and equitably, the paper and digital records of local real estate and as much as possible of the legal, taxation and ownership data attributes that pertain to each plot or parcel of land.

Note: although this use case is focused on software and data in relation to blockchain, the land registry use case is as much about functionality as it is 'software' (or solutions involving technology). A land registry could be operated by a single expert user on a spreadsheet or with a paper archive, for example. Discussions about land registries have to include other factors such as operations, business rules (smart contracts) and transparency.

Finally, it's worth noting that 'land' in this context (also referred to as 'property' in certain jurisdictions such as the United Kingdom) refers to apartments/flats, parking spaces, agricultural land and forests, road embankments, building plots and so on. Any geographical space that can be clearly segregated and identified is a valid 'land' entity that may be entered on a land registry.

The Paper Register

All land registries contain a significant paper element. It's the prima facie source material for most land. Even in a world of blockchain, for example, it's unlikely that paper will ever go away, not least because the legacy records of each specific plot will still need to be incorporated in the modern blockchain database as a historical record.

So even for new blockchain-powered land registries there is a requirement to scan, tag and categorise an archive of pre-existing paper records. Categorisation by date, location, owner, money value, taxation, price, debt charges and so on must be thorough and reliable. This means that there will need to be parallel services such as expert oversight and dispute settlement even before a new blockchain might be considered ready for wider public use.

The Plots

It goes without saying that a land registry has, as its core object of reference, land. Each individual land entity will vary in size, shape and position. Land parcels will usually have one or more unique paper records to go with them.

Land registries need to be localised, therefore. Local knowledge and expertise are required to maintain and validate the registry's accuracy and relevance. Keeping it local makes sense in any case, as the decisions required to buy, sell and develop land are usually decided locally too.

The Survey

Making sense of land, real estate or property is the domain of expert surveyors. Not just at a technical level: census information, which analyses population, is also part of land registry data.

New survey information is updated into a working land registry on an as-and-when basis. It's an ongoing, 'never-ending' process. This applies not just to new builds, for example. Where an older piece of land is re-surveyed it may contain new or updated data on utility supplies (such as gas and electricity, sewage or drains etc.), neighbouring plots of land and other information that will need to go into the land registry itself.

The Land Registry

Independent, trusted, and authoritative; reliable and with public access: a land registry must be accountable. For that reason, the land registries are usually overseen by local government and form part of a national network of government agencies that ensure consistency.

Access to the Land Registry

As with other blockchain use cases, it is access to underlying data (in this case, land data) that's key. Land registry access must be secure, equitable and transparent to all users. A land registry must be read-only because an editable land registry would not work.

We've seen in this section some of the core land registry functions and features. It's hard to generalise an overall type for land registries, not least because different countries, legal systems, economies etc. each operate their cadastres totally independently. But some features do recur: the predominance of paper, both legacy and modern; the need for neutrality/expertise; and a connection to local democracy are vital elements.

Key Land Registry Concepts

In this section we'll have a look at some key land registry concepts such as legal entities, actors, types, models and stresses/challenges. We'll later draw inference from these key land registry concepts into the way a blockchain operates, and the apparent advantages that it can offer over non-blockchain alternatives.

Legal Entities

The principal legal entities involved in land registries are as follows:

Land Registry

Obvious as it might seem, a key legal entity in the land registry is the land registry itself. The land registry entity has agency, i.e. the power and capacity to act on its own behalf, and is usually operating under charter or instruction from the local democratic institution that established it and oversees it.

Owner/Seller/Landlord and Buyer/Tenant

Bundled together here are the legal entities of owner, seller, landlord (on the 'credit' side of the ledger) and buyers and tenants (those not yet owning the land). These entities may be human/natural persons, as in you and me; or they may equally be legal persons (companies, governments, investors, trustees etc.).

Although these words (for example, landlord and tenant) are pejorative to some, they are embedded in law and legal documents. It's interesting to note that modern technology solutions such as Airbnb, for example, use less legal-sounding labels such as 'owner' and 'renter'.

Realtor/Real Estate Agent

Often with additional delegated responsibility over land/property, for example as a managing agent, the realtor or real estate agent is appointed to represent the owner/seller/landlord in real estate transactions including rental collections.

Realtors/real estate agents help sellers and buyers, landlords and tenants agree terms over buying and selling property and in renting.

The realtor/real estate agent has few direct dealings with the land registry, but the outcomes of their work do have a serious impact.

Bank or Finance Provider

The bank (including mortgage-type finance provider) is a legal entity in the context of a land registry and one of its main users/consumers.

For banks, as they are often the legal 'owner' of the title of a piece of real estate, the efficient, secure, equitable and accurate operation of a land registry is a crucial component to their business model and can even affect their profitability. We'll look in more detail at how banks can contribute to (and benefit from) land registry reform later in this use case chapter.

Surveyor

The surveyor, as an independent quality assurance entity, operates as a neutral and expert actor in the land registry.

Most surveyors are local and will have long exposure to plots of land, their owners, landlord and tenants etc. This means that the land registry becomes part of the surveyor's professional workbench. It's arguable that without surveyors, most land registries would cease to function fully or at all.

Local Government

We've talked elsewhere in this use case about the relevance of local democratic institutions to land registries. Local government, in all its varieties and roles, is the ultimate owner of the land registry.

Without local government involvement, most land registries would not work properly. In terms of blockchain, for example, this creates other questions: what if the local government itself is unreliable? State socialism cadastres of the former Eastern European countries after the fall of the Berlin Wall in the 1980s are a case in point. Seized land had to be returned to its original owners but, with a corrupted cadastre, the question is, returned to whom?

Actors in Land Registry Stack

In addition to the legal entities (above), land registries also engage with actors (both natural/human and legal) within the real estate and operating model as follows:

Land Registry Administrator

The land registry administrator manages and maintains the land registry itself. This ranges from 'standard' updates (such as purchase and sale transactions, boundary changes, tenancy and mortgage information) to more major edits, for example, new-build developments, planning application notices and outcomes, and critical infrastructure work such as new roads or railway development.

With blockchains, we might assume that some of the day-to-day work of a land registry administrator would be carried out by smart contracts, for example. We'll look at the impacts of this assumption later in this use case.

Auditor

The role of the auditor is that of independent audit of the land registry's accounts, books and records, and cash handling (if relevant). Whatever the technology used to underpin the land registry, it is assumed the role of auditor remains constant.

Types

The following are all types of common or frequent real estate, land/property scenarios that are found in land registry.

Scenario 1: Administering Existing Plots of Land

The majority of land registry scenarios/cases relate to the administration of existing plots of land, property or real estate. Existing plots of land come with legacy documentation on paper, a potentially detailed transaction, debt, tenancy and tax history, and a requirement for expert oversight for the resolution of complex updates and contentious matters.

Scenario 2: Setting Up and Administering New Builds

Property developers work with land registries for new-build development.

Whatever the designs put forward, and regardless of the granting of permission by the local authorities and/or the success of the project, the land registry will keep careful records of the plans proposed in its database for future reference.

Should the new-build project go forward to completion, then the new plots of land will also need to be fully established in the land registry and maintained.

Scenario 3: Large-scale Infrastructure Projects

New roads, railways, bridges, airports and urban developments require intensive use of a land registry, not only for mandatory purchase, clearance and demolition. Major infrastructure work includes redevelopment of sites, the design and approval of plots of land and (often) disputes.

Models

Not all land registry models are the same and we explore the differences here in more detail and set out the economic rationales for each.

Land Registry Model

The example here is the United Kingdom's 'HM Land Registry' agency:

> HM Land Registry registers the ownership of property. It is one of the largest property databases in Europe. At the peak of the property boom in 2007, £1 million worth of property was processed every minute in England and Wales.
>
> Like land registration organisations in other countries, HM Land Registry guarantees title to registered estates and interests in land. It records the ownership rights of freehold properties, and leasehold properties where the lease has been granted for a term exceeding seven years.
>
> The definition of land can include the buildings situated upon the land, particularly where parts of buildings at different levels (such as flats) are in different ownership. It is also possible to register the ownership of the mines and minerals which lie within the ground, as well as airspace above property where this is in separate ownership.
>
> HM Land Registry receives no government funding, being required to ensure that its income covers expenditure, and finances itself from registration and search fees. It provides online access to its database of titles (ownership and charges or interests by other parties) and most plans (maps). People need to pay a fee to access some information.
>
> Property owners whose property is not registered can make voluntary applications for registration. As of March 2016, there are 24.5 million registered titles representing 88% of the landmass of England and Wales. Registration of land under the Land Registration Act 2002 affords property owners some protection

against squatters as well as avoiding the need to produce old documents each time a property changes hands.[3]

Federal Cadastre Model

The example here is the German cadastral system:

Security of land tenure in Germany has a tradition of some centuries. The forms of land registration in former centuries had great variety because of the great number of independent states on the territory of the present Federal Republic of Germany. The basic laws have been quite different as well, because since the end of the 30-year war in 1648 states as Prussia or Saxonia have been completely independent.

At the beginning of the 19th century in some of the kingdoms cadastral systems were established for taxation purposes. Until 1876 the cadastre in Prussia was completed. Although the main purpose for establishing a cadastre was taxation of land, the idea of using maps and records for further purposes of governmental activities was implemented in the cadastral systems from the beginning.

After Germany was founded in 1871, the need of standardisation of the private law was evident. Since January 1, 1900 the common private law exists for the whole country. In connection with this law the land registration system for the whole country has been established. This land registration system (in German terms called 'Grundbuch') contains all rights of ownership and other rights on land and buildings. By establishing this Grundbuch system the importance of a good working cadastral system grew very fast. The description of the land parcels (parcel identifier and cadastral maps) became the official and legal register of parcels as a part of the land register. Cadastre developed from a system for taxation of land to a register that gives guarantee to the right of land tenure.

Since 1934 the results of the official soil assessment have been recorded in the cadastre. This was the first step in the direction of a multipurpose cadastre.

The constitution of the Federal Republic of Germany accords responsibility for legislation around the land register to the

Federal Republic whereas the states make the laws concerning the property cadastre. Interstate bodies (working groups of state survey agencies) ensure uniformity of the property cadastre.

These days the cadastre fulfils all legal demands and demands of administration and the private sector. It is a basic Land Information System (LIS) of great variety and flexibility in planning, environmental protection etc. Maps and cadastral records in most parts of Germany are stored in computer systems. Although cadastre in Germany is in the responsibility of the 16 states, the computerised systems are unique with some small exceptions. These systems are the automated cadastral map (ALK) and the automated property register (ALB).

This historical review of the development of cadastre in Germany shows that this system is not a static one. The modern form of cadastre is a multipurpose cadastre as it is described as well in the FIG Statement on the cadastre.

Even in developing countries cadastral systems should be designed to give options for using it as a basic Land Information System.[4]

Stresses in Land Registries

A land registry is not, by definition, a dynamic ledger. Although there can be contention, for example with boundary disputes, unreconciled property transactions, taxation assessment and survey issues, the bulk of the work of a land registry varies for each plot and actor.

Rather than generalise the stresses here, we refer readers to the specific caselets later in this use case chapter for real-life examples of land registry and cadastre stresses.

Challenges More Generally

In the modern era, land registries and cadastres do face some significant challenges as they adapt to ongoing and new issues. The following is a high-level view of that, and touches on the growing impact of the relative costs of real estate on today's land registry users.

Taxation

The role of the cadastre, in particular, is directly related to land taxation and the exercise of tax-charging and tax-collecting rights by government on real estate and landowners.

Shifting the focus of cadastres towards a more civic role (as well as supporting the needs of tax authorities), for example in respect of planning permission, development and marketing of new development and so on, is an important part of the future.

Tax reform itself isn't a compelling use case for converting cadastres to blockchain, but will appeal to governments and tax authorities.

Paper

Paper, the legacy standard of almost all land registries and cadastres, is a major challenge to the ongoing development and adoption of land registry/ cadastre technology.

Paper retains some advantages: it can be legally verified, accurate and acceptable, and is readily used in property litigation and notarised real estate transactions.

Ingesting paper into a new land registry blockchain (via scanning, tagging and categorisation, for example) is not a technology challenge, but will cost the land registry in terms of time and resource. There is also the issue that a lot of land and property paper is still held privately in the forms of personal deeds and may only be entered into the land registry during a transaction.

Tokenisation

Land registries and cadastres, through blockchain technology, will enable land and real estate owners to 'tokenise' their property.

What does this mean? One challenge is that 'tokenisation' means different things to different audiences. In our case, we are referring to tokenisation as a form of fractional or unitised securitisation of real estate and property.

Using a reliable, secure, immutable and equitably accessed land registry as a base, property owners and investors may decide, legally, to securitise their newly tokenised land.

The benefits are greater liquidity; fractional ownership options; tenancies that might be shared in nature; and collectivisation of land, real estate and property.

Summary and Opinion

Land registries and cadastres, for centuries buried under paper mountains, are devising new and evolutionary ways to increase their usefulness and relevance to modern, digital societies.

Along the way, new designs for land registries and cadastres will need to walk a delicate tightrope: make technological advances, for example using blockchain and encouraging tokenisation of land, but also ensure accurate and reliable legacy paper records are also incorporated in their new models.

How Land Registries Use Ledgers Currently

Land registries operate on a distributed range of systems, in local currencies, in separate taxation jurisdictions and – largely – in a single language base.

Land registries are localised, specialised, legacy archives connected to a range of third parties, for example, court and taxation systems, surveyors and bank/finance houses, and tenancy systems.

Land registries use a range of customised and home-made software and databases and ledgers.

How Land Registries Would be Different Using Blockchains

Land registries are an ideal use case for distributed ledger technology and could be reshaped by blockchains.

There are three standard tests for the usefulness or relevance of blockchains in a specific industry, for example:

■ What's the asset to be tokenised? In a land registry, it's the subject of the registry – plots of real estate, property or land.

∎ Is there a requirement for a proxy for trust? Yes. In land registries, trust is paramount, which is often why the land registry or cadastre itself is under the control and supervision of local government (including via the taxation authority, as is the case usually with cadastres).

∎ Will there be equitable access? Yes. Equitable access, in the case of land registries, means that all the actors, legal entities, types and in all scenarios should have equal and secure access to the data held in the land registry itself.

Let's assume that most land registries and cadastres are bound to a greater or lesser extent by legacy paper and non-digital processes. Going digital is a big step forward for land registries; going to blockchain is a paradigm shift.

In other words, designing, building and deploying a land registry/cadastral blockchain solution is always going to be a revolution, not just an incremental development.

Land Registry Demonstration Problems and Use Case

The use case here is for the land registry in a developed economy and a subsequent 'greenfield' land registry/cadastre in a developing country.

In the first fictional use case, we imagine an ownership update made to a plot of land on the United Kingdom's land registry, HM Land Registry.

In the second, we look at the cadastre of the Republic of Bangladesh, where there is a 'transition' stage status for the land registry/cadastre in a developing country.

Caselet 1: 'Location, Location, Location'

Current state: A combination of paper, email, end-user computing and manual updates determines the daily life of professionals who use the UK's land registry, HM Land Registry.

For the past six months Martina Mendes has been finalising the sale of her flat in Bath Street, Hereford (a small market town on the England/Wales border in the United Kingdom). Martina is Chilean and is separated. She works in Hereford on a two-year field assignment as an agricultural scientist via the Chilean government.

Martina has been using a local firm of estate agents (realtors) to market her flat although the buyer, Tonya Wilmot, found the flat for sale using an online property app. Martina is using a firm of solicitors (attorneys) in the nearby large city of Birmingham to process the sale transaction. The solicitors were recommended to Martina by a friend.

Now, Martina is ready to finish the paperwork and complete her own sale transaction. Martina's mortgage bank, HSBC, is working with the solicitors, the buyer's solicitors and the estate agent to process all the necessary updates. There is a substantial mortgage outstanding on Martina's flat and the bank has the right, as the mortgagor, to be a significant part of the transaction.

The buyer's solicitors advise Martina's solicitors that Ms Wilmot's money is ready to be transferred to Martina's solicitors' client money account, but only following receipt by them of a satisfactory report from the land registry as to the title of the flat etc.

Martina's solicitors, acting for both Martina and her mortgage bank (HSBC) open a land registry case at HM Land Registry and request, for a fee, the relevant report. The land registry staff receive the request and process the relevant report, which is derived from a combination of paper, spreadsheet, image library and database elements. After a short pause, the draft report is ready and is made available to Martina's solicitors.

Martina's solicitors physically receive the report from HM Land Registry, check it and share it manually (i.e. via email) with all the interested and legally entitled stakeholders, including Martina and Tonya, Tonya's solicitors and HSBC.

Tonya's solicitors dispute a technical element of the land registry report and request an independent surveyor to attend the flat and make an inspection.

Martina's solicitors and Tonya's solicitors agree to jointly appoint an independent local surveyor, Natalie Bowden. Ms Bowden attends Martina's flat, makes her professional inspection and drafts and submits her official report to the parties.

After a pause, Martina's solicitors receive an update from Tonya's solicitors that they are now satisfied with the technical aspects of the flat and are ready to sign the purchase agreement, exchange deeds for money and complete the sale. Exchange and completion happens a week later with the parties (banks and solicitors) reconciling and confirming all aspects.

Minus the outstanding mortgage repayment balance, Martina receives the surplus money from the real estate sale transaction proceeds and, on the other side, it is Tonya Wilmot's name that appears in the records (the deeds) of HM Land Registry as the new owner of the flat.

All parties, culminating in HM Land Registry, update their records accordingly and the sale transaction is marked as 'closed'.

Future state: A combination of paper, email, end-user computing and manual updates determines the daily life of professionals who use the UK's land registry, HM Land Registry.

For the past six months Martina Mendes has been finalising the sale of her flat in Bath Street, Hereford (a small market town on the England/Wales border in the United Kingdom). Martina is Chilean and is separated. She works in Hereford on a two-year field assignment as an agricultural scientist via the Chilean government.

Martina, the buyer (Tonya Wilmot), the realtor (estate agent), the banks, solicitors, surveyors and the land registry itself are using a phone-distributed blockchain and smart contract 'proof of concept' (POC) model, launched by HM Land Registry recently, to process the transaction. In this specific case, the transaction qualifies because HM Land Registry has previously migrated Martina's property records to their new POC blockchain, in part because Martina's flat is a 'new build'.

As nodes, and in anticipation of Martina and Tonya's smart-contract-originated rule update requesting sale and purchase, respectively, each of the bank, the solicitors and the surveyor are requested to grant their approval or updates to the blockchain database for this specific plot of land.

Because Tonya's solicitors elect for a new survey, the local surveyor Natalie Bowden is alerted by phone to complete a specific rule on the flat. Ms Bowden attends immediately, takes photos and updates the rule (via her phone) to indicate she is professionally satisfied and that the sale can complete.

All the parties therefore receive an alert on their blockchain-powered phone app to say 'Exchange and complete'; and as the various actors confirm this for deeds/title, registry records updated, money paid/received, survey approved, mortgage repayment made, surplus funds transferred/received etc., then HM Land Registry issues a new (material) block with all of the above.

The new status of (now Tonya's) flat is therefore updated accurately on the public record without contention or reconciliation required in a quicker timescale than with the previous system.

Caselet 2: 'Bangladesh Opens a New Cadastre'

Current state: Bangladesh operates a land registry system that is typical of the developing world: a combination of paper, tax and local authority records but no single, centralised or decentralised service or database.

Nazrul Islam, a 40-something Dhaka property developer, is considering buying a plot of land for potential development in Titas (Bengali: তিতাস), an Upazila of Comilla District in the Division of Chittagong, Bangladesh. The Titas Upazila was founded in 2004, although real estate in the area has been bought and sold for generations previously.

Nazrul enquires of the current owner as to his intentions for sale etc. The current owner, Ahmed A. Jamal, agrees a sale price readily as he wants to move back to his elderly mother in Dhaka city centre, and so is happy to sell this real estate to provide money for him to make the move.

The title deeds of the property appear to be in good order and are found, after a time-consuming search, at the relevant archive in the offices of the responsible Sub Registry. The title deeds are in paper form and, because the owner has owned the property for decades, require updating as to the (more recent) establishment of the administrative area details.

After a long pause, Nazrul and Ahmed make the transfer with cash and Nazrul agrees to pay for the full update of the title deeds in the correct Sub Registry of the new Titas Upazila.

Ahmed moves back to his family home in central Dhaka but, due to planning approval complexities, Nazrul is significantly delayed in starting his development project and decides to leave the plot of land undeveloped for the time being while he considers his options. In the meantime, the value of the plot increases steadily.

Future state: Bangladesh designs and deploys a phone- and blockchain-powered new land registry/cadastre database for all new land transactions and devises a staged legacy migration from paper records to digitalisation over ten years.

Nazrul Islam, a Dhaka property developer, is considering buying a plot of land for potential development in Titas (Bengali: তিতাস), an Upazila of Comilla District in the Division of Chittagong, Bangladesh. The Titas Upazila was founded in 2004, although real estate in the area has been bought and sold for generations previously.

Nazrul enquires of the current owner as to his intentions for sale etc. The current owner, Ahmed A. Jamal, agrees a sale price readily as he wants to move back to his elderly mother in Dhaka city centre, and so is happy to sell this real estate to provide money for him to make the move.

Titas Upazila is one of the first administrative areas to be adopted by the newly formed Bangladesh Blockchain Land Rights Service (BBLRS) and on that basis has had all of its plots of land within the Upazila boundary digitally mapped and all available paper records consolidated to current definitions (for example, Titas Upazila was only formed as an administrative region in 2004), scanned, tagged and categorised.

All real estate owners in the newly digitised Titas Upazila are educated on a new BBLRS (Beta) phone app and are asked to confirm their ownership details using the app itself.

Nazrul, as a potential buyer, is also able to install and open the BBLRS app on his own phone and can see the specific details of the plot, its ownership status and the correct (and current) administrative status too.

Following a short negotiation, Nazrul and Ahmed agree terms for the purchase and, by mutual agreement (and following the safe receipt of the purchase money), both submit the relevant instructions on the BBLRS app to confirm their respective status as 'owner' and 'former owner', along with the listed sale price and the relevant tax information.

Nazrul, as the new owner, is able to submit a digital planning application to the local authority who (using their own desk-based app access) update the BBLRS blockchain with approval for Nazrul's development.

The caselets give a specific, practical example of the benefits of enterprise-level blockchain in land registries. In addition, there are other benefits in a future-state (blockchain-powered) land registry solution as follows:

- **Property development and planning**. As can be inferred from the Bangladesh caselet, above, better land registry records imply a more efficient, fairer and transparent land development planning applications process, with options for neighbours to engage, as well as validated new valuations and contingent planning capacity (for example, utilities or transport planning).
- **Simpler and fairer taxation**. Property sale, inheritance/probate, estate management and access to future planning for taxation purposes are all potentially enhanced with a fully digitised land registry and cadastre. When the tax authority is a node on a cadastral blockchain, there is less contention and fewer surprises for estate planners, for example.

■ **Population analysis is easier** and simpler to access where there is a land registry of significant coverage in both rural and urban areas. Immigration, the provision of local infrastructure such as education and healthcare, for example, might all connect with land registry data for more accurate decision making.

There is no single or common standard required or even possible for land registries. As the surface of the earth is infinitely variable, so the related land registries are different and see implementation locally as a custom solution.

There is, however, a common set of requirements that blockchain-powered land registries and cadastres can offer which will not only offer the benefits of trust, security, immutability, equity of access and transparency but also provide important secondary benefits such as better planning, the securitisation/tokenisation of land rights and ownership, and more democracy for potentially contentious areas such as planning law.

Digitising land registries may never be complete, as dusty paper records, or simply an absence of any sort of accurate title deeds or litigation papers, will preclude a small but significant minority of land records from entering the domain of scanned and digitised information.

Summary and Conclusion

In both the developed and developing world, the improvement of land rights (via a well-constructed and -operated land registry) is a vital step forward and an obvious use case for blockchain.

The extent and scale of the process of digitisation – and the pace at which such a change might occur – is a function of local and national appetites for change, and not a constraint of technology or deployment experience. As this chapter use case has shown, there remains a considerable 'development deficit' in respect of analysing and defining common standards for a blockchain-powered land registry and its required/related smart contracts; however, we believe that the majority of these can be readily identified and deployed and, when done, this will cover most land transactions and information requirements.

Before You Go On

- Consider the headwinds to registry digitisation – paper records, contentious litigation over property and a resistance to engage with the perception of a taxation-driven cadastre.
- Reflect on the definition of the majority of common rules that might be applicable as both user experience functions (e.g. transaction, planning application, taxation etc.) and through yet-to-be defined land registry-specific smart contracts.
- Remember that the technology already exists. It's the 'how' rather than the 'what' that is an open and tricky question currently.

Notes

1 Wikipedia. Land registration article. https://en.wikipedia.org/wiki/Land_registration.
2 International Federation of Surveyors (FIG). FIG Publication No. 11 / FIG Statement on the Cadastre. www.fig.net/resources/publications/figpub/pub11/figpub11.asp.
3 Wikipedia, Her Majesty's (UK) Land Registry article. https://en.wikipedia.org/wiki/HM_Land_Registry.
4 www.fig.net/organisation/comm/7/Library/reports/events/penang97/penang9710.htm.

Further Reading

http://ica-it.org/pdf/Blockchain_Landregistry_Report.pdf
www.elra.eu/wp-content/uploads/2017/02/10.-Jacques-Vos-Blockchain-based-Land-Registry.pdf
www.oecd.org/corruption/integrity-forum/academic-papers/Georg%20Eder-%20Blockchain%20-%20Ghana_verified.pdf

Chapter 11

Central Bank Currency Use Case

The privilege of creating and issuing money is not only the supreme prerogative of government, but it is the government's greatest creative opportunity.

Abraham Lincoln[1]

James Gillray, Political Ravishment: The Old Lady of Threadneedle Street in Danger, 1797. www.bankofengland.co.uk/museum/online-collections/artworks/ cartoons-and-caricatures

DOI: 10.4324/9781003132592-11

Summary

This entire chapter is a use case, a case study. At the end of this chapter you'll be able to

- Understand and have an overview of central banks and their relation to blockchains;
- Know how central banks work in real life;
- Define the central bank and main economic system component key legal entities and actors;
- Know about the different types of central bank deployments;
- Compare blockchains in central banks to current solutions;
- Get an understanding of a specific central bank use case (a case history);
- Understand the positives and potential negatives in the central bank use case; and
- Understand the likely future direction of central banks.

Chapter Overview

Central banks – for example, the United States Federal Reserve System ('the Fed'), the Bank of Japan ('Nichigin'), the European Central Bank ('the ECB', which is the central bank of the 19 European Union countries which have adopted the euro) and the Bank of England ('The Old Lady of Threadneedle Street') – have a rich and varied history.

Central banks today are highly relevant and continue in their role of currency management and issue, banking system regulators and implementers of government-directed policy and economic directives.

Central banks are investigating and analysing blockchains, not only for research purposes (and not only in the context of cryptocurrencies) but also in consideration of the potential 'continuity' role of blockchains with regard to economic change, government and political policy, and the way in which cash, payments and trade finance are used in society at large – whose economic stability is the core responsibility of central banks in any case.

> According to a January 2019 report by the Bank for International Settlements (BIS) in Basel, Switzerland, at least 40 central banks around the world are currently, or soon will be, researching and

experimenting with central bank digital currency ... which has attracted much interest within the central banking community for its potential to address long-standing challenges such as financial inclusion, payments efficiency, and a payment system [sic] operational and cyber resilience.[2]

Understanding how central banks work and the relationship between currency, blockchain and the economic wellbeing of all of us is critical for all bankers, economists, policy makers, researchers and strategic analysts.

■ In this chapter we will examine the central banking use case and smaller 'caselets'.
■ The chapter will explain the main features, challenges and benefits of central banks for the potential use and adoption of blockchains in their economic models and strategy.
■ This chapter will cover typical central bank entities and actors such as government/treasury, regulators, local authorities and governments, retail and institutional banks, trade and commercial actors and other/ international banks and banking systems.
■ The chapter will also include a detailed look at how blockchain provides a robust, efficient and cost-effective solution for central banks, their currencies and the policies they are tasked with implementing.

Central Banks in More Detail

The Oxford English Dictionary defines a central bank as 'a national bank that provides financial and banking services for its country's government and commercial banking system, as well as implementing the government's monetary policy and issuing currency'.[3] The examples previously given (the US Federal Reserve, the ECB, the Bank of Japan and the Bank of England) are classic central banks.

The core functions of central banks and banking are for the processing of payments and settlements (principally cash-to-cash and cash-to-security), currency issuance and management, economic policy implementation (for example, interest rates and inflation), the issuance and maintenance of government bonds, retail/investment/custodian bank regulation/supervision, and the production, publication and maintenance of economic and banking data in a secure and transparent way.

Central Bank Software

In most of the developed world (and a significant proportion of the developing world) central banks share a common (core) system solution for payments and settlements: the Real Time Gross Settlements (RTGS) system. The working definition of a standard RTGS system is

> Real-time gross settlement (RTGS) systems are specialist funds [cash] transfer systems where the transfer of money or securities takes place from one bank to any other bank on a 'real time' and on a 'gross' basis. Settlement in 'real time' means a payment transaction is not subjected to any waiting period, with transactions being settled as soon as they are processed. 'Gross settlement' means the transaction is settled on a one-to-one basis without bundling or netting with any other transaction. 'Settlement' means that once processed, payments are final and irrevocable.
>
> RTGS systems are typically used for high-value transactions that require and receive immediate clearing. In some countries the RTGS systems may be the only way to get same-day cleared funds [cash] and so may be used when payments need to be settled urgently. However, most regular payments would not use an RTGS system, but instead would use a national payment system or automated clearing house that allows participants to batch and net payments. RTGS payments typically incur higher transaction costs and are usually operated by a country's central bank.[4]

What this means in practice is – usually – an old FORTRAN-operated greenscreen mainframe buried deep in the basement of the central bank's operations building and which processes transactions day in and day out.

In the United Kingdom, for example, the RTGS system is further defined by the two main functional or payment 'pipes' travelling through it: CHAPS (cash-to-cash and the UK's high-value settlement system) and CREST (cash-to-equity, the UK's securities settlement system).[5]

Central Bank Policy

Central bank policy is a mixture of the bank's own strategic and goal-oriented policies (for example, the historical and ongoing management of the issuance and exchange of currency) together with the political policies and obligations put upon the bank from government and treaty actors from time to time (the example in the EU are directives that are subsequently enshrined in secondary legislation, thereby becoming national law in member states and for the central bank to implement).

In reality, central banks are fully engaged in the shaping and determination of policy and strategy relating to money, the economy, interest/inflation rates and so on. The influence of central banks over government, other international actors and their own research and development units is significant.

Central Banks in the Real World

In the global financial crisis of 2008/9, the central banks of the world came to the attention of all of us in ways that we had not, in living memory, seen before. In effect, the actions and reactions of central banks to the unfolding global crisis were both unprecedented and critical; but the actual outcomes engineered by central banks in the real world were largely taken from textbook precedent and implemented accordingly.

In the real world, i.e. the more mundane, non-crisis reality of the day-to-day, central banks are constrained by political reality, government policy, international relations and events.

The Role of Other Banks in Central Banking

Central banks rarely act alone because the international financial system is interrelated. Unilateral financial action would potentially be self-defeating in the modern era in any case, and the political implications of 'going it alone' would be severe, both at home and abroad.

Central banks are not, of course, retail or investment (or custody) banks; they therefore occupy a position in the international economic framework as if they were in the state/executive, and therefore central banks tend to interact via treaty, directive, formal (and public) agreement, so not unexpectedly nor without prior discussion or dialogue with their peers.

Blockchains in Central Banks

Central banks around the world are already paying close attention to blockchains and are assessing, either alone or in concert, the potential risks and benefits that blockchains might bring to their own national currency

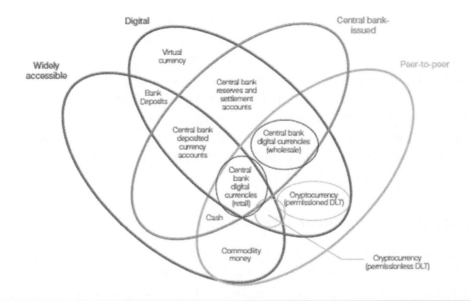

Figure 11.1   The 'Money Flower' – categories of money in the central bank/blockchain sphere of influence.

Source: Adapted from M. Bech and R. Garratt, 'Central Bank Cryptocurrencies'. BIS Quarterly Review, *September 2017, pp. 55–70. As seen in 'Cryptocurrencies: Looking Beyond the Hype'.* BIS Annual Economic Report *2019, p. 94*

and banking systems. Figure 11.1 provides a diagrammatic representation of central bank interest in blockchains.

An important distinction needs to be drawn here between cryptocurrencies and blockchain. There are two potentially significant (and potentially parallel) routes through which the influence of blockchains on central banks may be expressed:

1   In the central bank's issuing a newly tokenised version of a national currency, such as the Swedish eKrona proof-of-concept experiment; and
2   In the central bank's using the core blockchain decentralised ledger as an underlying database in its own payment and settlement systems and architecture.

We will touch on both of these options in discussing the central bank use case in this chapter in more detail.

What is a Central Bank?

A central bank has been formally defined earlier in this chapter. The central bank's primary role is in the day-to-day and strategic management of the national currency and economic factors that are related to that, for example, inflation/interest rates, growth stimuli, regulation of banks and so on. Figure 11.2 illustrates how the US Federal Reserve System is organised by entities.

A central bank is loosely made up of the following functional areas and associated actors.

The Treasury

The Treasury is the formal department of government that deals with national, federal, devolved/state and regional financial policy and economic strategy.

The financial ministry is usually the sponsoring democratic entity overseeing the Treasury or treasury function. It'll be the task of the Treasury to extensively model the economy, assess the economic outlook and interact with existing constraints and parameters such as government debt/ the national debt, interest and coupon payments on government bonds, wage and growth objectives and so on.

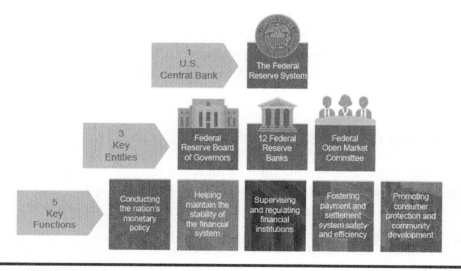

Figure 11.2   About the Federal Reserve System.

The Mint

The mint is the central bank entity tasked with the responsibility of printing and managing the national currency.

This is a practical role. In reality, modern mints often outsource or collaborate on the physical production of currency as the cost and effort required, especially for smaller or developing countries, can be onerous.

The Banking Regulator

The role of banking regulation is typically delegated to the central bank given its proximity to the banking activity in general and its direct/market relationship with the participant banks themselves.

Banking regulation policy is set by government in law and implemented by central bankers in coordination with other factors such as international relations and economic activity in general.

Payment Processing and Settlement

Central banks were originally invented to support and develop government borrowing on a formal basis, following the development of fungible securities and the ongoing requirement to issue and maintain a reliable national currency.

Payment processing and settlement is an adopted role within central banks as the development of payments and settlement software has grown since the 1950s. Today, as the provider of liquidity, payments processing and settlement is a core responsibility of central banking, both in terms of domestic payments/settlement and foreign exchange and international settlement.

Access to the Central Bank

In the modern era, access to central bank accounts (i.e. who can be an account holder) is focused on wholesale actors, for example, head offices of large, systemic retail banks and the clearing/payment accounts of investment and corporate banks.

In a decentralised world, such as blockchain-powered (tokenised) fiat currencies, there is the further potential to offer all currency holders a permissioned central bank account, meaning that a tokenised fiat currency might have millions (or even billions) of central bank 'account' (participating entities) holders engaged. We will explore this in more detail in the caselets of this chapter.

Key Central Bank Concepts

In this section we'll have a look at some key central bank concepts such as legal entities, actors, types, models and stresses/challenges.

Legal Entities

There are several key principal legal entities involved in central banks as follows:

Central Bank

Each central bank is established and designated as a discrete legal entity separate from government. However, the central bank itself is not usually a for-profit organisation (although this is often the historical provenance of most central banks); surpluses are returned to working capital via the operations model of the central bank.

Payment Clearance

Payment clearance is a separate 'legal entity' on the basis that counterparties in cash-to-cash and/or cash-to-security transactions require legal certainty that their gross (i.e. immediate) payments are settled and cannot be revoked or subject to a cash or stock break.

In this sense the central bank itself is the material legal entity standing behind the liquidity of each transaction, thereby ensuring settlement.

Economic Oversight

Economic oversight is not a specific legal entity per se, but the exercise of government policy through the levers of central banks: inflation rates, interest rates, currency supply and the control of banking activity, capital adequacy and so forth.

The consequences of active economic oversight are real. High interest rates, for example, can make mortgages and loans unaffordable.

Banking System Regulator

The banking system regulator may not be a specific legal entity per se, but is the agency needed to enforce the central bank's powers to oversee, inspect and enforce decisions and rulings.

So even in an environment where the central bank is active in currency issuance/management, payments processing and settlement, and strategy, there will also be a unit or division of the central bank that can carry out oversight and enforcement.

Government

Government is a legal entity, although its effects are usually made via legal instruments such as new and revised laws that are enforced in the courts, or as economic policies and directives that are applied through the daily activities of commerce and finance.

Actors in the Central Bank Stack

The central bank stack is a combination of technology, infrastructure, legal entities, operating models, third parties and more. The following is a high-level attempt to set out some of the major parts of the central bank stack and to outline how and why the various different elements have a potential bearing on the use cases.

Central Banker

The central banker is both a natural and legal actor in the central bank stack, and acts through a combination of policy execution, payments and settlement, and liquidity controls (including the issuance of fiat and digital currency).

Regulator

The regulator in the central bank stack has an ability to intervene in the daily and strategic processes of banking, for example, buying retail and commercial bank shares in the global financial crisis of 2008/9 or creating a money supply through the decade-long cycle of quantitative easing post 2010.

Cashier

'Cashier' is the generic central bank label applied to the management of currency, its issuance, maintenance, supply/contraction and so on. Whether currency is digital or more traditional fiat currency, there is a key role in the central bank stack to turn on/off the taps of money supply.

Auditor

Even central banks are audited. Control of third-party liquidity and capital adequacy deposits is an activity requiring detailed and reliable audit, not only for the purposes of banking but also in respect of the delivery of central bank control – for example, tightening liquidity in times of crisis.

Types

The following are all types of common or frequent central bank scenarios that are illustrative, not as use cases in their own right, but as general circumstances affecting the process and decisions of typical central banks.

Scenario 1 – The Inflation Rate Target

In 1997 the UK finance minister, the Chancellor of the Exchequer, granted the Bank of England independence (it had previously been a department of government), with a proviso: that the inflation rate target would be 2.5% annually, with deviance from that reportable in the form of a handwritten letter from the Governor to the Chancellor.

Since then, although the sleeve inflation rate targeted has been breached on occasions, the overall outcome – in terms of inflation – seems to have been achieved. In this scenario, therefore, government policy of controlling the damaging effects of too-high inflation seems to have been contained by the apparently contrarian act of liberating the bank from direct control.

Scenario 2 – Increase or Reduce the Money Supply

This is a day-to-day scenario for central banks. Through their execution of money supply – the 'printing' of fiat and/or digital currency – central banks are able to directly and immediately influence the amount of money in circulation and thereby the overall money supply.

Under normal circumstances, this measurable activity is sufficient to influence and implement the government policy of the day; however, as was witnessed in the global financial crisis of 2008/9, extreme circumstances call for tougher measures and hence the more drastic action taken in reducing interest rates to zero or negative rates and the massive scale of quantitative easing undertaken at that time.

Scenario 3 – Convergence

The example here are pre-accession European Union Eurozone countries (there are currently 19 EU member states in this category). During an agreed and set period of Eurozone accession, member states seeking to adopt the euro as their currency must shadow and peg their home currency to the euro itself and also, at the same time, manage or reduce their levels and ratios of debt accordingly.

Once Eurozone accession has been achieved, and full 'convergence' delivered, this scenario passes.

Stresses in Central Banks

The age-old saying, 'if you owe the bank a small amount, it's your problem; but if you owe the bank a large amount, it's the bank's problem' applies equally to central and retail/investment banks and their customers.

Additionally, central banks experience further stress as they must apply government policy without overstepping (or sidestepping) the outcome; in other words, by being the engine of payments, currency and policy, central banks must also ensure the general banking marketplace remains as free to act commercially as much as possible. A delicate tightrope to walk.

Challenges More Generally

When we speak of central bank challenges, we refer (in this specific use case) to those challenges and issues that might best be resolved with the use and adoption of more efficient, transparent, secure, equitably accessed and dynamic software, systems and databases such as blockchains, for example.

Challenge 1: Less Cash, But More Digital Cash?

Digital currencies are here and many consumers are using digital (though not necessarily blockchain-powered) cash alternatives already.

So the challenge is, how will central banks deploy 'stablecoins' (fiat currency in a token form, backed and collateralised by government etc.) in a way that fits consumer requirements, so for example, usable on the phone smartwallet, and via the payment card and on the banking app) without sacrificing control over currency and economic targets and policy, for example.

Challenge 2: Financial Inclusion?

The lower margins and access restrictions to bank accounts for the less affluent and the unbanked is not new.

However, mobile financial services may in fact make payments more expensive for both the banked (mobile financial services charge a materially high per-transaction fee, for example) and the unbanked.

And if a central bank currency is only available digitally, and/or via a phone, then those vulnerable or already-excluded consumers might suffer again from lack of access and see a second, more serious, financial exclusion.

Challenge 3 Tokenisation?

Tokenisation is happening for securities and cash (two areas of direct relevance for central banks).

The challenge for central banks will be to maintain their ability to oversee and regulate these tokenised markets. On one hand, for example, there is the likelihood that central banks themselves will continue in their role of 'platform' for payment, settlement and reconciliation. If there is a permissioned central bank blockchain in deployment, for example, then the role and expectation of the central bank will remain clear.

But what if central banks suffer the same fate as fixed-line telecommunications did at the advent of the (decentralised) networks of mobile phones? Tokenisation of cash and securities might deliver a decentralisation (P2P and DLT) and thereby cut central banks out of the loop altogether.

A cumulative effect of that might also start to encroach on – for example – the role of the US dollar as the global reserve currency. Do central banks have a blockchain model that has addressed these (admittedly, outlier) consequences of the digitisation of fiat currency?

Summary and Opinion

Central banks are both attracted to and repelled by the prospect of digital currency. It's not the technology that's a concern: if anything, blockchains are far more efficient and adoptable than current tech.

The concern is around the paradigm change and consequences. The reason a central bank exists is to control the currency and economy, two things against which the decentralisation ethos of blockchain speaks directly.

How Central Banks Use Ledgers Currently

Central banks use a complex data and applications infrastructure that is designed for security, resilience, speed and accuracy. Integrating central bank technology to internal (including government) and external (including international) central and retail banking systems is a key feature of the way that central banks use ledgers currently.

The question is: what concept of ledgers do central banks hold/operate or process, and how is that materially different to other banking ledger deployments?

There's a significant variance between the day-to-day activities of a central bank vs. a retail or investment bank: a central bank has no main commercial operations (there may be some outsourcing, for example), its balance sheet is different, it is the provider of liquidity and lender of the last resort etc.

But at a data level, a central bank can be characterised as being centralised, secure, private, resilient and responsive to policy.

How Central Banks Would be Different Using Blockchains

The first question or challenge for central bankers interested in shifting to a blockchain-powered model is that of centralisation vs. decentralisation. In a blockchain architecture, decentralisation is a key factor (in fact, *the* key factor) in the design and delivery of the data to the users.

Decentralisation would work well for a distributed stablecoin cryptocurrency – for example, if the euro or dollar were also issued on an ECB- or Fed-maintained blockchain then it would be decentralised. But not in terms of money supply or liquidity: as each USD or EUR token was digitally issued, the corresponding 'real' or fiat currency (notes, coins and electronic currency) would be withdrawn, meaning no overall change in the money supply. So decentralisation here is in the context of *data* decentralisation, not money control or ownership of access to it, for example.

There are three standard tests for the usefulness or relevance of blockchains in a specific industry, for example:

- What's the asset to be tokenised? In a central bank, the asset to be tokenised is the currency and, additionally, the processes of payment and settlement.
- Is there a requirement for a proxy for trust? Yes. In a central bank, as the issuer of currency and lender of the last resort, trust is of paramount relevance.
- Will there be equitable access? Yes. Equitable access, in a central bank, means if a digitised currency were issued, then everyone who wanted access to that would need it for the usefulness and salience of the new currency to be valid.

Not all central banking scenarios are applicable as blockchain use cases, for example, the delivery and execution of economic policy or the practical activities of the mint. And central banks may have an aversion to some of the core concepts of blockchain features, for example, mining, gas (the cost necessary to perform a transaction on the network) and anonymity.

Central Bank Demonstration Problems and Use Case

The use case here imagines the central bank 'as is' with a future-state, blockchain-powered central bank digital currency. It's a fictional use case, articulated in a single caselet to allow us to focus on the explicit features of the potential blockchain solution.

Caselet 1: 'A Day in the Life of Pounds Sterling'

Current state: The Bank of England, the UK's central bank, is mandated to issue and operate the national currency, pounds sterling ('pounds', 'GBP' and '£'). Electronic £ payments and settlements made in pounds on each working day (e.g. via debit cards, internet banking etc.) are processed and settled via the central bank accounts of the main retail banks.

Martin wants to pay Stuart the £30 he owes Stuart for Martin's share of their work dinner last week. Stuart sends Martin the relevant UK bank account details (sort code and bank account number) by WhatsApp. Martin receives the details and logs onto his phone banking app. He sets up the payment and sends Stuart the £30. It is Friday afternoon, around 5pm. Stuart is alerted by his banking app that he has received £30 and so Stuart immediately withdraws this from an ATM as he is going home and wants a taxi.

Martin's bank receives the payment instruction and, because the Bank of England is now closed for business (opening hours 9am to 4pm London time), his bank creates a ledger entry for payments in its internal systems.

At the end of each business day every UK retail bank posts its ledger balances as a report to the Bank of England (BoE). If the following day is a non-working day, then retail banks, as institutional bank account holders at the BoE, are obliged to arrange their finances so that all credits and debits can be paid and settled on a gross basis on the next available working day. Martin's bank therefore creates a liability of £30 in its BoE account on behalf of Martin's approved internet bank transaction.

Stuart's bank therefore creates a credit expectation of £30 in its BoE account, the receiving part of Martin's internet banking transaction.

On Monday at 9am in London, when the BoE opens for clearing, Martin's bank reconciles all of its credits and debits with Stuart's bank and they agree a net (in reality, 'gross') balance transfer between their respective BoE accounts as full settlement. Both banks update their internal ledger records accordingly.

Future state: The Bank of England, the UK's central bank, is mandated to issue and operate the national currency, pounds sterling ('pounds', 'GBP' and '£'). Now, GBP is a blockchain-powered stablecoin and is available also as a token that may be transferred between Bank of England (BoE)-provided ERC20 wallets, as well as all of the traditional paper/coin currency, cards and as electronic (internet banking etc.) payments.

Martin wants to pay Stuart the £30 he owes Stuart for Martin's share of their work dinner last week. Stuart sends Martin the details of his GBP token wallet securely on their shared token app, Tokenbase. Martin logs onto his Tokenbase app and sends to Stuart's wallet the £30 in tokens.

Stuart immediately receives the £30 in tokens into his wallet. He orders the taxi ride home and pays the taxi driver by transferring the same £30 to the taxi firm's pooled token wallet.

The BoE issues a new block in the GBP blockchain and, as all of the actors (Martin, Stuart, Tokenbase and the taxi firm) are BoE token account holders, all of the transactions are recorded as settled gross and fully reconciled.

The caselet gives a specific, practical example of the benefits of enterprise-level blockchain in central banks. In addition, there are other benefits that pertain to the future-state (blockchain-powered) central bank payment and settlement solutions as follows:

- Less liquidity required to be held internally by 'retail banks';
- Less capital adequacy required to be held at the central bank by participating banks and other financial institutions;
- Immediate reporting and money supply updates by the central bank; and
- Greater transparency between payment counterparties and faster gross settlement.

Central banking thrives on reliable, resilient, secure and immediate ('gross') payments and settlement. Delivering all of those attributes through a decentralised, permissioned, efficient and 'thin stack' blockchain infrastructure will work immediately from a technological perspective.

A major issue for central banks in looking at blockchain options will be the role and future status of incumbents (like retail banks, for example); the execution of economic policy and practical parameters such as interest rates and inflation targets; and the consequences.

Practical benefits stand out from potentially using blockchain in the central bank use case and not just the consumer benefits articulated here. All actors in the central bank stack can see a reward from faster and more accurate gross settlement, decentralised account holders, and less liquidity and capital standing idle.

Summary and Conclusion

Central banks throughout the world are looking closely at the potential changes and benefits that blockchain technology can bring them, consumers, businesses, industry and governments, both national and international.

It is clear that one of the major challenges facing central banks in their analysis and potential deployment of blockchains is centred around the 'category' problem of cryptocurrencies; certainly no central bank is a fan and would rather not have any connection with a decentralised coin like bitcoin etc.

But a correctly permissioned, tokenised and properly backed fiat currency, issued and managed as currency by the central bank under its current legal and statutory obligations, is appealing to users, businesses and regulators alike. Even existing retail and investment banks, although they might lose some more of their primary role as payment providers, would see improvements in their balance sheet and reconciliation processes, for example, that may mean wider opportunities.

The use case we have explored here is a basic but important example of how changes brought by blockchain might be seen in practical terms. However, it will be central banks themselves that will make the inevitable changes and we anticipate their acting in union in the near future to that effect.

Before You Go On

- Consider that central banking is a mixture of policy, payments and practical enforcement of the government rules, and not just a commercial or retail activity.
- Reflect on the way that 'electronic' money was originally introduced – e.g. internet banking, payment apps and debit cards. The likelihood

is that a stablecoin national currency would follow a similar evolutionary path.

■ Remember that most central banks act in unison with others or at the very least, with the full knowledge and approval of other governments. Any significant tokenisation of national currency would likely be the same in origin and deployment.

Notes

1 https://en.wikiquote.org/wiki/Talk:Money.
2 World Economic Forum, 'Central Banks and Distributed Ledger Technology: How Are Central Banks Exploring Blockchain Today?' White Paper published 3 April 2019. www.weforum.org/whitepapers/central-banks-and-distributed-ledger-technology-how-are-central-banks-exploring-blockchain-today.
3 Oxford English Dictionary, Definition of central bank. www.lexico.com/definition/central_bank.
4 Wikipedia, Real Time Gross Settlement (RTGS) article. https://en.wikipedia.org/wiki/Real-time_gross_settlement.
5 Bank for International Settlements, BIS Paper on UK payment and settlement systems. www.bis.org/cpmi/publ/d105_uk.pdf.

Further Reading

www.pwc.com/gx/en/financial-services/pdf/the-rise-of-central-bank-digital-currencies.pdf
www.bis.org/cpmi/publ/d174.pdf
https://publications.banque-france.fr/sites/default/files/media/2020/02/04/central-bank-digital-currency_cbdc_2020_02_03.pdf

Chapter 12

Fund Management Use Case

Someone's sitting in the shade today because someone planted a
tree a long time ago.

Warren Buffett[1]

© *Economist cartoon*

Summary

This entire chapter is a use case, a case study. At the end of this chapter
you'll be able to

DOI: 10.4324/9781003132592-12

- Understand and have an overview of fund management and its relation to blockchains;
- Know how fund management and mutual and exchange-traded funds work in real life;
- Define fund management and main economic system component key legal entities and actors;
- Know about the different types of potential fund management deployments;
- Compare blockchains in fund management to current solutions;
- Get an understanding of a specific fund management use case (a case history);
- Understand the positives and potential negatives in the fund management use case; and
- Understand the likely future direction of fund management, funds and the overall industry.

Chapter Overview

The mutual fund management industry is a global industry of scale and structural importance.

> In 2019, total assets under management (AuM) grew by 15%, to $89 trillion. Retail clients were the fastest-growing segment, with assets rising by 19%, while institutional client assets grew by 13%. North America, the world's largest asset management region, showed the strongest growth at 19%, or $7 trillion in value, due to a combination of strong consumer spending, historically low unemployment, and quantitative easing.[2]

Mutual fund management is a service industry dedicated to investing, managing and administering the life savings and retirement investments of the world's consumers and savers. There are also institutional (B2B) mutual funds, as well as the more common user retail funds.

Mutual funds, in all their different guises (mutual funds, unit trusts, investment trusts, exchange traded funds (ETFs), passive vs active funds, hedge funds and more) are the staple of a typical retail investment portfolio, which usually comprises 60% funds and 40% non-funds such as exchange-traded instruments (e.g. stocks/equities and cash).

A mutual fund is a legal vehicle for pooled investments, from a range of subscribers, managed by a professional fund manager and whose stated goal is to grow the capital and income offered by the fund for the benefit of its subscribers. Most mutual funds have an 'open-ended' style, i.e. there are an unlimited number of subscribers and units available; a smaller number of funds operate on the much older fund model of a fixed number of shares or units in issue.

All mutual funds require extensive management and administration – for example, of the underlying investments, the pooled and individual portfolios, the performance measurement of the fund itself and the trading, settlement and unit/share issuance activities. Figure 12.1 illustrates the most popular domiciles of worldwide fund assets.
A huge market, the global fund management industry is dominated by wealthy countries such as the USA, the developed world nations such as the EU, Japan, Australia and the UK, and major developing countries with an emerging middle class such as China and Brazil.

Understanding how fund management works is critical for the case study in how blockchains might reform and revolutionise this industry.

■ In this chapter we will examine the fund management use case and smaller 'caselets'.

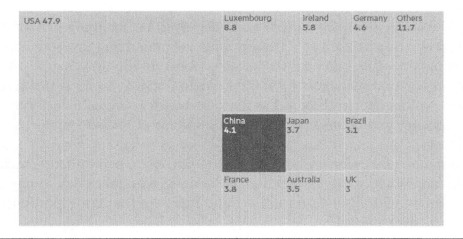

Figure 12.1   Top 10 domiciles of worldwide fund assets.

Source: European Fund and Asset Management Association; Investment Company Institute © FT

■ The chapter will explain the main features, challenges and benefits of fund management.

■ This chapter will cover typical fund management entities and actors such as fund managers, financial advisers, investors (both retail and institutional/wholesale), fund distributors and fund administration entities.

■ The chapter will also include a detailed look at how blockchain provides a robust, efficient and cost-effective solution for the fund management industry.

The Fund Management Industry in More Detail

Fund management is a traditional and conservative industry that has, for decades, lagged behind the digital progress made in the related banking and retail investment management industries.

Fund managers, sometimes referred to as the 'buy side', operate with discretion over their subscribers' pooled capital in the mutual fund to buy and sell underlying investments which are typically securities, exchange-traded instruments (ETIs), fixed-income bonds and cash or near-cash. Fund managers deal or trade (in reality, the same thing) from market counterparties such as investment banks, other funds, hedge funds, government treasury departments and financial services providers – the 'sell side'.

Fund management is a narrow and deep practice, meaning that a fund will typically restrict itself to a certain range of underlying investments or to seeking a specific outcome for its subscribers. In the universe of 'retail investments', fund managers form the kernel of activity as most financial advisers will recommend a fund as the best way for a retail investor to gain exposure to a diversified, managed portfolio of investments on a risk-rated basis.

'Fund manager' refers to both the single-purpose open-ended company and the appointed, professional human being(s) who takes day-to-day responsibility with discretion to select and maintain the fund's portfolio of underlying investments.

A fund manager is responsible for implementing a fund's investing strategy and managing its portfolio trading activities. The fund can be managed by one person, by two people as co-managers, or by a team of three or more people. Fund managers are paid a fee for their work, which is a percentage of the fund's average assets under management (AUM). They can be found working in fund management with mutual funds, pension funds, trust funds, and hedge funds. Investors should fully review the investment style of fund managers before they consider investing in a fund.[3]

Fund manager firms are often, directly or indirectly, from a long line of ancestors and some are quite old (especially in financial services terms). Some of the oldest acknowledged fund managers are

■ Foreign & Colonial Investment Trust (152 years old);
■ Dunedin Income Growth Investment Trust (148 years old);
■ Scottish American (146 years old);
■ JPMorgan American Investment Trust (136 years old); and
■ The Mercantile Investment Trust (133 years old).

This is relevant because some of the stuffy and traditional practices and assumptions made and continued by the fund management industry at large stem from the past. For example, the phrase 'fund manager's box', which refers to the daily valuation of the net present value (NPV) of the fund's underlying investments and therefore the number of units or shares available and their prices, harks back to the days when fund managers would handle paper share certificates in a wooden box in order to administer the fund itself.

As we shall see, this means that some areas of the fund management industry are especially ripe for digitalisation. Fund managers are some of the best-placed financial services industry actors who might benefit from a 'species jump' to blockchain as the decentralised ledger and smart contracts would add efficiency and transparency to legacy fund manager operations while simultaneously slashing costs.

Fund Management Software

Many fund managers use the services of an outsourced 'fund administration' service provider to run their funds on a day-to-day basis:

These [fund] administrative activities may include the following administrative functions, which may include 'fund accounting' functions. Some of these items may be specific to fund operations in the US, and some pertain only if the fund is an SEC-registered fund:

- Calculation of the net asset value (NAV), including the calculation of the fund's income and expense accruals and the pricing of securities at current market value, is a core administrator task, because it is the price at which investors buy and sell shares in the fund. This involves trade capture; security valuation (for highly illiquid securities, considerations include whether counterparty valuations are available and/or appropriate and whether the securities can be valued by independent vendors); reconciliations; expense calculation; and NAV calculation and reporting. The accurate and timely calculation of NAV by the administrator is vital.
- Preparation of semi-annual and annual reports to shareholders.
- Maintenance and filing of the fund's financial books and records as the fund accountant, including reconcilement of holdings with custody and broker records.
- Payment of fund expenses.
- Settlement of daily purchases and sales of securities, ensuring collection of dividends and interests.
- Calculation and payment to the transfer agent of dividends and distributions (if required).
- Preparation and filing of the fund's prospectus.
- Preparation and filing of other regulatory filings/reports.
- Calculation of the total returns and other performance measures of the fund.
- Monitoring investment compliance with the regulator.
- Supervision of the [orderly corporate actions e.g.] liquidation and dissolution of the fund (if required).[4]

Fund administration is a complex and perpetually ongoing aspect of fund management.

Fund managers will themselves carry out their own 'front office' fund administration, for example, portfolio construction and strategy, and performance reporting and risk rating of the underlying investments.

Fund Management Policy

Most economies have a fund management policy and encourage the activities of funds on the grounds that a well-regulated, active and passive fund management industry is beneficial for savers and investors, advisers, regulators and governments.

Policy towards fund managers encourages greater transparency, accountability, value for money and resilience. For example, in the UK, the Financial Conduct Authority's (FCA) banned trail commission on 31st December 2012:

> Trail commission was an annual fee paid to financial advisers by their customers over the lifetime of products such as pensions, with-profits bonds and unit trusts.
>
> It was also paid to intermediaries, such as discount brokers and fund platforms, that recommended or enabled the purchase of funds or other investments.
>
> Trail commission was a percentage fee, typically 0.5%, taken out of the sum of your investment each year. It was usually included in the annual management charge, so it was not always clear that you were paying it or how much it cost you.
>
> The trail commission may have been intended to cover an ongoing service, but was often paid to advisers each year without them reviewing their customers' investments or providing further advice.[5]

Other major fund and financial services regulators, such as the European Securities and Markets Authority (ESMA) and the Securities and Exchange Commission (SEC) in the USA, are also proponents of a policy of thematic reviews of their fund management industries to promote strong collective investment governance frameworks.

Fund Management in the Real World

Fund management occupies an important role in the real world. Many readers in developed world economies will also be savers and – via their pension savings – likely investors in mutual funds as well.

Fund management has a direct and indirect impact on the ability of working people to retire and to continue to receive the benefits they are hoping for well into that retirement. A poorly performing, inefficient or technologically complex fund management industry will create headwinds for the good outcomes expected by the tens of millions of investors in funds.

Fund management is also a major investor in publicly quoted (and, in the hedge fund sector, non-quoted) businesses and firms. This is a real-world benefit for millions of workers both directly and indirectly employed by the businesses and governments that funds invest in.

The Role of Business in Fund Management

Fund managers are in business to earn, for themselves, management fees. These must be declared to fund subscribers up front, and range from a fee potentially paid to a regulated financial adviser for recommending the fund to annual fund management fees and (less commonly) for exit fees or fees charged for 'life events' such as when a subscriber becomes deceased, divorced, bankrupt etc.

Fund management is a profitable business that enjoys recurring income from long-term customers, sometimes over decades. However, fund management is relatively expensive and a fund management firm is often owned by a larger institution, for example a bank or an insurance company, as part of a group of businesses.

Blockchains in Fund Management

Fund management is a relatively conservative, traditional industry that is (at best) a late adopter of new technology. This applies in the case of blockchain and fund managers: many fund managers are curious about blockchain but unwilling to change their own fund management technology and architecture alone.

Paradoxically, fund management is an ideal candidate for blockchain adoption. Funds are ledger-driven, with multiple, distributed subscribers on the one hand, and a diversified and wide range of securities and cash in the main fund portfolios on the other. In such a case the potential benefits of a decentralised ledger, such as a blockchain, with its immutability, transparency and efficiency, are obvious and directly applicable.

What is Fund Management?

On a day-to-day basis a fund manager, both the fund itself (as a legal entity) and the professional human fund managers who run the fund, are focused on money, portfolio configuration, the underlying investments and the hundreds of thousands (sometime millions) of fund subscribers.

The Fund Management Company

The fund management company is the commercial entity that runs a fund. Usually, a fund management company may run several different funds, although these funds are kept strictly segregated from each other legally, financially and in terms of each fund's objectives, risk rating and performance.

A fund management company is often an arm or division of a much larger financial services industry firm, such as a retail bank, an insurance company or even a financial advice firm.

Some fund management companies in the UK are referred to as 'discretionary fund managers', meaning they are professional (i.e. regulated) financial advisory firms that enjoy an extra, formal, power of attorney from their retail clients to select and manage their clients cash and underlying investments on their behalf.

The Mutual Fund

A mutual fund is a collective investment vehicle, similar to a limited liability company, that pools its subscribers' cash investments, and aims to provide subscribers, after professional fund management costs are deducted, with benefits such as an income from the profits of the fund or a reinvestment of those profits for capital growth.

The mutual fund has had several different incarnations over its long history, for example closed-ended funds are now quite rare (as most mutual funds are now open-ended) and commission for selling a fund investment is now generally disallowed by regulators. However, at a high level, the mutual fund has remained a relatively stable and predictable investment vehicle and adopts innovation only slowly compared to other types of financial product.

Mutual funds may be either 'active' or 'passive'. An active fund is typically more expensive than a passive fund as it is looked after dynamically by a professional human fund manager who is qualified as a professional investor. A passive fund (also sometimes referred to as an 'index' fund) is algorithmic in design and tends to 'track' a specific market or sector of one or more global economies.

There is significant debate over the merits and demerits of active vs. passive funds:

> In 2007, Warren Buffett made a bet against hedge-fund manager Ted Seides that a simple S&P 500 index [passive] fund would outperform a basket of at least five hedge [active] funds over the course of a decade. The bet's time frame started in January 2008 and concluded at the end of 2017. It's now [2018] official – Buffett is the winner, and by a large margin.[6]

Most mutual funds are traded in units or shares and are not, strictly speaking, available on stock markets like other fungible securities such as equities/stocks and fixed income bonds. Most mutual funds have a daily net asset valuation (NAV) carried out and the resulting number of units/shares and unit/share price issued by their fund manager.

The Exchange-Traded Fund (ETF)

An exchange-traded fund (EFT) is a mutual fund (and may be active and passive, although the vast majority are algorithm-driven passive/index ETFs) that is characterised by its behaviour as an exchange-traded instrument.

Thus, unlike a more traditional mutual fund, an ETF may be bought and sold as-and-when on a stock market or exchange, like an equity/stock or a fixed income bond, for example. ETFs are perceived as more accessible and transparent for these reasons and have therefore seen a huge growth in recent years, especially as self-service retail investment solutions, apps and 'day trading' have gained in popularity.

The Hedge Fund

A hedge fund is a collective investment vehicle, similar to a mutual fund, but typically with a more flexible investment philosophy (for example, the ability to take long and short positions), more aggressive investment return expectations, and much more active fund management.

Hedge funds are also usually more expensive, charging higher annual fund management fees and, depending on the fund, a levy (for example, 20%) on any profits made by the hedge fund in a year.

The Fund Management Regulator

The fund management regulator is usually part of a territory's general financial regulatory framework – for example, in the UK the fund management regulator is the Financial Conduct Authority (FCA).

In the EU, there exists a fund management regulator in the form of the European Securities and Markets Authority (ESMA). EU-wide fund regulation extends into policy too – for example, creating EU-wide directives such as the 'undertakings for collective investment in transferable securities' (UCITS) that have been successful outside the Union and are now partly a global standard for fund management regulation.

Fund Management Processing and Settlement

Mutual fund trading differs from stock trading in many ways, but the most important difference has to do with timing. In nearly all cases, mutual fund trades execute once every day after the financial markets close. If you miss the trading deadline for a particular day, your mutual fund trade won't get executed until the following day.

This difference in how mutual fund shares get handled also helps speed the settlement process. With most mutual fund trades, the fund is able to settle the transaction on the next business day. By contrast, stock trades typically take three business days to settle. Occasionally, a fund might have provisions in its shareholder agreement that give it more time to settle transactions. However long the settlement period is, fund buyers have to make sure they have cash available to make the purchase by the settlement date, and fund sellers won't be able to use cash proceeds for other purposes until the trade settles.

Money-market mutual fund transactions follow special rules. Because money-market mutual funds are designed to be especially liquid, fund transactions settle on the same day that the trade is effective. That allows shareholders to use money-market mutual funds as sweep options for brokerage accounts without having to wait an extra day to clear purchases and sales.

Finally, bear in mind that other types of funds that are governed by some similar rules to mutual funds nevertheless have different settlement rules. Exchange-traded funds, for instance, have a lot in common with mutual funds, but ETFs follow the same rules as stocks and take three days to settle. Closed-end funds work similarly, as their shares trade on secondary markets rather than directly through the fund company and thus have a three-day settlement period.

The differences in mutual fund settlement rules can make them an important source of cash that's faster than selling stock. Knowing those rules will help you avoid unfortunate mistakes in not having cash on hand in time for a purchase to settle.[7]

Managing Funds

Funds are managed on a day-to-day basis by professional fund managers and their associated specialist and support teams.

A fund manager is usually a qualified professional, sometimes with the Chartered Financial Analyst (CFA) qualification. Fund managers are backed up by specialist quantitative analysts, portfolio, risk and product analysts, securities traders (also known as 'dealers' and 'brokers') and teams of dedicated technology and information specialists. Together, these teams are usually referred to as the fund manager's 'front office'.

Fund managers are also supported by significant numbers of skilled, professional administrators who typically work in the fund manager's 'back office'. These teams include people experienced in order management, settlement, reconciliation, reporting, cash management, product management, risk, tax and compliance, change and transformation, and a dedicated team of in-house legal counsel.

Key Fund Management Concepts

In this section we'll have a look at some key fund management concepts such as legal entities, actors, types, models and stresses/challenges.

Fund management is not a homogeneous industry, and all funds are different in either subtle or major ways. This section will deal with the most typical fund management concepts, pointing out common deviances as we go along.

Legal Entities

There are several key principal legal entities involved in fund management as follows:

The Fund Manager

The fund manager is both the firm that is managing a fund vehicle and the professional human being who is employed by that firm to specifically manage an individual fund.

The Fund

A fund is a limited liability company, usually with a variable number of shares or units (and shareholders or unitholders). The fund company is established with directors, either legal or physical persons, and publishes a prospectus, terms and conditions, and other legal foundation paperwork for the benefit of its prospective investors.

Fund companies are therefore legal entities in their own right and, while they otherwise are not hugely similar to ordinary limited liability companies, fund companies are subject to some of the same rules that govern day-to-day commerce.

However, unlike non-fund companies, funds are regulated entities and must file extended reports and information with the tax authorities, the financial regulator and – in some cases – the central bank.

Exchange-traded funds (ETFs), mutual funds, investment trusts and hedge funds are not the same, but originate from the same limited liability fund root.

The Fund Shareholder/Unitholder

Retail investors in a fund are the fund's shareholders (or unitholders). This is not the same role as played by a shareholder in a non-fund limited liability company – for example, there is unlikely to be a shareholders' agreement, voting rights or any of the other normal artefacts that are issued and agreed between shareholders in a non-fund limited liability company.

Share-/unitholders in a fund are entitled to share in the profits of the fund and their rights and responsibilities are usually set out in the fund's various legal documents such as prospectus, terms and conditions, and so on.

The Underlying

Funds receive cash from their subscribers. In return, the fund issues subscribers with shares and/or units. The cash is then invested by the fund manager into an underlying of exchange-traded securities (for example, equities/stocks, fixed income bonds, ETFs), other funds, and cash and cash-like securities.

This range of securities is collectively referred to as the 'underlying investments'. Managing the underlying is the key day-to-day job of the fund manager and requires professional training and qualifications.

The Investment Manager

Within a fund there is a specialist function known as the investment manager. The investment manager is sometimes separate from the fund manager and the investment manager's roles and responsibilities are usually formally set out in the fund prospectus itself.

The investment manager oversees the selection, distribution, risk assessment and portfolio construction of the underlying investments in the fund.

The Custodian

The underlying investments of the fund, once bought, are kept for safekeeping with a regulated custodian.

The role of the custodian is to hold the underlying investments, in electronic form, in the event that the fund and/or the fund manager becomes insolvent. In these circumstances, which are less frequent than with a non-fund limited liability company, the custodian will communicate with the fund subscriber directly and will work with the liquidators to return as much of the fund's assets to investors as possible.

The Bank

Fund managers are not deposit takers. On that basis, each fund manager requires a bank to hold and segregate its corporate cash from the cash of the investors (in the form of subscriptions and withdrawals) and the cash of the fund portfolios (most funds have an allocation of cash within the underlying investments).

Banks are the custodians of the cash in the fund (mirroring the role of the custodian, which has custody of the securities in the fund).

Actors in the Fund Management Stack

The fund management stack is the logical arrangement of technology applications, legal entities, people and processes, and business rules that together make up the functional structure of a fund management business.

We refer to a stack in the logical sense – in other words, the professional definition of architecture domains, e.g. business, data, applications and technical.

Business Architecture

Fund manager business architecture is a mature and established model of roles and responsibilities, people and processes, and defining and setting clear boundaries between who does what within the fund manager operating model itself.

Almost all funds issue a prospectus of one form or another. This is a legally binding agreement document, not too dissimilar to a private company shareholders' agreement. As such, the fund prospectus sets out how and when shares/units may be valued, bought, transferred, cancelled etc.; it also determines how shareholder or unitholder benefits might be distributed among owners.

A fund is a legal entity governed entirely by its own legally binding rules and the oversight and rules of the fund regulator, auditors, tax authorities and client money rules.

Data Architecture

Fund manager data architecture follows, in most cases, the business architecture. For example, if a fund is domiciled in the European Union, it is likely to require that personal data on the share-/unitholders be maintained within the European Economic Area.

The data for underlying investments, transactions, cash management, performance and reporting will be determined by the local regulatory standards in place, fund manager policies and client requirements.

Fund managers are not typically innovators on their data, although trends such as AI, risk management, environmental, social and corporate governance (ESG), algorithmic trading, and detailed fund performance measurement do drive data architecture innovation and this will be a continual process of improvement.

Application Architecture

An application architecture describes the patterns and techniques used to design and build an application. The architecture gives you a roadmap and best practices to follow when building an application, so that you end up with a well-structured app.

Software design patterns can help you to build an application. A pattern describes a repeatable solution to a problem.

Patterns can be linked together to create more generic application architectures. Instead of completely creating the architecture yourself, you can use existing design patterns, which also ensure that things will work the way they're supposed to.

As part of an application architecture, there will be both front-end and back-end services. Front-end development is concerned with the user experience of the app, while back-end development focuses on providing access to the data, services, and other existing systems that make the app work.[8]

For fund managers, most application architectures are based on existing patterns in financial services industries and are not expected – or even desired – to be innovative.

In the past decade, fund management has seen some focus on 'auto' investing, and smaller, more nimble start-ups have drawn new clients to fund and collective investing with their easy-to-use mobile phone interfaces and online joining and verification.

Technical Architecture

It is important to define the [technical] architecture before building a software application. The technical architecture typically defines the communication networks, security, hardware, and software that are used by the application. This ensures that all new systems are compatible with the existing computer devices and equipment used in the company.[9]

Fund management technical architecture is largely standardised. Many fund managers share the same commercial platform as their core technology.

Types

The following are all types of common or frequent fund management scenarios that are experienced in the fund management industry on a regular basis.

Scenario 1 – Net Asset Value (NAV)

Most funds calculate and publish a daily net asset value (NAV) valuation of their combined cash and underlying investments, and use this NAV to further calculate the number of shares or units in issue and their (daily) price.

NAVs can be both time-consuming and complex to administer and calculate. A NAV is not frequently missed but, when it is, this causes related issues for portfolio managers and advisers and end-clients, none of whom may see a true valuation of their unit holding in the fund until the NAV is re-calculated.

Scenario 2 – Fund Rebalancing

Fund rebalancing is the process of administering the make-up of a fund's underlying investments, based on factors such as risk, market volatility, in-house investment philosophy and analysis.

Fund rebalancing can be fraught with challenges, such as in-flight share and unit transactions (and underlying transactions) and transfers, market volatility, fees and charges, and liquidity. Additionally, fund managers must constantly assess and react to the distribution and concentration of their underlying investments and are obliged by their fund prospectus and other documentation – and the principles of active fund management rules and policies – to rebalance.

Scenario 3 – Corporate Action

A fund corporate action (for example, a fund merger, closure or part-closure of the fund, distribution of cash or other formal benefits etc.) requires approval and legal consensus to be achieved by the fund manager from the various share- and unitholders of the fund.

In a largely paper and distributed technology model, which historically has been the case, fund managers are not always immediately aware of the exact ownership and intentions of the share- and unitholders in their fund. Collecting and validating the approval or rejection for a specific corporate action from the share- and unitholders in the fund is a formal requirement for fund managers and takes significant time, effort, resources and costs to complete.

Models

Not all fund management models are the same and we explore the differences here in more detail and set out the economic rationales for each.

Model 1 – Active Fund Management

Active fund managers are the most common types of fund manager – far larger a sector than non-active (i.e. passive funds, index-tracker funds, ETFs, hedge funds etc.). The split between retail (i.e. for consumers) and institutional (for sell-side and corporate investors) is relatively equal and consistent. Figure 12.2 illustrates the split of global assets under management.

Active fund managers predominate in part due to the desire of fund share- or unitholders to 'delegate' the management of the underlying and the overall investment strategy to a professionally qualified and regulated fund manager. Despite overwhelming evidence that (a) active fund managers do not (in total) outperform other, non-active, funds and (b) fund

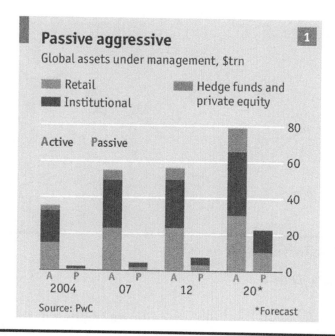

Figure 12.2   Global assets under management.

Source: PwC Economist Funds Breakdown

managers are many times more expensive than passives, most retail and institutional share- and unitholders persist with their preference for active over passive fund management.

Model 2 – Passive Fund Management

Passive fund management, by and large, is more mechanically simple and less complex than the people, processes and technology required for active fund management. As a result, passive fund management costs are noticeably less than active fund management and its performance, over time, remarkably similar.

Passive fund management has increased in size, popularity and product range in recent years (Figure 12.3), driven by the rise of execution-only (self-invested or 'day trader') types of investors and as a by-product of the large and fast-growing ETF marketplace. Retail consumers, in particular, feel an affinity with passive funds as they are transparent and easy to understand.

In times of market volatility, however, and unlike active funds, passive funds offer only a very limited 'downside protection'. Losses in passive or

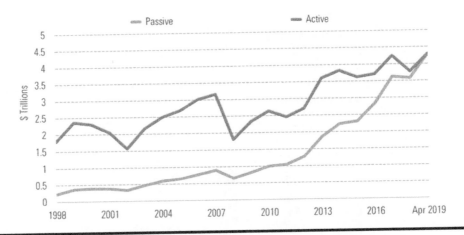

Figure 12.3   US active vs. passive funds.

Source: Morningstar Direct

index tracker funds would require a significant change in the market itself for a reversal of negative activity to take place.

Stresses in Fund Management

Fund management is a profitable business, in general terms. Growth of funds under management (FUM, also known as assets under management, AUM) has been affected even before the as-yet unknown but assumed-to-be-serious consequences of COVID 19 are considered:

> The asset management industry may have to revise projected growth in assets under management (AuM) due to the economic slowdown of recent years. In Funds Europe's Global Industry Report [they] revisit a projection from PwC in 2015 that predicted AuM in the global asset management industry would reach a record $101.7 trillion by 2020 from a 2012 total of $63.9 trillion. The report, 'Asset Management 2020: A brave new world', also predicted a compound annual growth rate for AuM of nearly 6%. But a slowdown in the world's economy since the report was published looks to have dented those heady predictions. According to a report from Willis Towers Watson the global AuM of the world's 500 largest fund managers fell 3% in 2018 to $91.5 trillion. Steve Edgley, head of institutional for Europe at Fidelity

International, now expects a base growth rate of between 1% and 3% a year over the medium to long term.[10]

Challenges More Generally

Fund management does face some more general (and specific) challenges aside from the macro-economic factors facing business and governments globally. Cost-to-serve ratios, evergreen regulatory overheads, and thriving (but immature) new fund manager competition – especially in the digital and fintech sectors – all conspire to threaten tightening profit and operating margins.

Challenge 1

'Cost-to-serve' ratios, i.e. the costs faced by financial advisers who typically recommend and therefore distribute mutual funds to their wealthy clients, are relatively high.

This is a function of the underlying lack of process automation in financial and wealth advisory firms, which can often see the most expensive and time-poor staff, the qualified and regulated advisers themselves, occupied with more mundane tasks such as assisting prospective and existing clients with onerous paperwork.

The obvious solution to the problem (process automation) looks some way off as the main platforms supporting the distribution of financial advice and fund portfolios are expensive, cumbersome and in a dominant position due to immature competition and regulatory pressures.

Challenge 2

Fund management is a highly regulated industry with a range of evergreen and new regulatory and thematic reviews constantly threatening the more profitable parts of the fund management business.

Commission, high annual management charges, opaque 'platform' charges and recurring ancillary revenues have all either been reduced or are in review by national and supranational government agencies and regulators.

Firms operating in regulated industries are not a new or especially unique category. However, fund management, with its decades-long trajectory of product design and its dependence on third-party distribution (which itself is heavily regulated) sometimes appears to be fighting for profitability with both hands tied behind its back.

Challenge 3

Incumbents in the fund management industry appear, in the minds of challenger entrepreneurs and investors, to be complacent, inefficient and ripe for disruption.

The truth is a little more nuanced, however. Not all traditional fund managers are dinosaurs; and not all new entrants are nimble and profitable either. With the arrival of fashionable fintech entrants, fund management seems to be seeing a real wave of change with optionality for retail and institutional clients alike.

For now, the new entrants look good and offer attractive pricing and compelling benefits. But when periodic market volatility strikes, as it inevitably does, retail and institutional investors will often question more closely the ability of new fund managers to weather the storm. In these circumstances, amidst uniform outflows, traditional brands with big corporate backing can win out against the newcomers.

Summary and Opinion

Fund management is a relatively straightforward proposition for wealthy retail and institutional investors to understand and to consider in their savings and investment portfolios.

As with retail banks, the recurrent fund management issues are not so much with the *proposition* but rather the *execution* of fund management: expensive staff not able to work at their most efficient; sometimes clunky and expensive underlying technology; and a variable picture of fund manager market health which not always flatters the outcomes for the consumer all conspire to cloud the view of the sector.

How Fund Managers Use Ledgers Currently

Fund management, like multiple financial services industries, has used ledgers (and continues to use ledgers) continually since its invention.

Funds themselves are ledger-bound: calculating the share- or unitholders, the value(s) of the underlying investments and cash (the NAV), the outflows and inflows to the fund, corporate actions, dividends, interest payments, price changes through market volatility and other factors must all be carefully kept and reconciled within multiple ledgers and maintained continually.

Innovation in fund management is constrained by the use of, and requirement for, traditional double-sided ledgers for cash, investments, prices and more.

How Fund Management Would be Different Using Blockchains

Centralised ledgers are a core part of the fund management industry today. Their defenders, of which there are many and rightly so, would recommend their continued use: 'if it ain't broke, don't fix it', as they are reliable, relatively low-cost and a known quantity.

There are three standard tests for the usefulness or relevance of blockchains in a specific industry, for example:

■ What's the asset to be tokenised? In fund management, the asset to be tokenised is the cash and instruments of the fund, its NAV and the assets and liabilities of the investments and benefits received from, and due to, the fund share- and unitholders themselves.
■ Is there a requirement for a proxy for trust? Yes. In fund management there is a pooled risk and reward. Nothing is more important in the minds and hearts of the fund share- and unitholders than knowing – and trusting – that there is an accurate and reliable NAV and fund administration in place.
■ Will there be equitable access? Yes. Equitable access, in fund management, means that all share- and unitholders, the underlying instrument issuers, regulators and fund distributors may have equal and transparent access to the core information, and data about the fund and that the rules of the fund are applied consistently and equally across all actors and interests.

On the face of it, the fund management industry is a perfect use case for blockchains and the following sections will set that out in more detail for comparison purposes.

Fund Management Demonstration Problems and Use Case

The use case here relates to the day-to-day management of the fund's NAV and its distribution to prospective and existing clients (both retail and institutional) via financial advisers. In this fictional use case, we have invented a new international fund manager based in New York, Dublin, Luxembourg and Singapore, Hardwood Funds, and a made-up firm of financial advisers, Sterling & Co.

Caselet 1: 'The NAV is Wrong – Often'

Current state: In the current state, Hardwood Funds are struggling to get the NAV for its funds accurate on a monthly basis, meaning, on certain days in the month, the fund failed to publish the required NAV by the published time each day, in this case, 12 noon. Where this happens, the funds share- and unitholders (and their advisers) must wait until the next working day for the correct price and NAV to be disseminated. This causes non-trivial issues such as performance calculation issues, reconciliation breaches and client care and conduct issues for distributors.

Hardwood analyse the issues and realise that their current, unfit-for-purposes NAV processes are inefficient and cumbersome and are the real cause of the delays. Different databases in different parts of the world (corresponding to where the fund's various underlying investments are in custody) are in different time zones with different currency, volatility and regulatory rules in place, making a once-a-day NAV tricky even with Hardwood's expert and committed staff.

Future state: Hardwood model a new Ethereum-powered decentralised ledger as the new core database and smart contract of the fund's NAV and other administration functions.

In the new blockchain, each of Hardwood's international centres (New York, Dublin, Luxembourg and Singapore) are nodes on the blockchain, as are each of the local regulators, major fund distributors, nominee owners of the shares or units (for retail) and institutional owners.

Hardwood also devised their own bespoke smart contracts. Now, for the first time, distributors can set rules that allow for the distribution and reconciliation of new share- and unitholders within the blockchain itself.

Hardwood link the issuance of new and updated share and unit holdings to triggers derived from the daily calculation of new cash and instrument holdings within the fund, which is also recorded onto the blockchain by the back-office administration nodes within Hardwood itself.

The outcome of this work is to streamline the Hardwood fund NAV calculation in a smart-contract framework. Now, a daily smart contract runs in the Hardwood blockchain that looks at all the transactions recorded within the fund for that day, taking into account the previous positions recorded on previous blocks, and also the to-date share- and unitholders' subscriptions, and calculates a new NAV for the fund itself.

The new NAV process is fast, efficient and mechanical, and is derived from immutable data from the previous cumulative periods.

Caselet 2: 'We're Advisers – We Need Accurate Information'

Current state: Sterling & Co, a well-known firm of London-based independent financial advisers, are a major distributor of Hardwood Funds to its wealth clients. The 'onboarding' process for a new Sterling & Co client is time consuming on some of Sterling's most qualified and expensive people: their advisers. In an effort to reduce this 'cost to serve', Sterling & Co initiate a strategic review of their portfolio system, which holds principally fund shares and units (aside from cash), to see if there can be a better way to deliver good outcomes for their clients.

Future state: Sterling & Co decide to test a new Ethereum blockchain, offered to them by Hardwood Funds who are themselves testing the technology for their own funds. Sterling becomes a new 'node' on the Hardwood Funds blockchain, and effectively opens one or more wallets for Hardwood Fund tokens on the blockchain.

Sterling link their own portfolio system via access to the Hardwood Funds blockchain to carry out transactions between wallets on the blockchain to investors' ownership. On that basis, Sterling & Co can reflect the relevant positions in their own, non-blockchain, portfolio management system, thereby avoiding the need to change their investment manager staff and client access tools.

Sterling now get an accurate and timely NAV into their portfolio system every day from the Hardwood Funds blockchain for each and all of Sterling's investors.

Because Hardwood Funds can now see all of Sterling & Co's client transactions and wallet ownerships of the Hardwood Funds shares and units, Hardwood Funds can offer easier and more efficient fund distributions, corporate actions and so on than previously.

Sterling & Co's portfolio system is also able to read the Hardwood Funds blockchain data directly – meaning that transactions made in the underlying of the Hardwood Fund, also stored on the Hardwood blockchain, are in near real time and can be displayed as such on the Sterling & Co investment manager systems (for performance and risk purposes) and to the end-clients.

The caselets give a specific, practical example of the benefits of enterprise-level blockchain in fund management. In addition, there are other benefits that pertain to the future-state (blockchain-powered) fund management solution, for example:

■ **Transparency**. Blockchains offer a reconciliation-free record of all a fund's transactions over time. This means that the true performance of the fund, including the effects of fees and charges, can be seen by all nodes at all times.
■ **Reduced cost**. Faster transactions, more accurate NAVs, easier access to data on the underlying investments and a wallet = portfolio mapping means that a blockchain-powered fund is simple to operate and easier for regulators to understand, lowering costs and risks simultaneously.
■ **Fewer intermediation**. Fewer layers in the fund management stack, in all domains (business, data, application and technical) means less intermediation, creating a simpler and more efficient fund management industry in general. This levelling of the playing field between entrenched and disruptive fund managers creates better choice for distributors and end clients alike.

Summary and Conclusion

Blockchains and fund management are – on the face of it – a good match. Functional efficiency, equitable access, transparency, reduced costs and fewer moving parts (i.e. intermediation) provide a better chance for customer choice, good outcomes and competition to thrive.

Before You Go On

■ Consider why the fund management industry might be reluctant to experiment with blockchains. Incumbent providers have much to lose and little to gain from more efficient fund management.

■ Reflect on the reasons why collectivised, pooled investments like funds, for example, might be well suited to decentralised, node-driven technologies such as blockchain. Is this a case of a square peg in a square hole?

■ Remember that only a very few fund managers have yet to try to deploy blockchains in their operations. Those that have often used proxies (tokens) in place of existing parts of their operating models. We have yet to see an end-to-end prototype.

Notes

1   www.forbes.com/sites/zackfriedman/2018/10/04/warren-buffett-best-quotes/.

2   Lubasha Heredia, Simon Bartletta, Joe Carrubba, Dean Frankle, Katsuyoshi Kurihara, Benoît Macé, Edoardo Palmisani, Neil Pardasani, Thomas Schulte, Ben Sheridan, and Qin Xu, 'Global Asset Management 2020: Protect, Adapt, and Innovate'. Boston Consulting Group, May 19 2020. www.bcg.com/en-gb/publications/2020/global-asset-management-protect-adapt-innovate.aspx.

3   James Chen, 'Fund Manager'. Reviewed by Gordon Scott. Updated Feb 17, 2021. www.investopedia.com/terms/f/fundmanager.asp.

4   Wikipedia. Fund Administration article. https://en.wikipedia.org/wiki/Fund_administration#:~:text=Fund%20administration%20is%20the%20name,trust%2C%20or%20something%20in%20between.

5   Financial Conduct Authority (FCA) press release, 'FCA Reviews How Fund Charges are Set Out'. First published May 13, 2014. www.fca.org.uk/news/press-releases/fca-reviews-how-fund-charges-are-set-out.

6   Matthew Frankel, CFP (TMFMathGuy), 'Warren Buffett Just Officially Won His Million-Dollar Bet'. The Motley Fool, Jan 3, 2018. www.fool.com/investing/2018/01/03/warren-buffett-just-officially-won-his-million-dol.aspx.

7   Motley Fool Staff, 'What Are Mutual Fund Settlement Rules?' The Motley Fool, updated Dec 23, 2016. www.fool.com/knowledge-center/mutual-fund-settlement-rules.aspx.

8   Red Hat, Inc., 'What is an Application Architecture?' www.redhat.com/en/topics/cloud-native-apps/what-is-an-application-architecture.

9   Troy Holmes, 'Wisegeek/Conjecture Corporation'. Last modified Jan 11, 2021. www.wisegeek.com/what-is-technical-architecture.htm.

10 Mark Latham, 'Global Industry Report: Asset Managers Revise AUM Growth', *Funds Europe*, Feb 10, 2020. www.funds-europe.com/news/global-industry-report-asset-managers-revise-aum-growth.

Further Reading

https://financialit.net/blog/blockchain/how-blockchain-could-restore-trust-fund-management-and-audit-industries

www.ft.com/content/b6171016-171f-11e8-9e9c-25c814761640

www.accountancyage.com/2019/10/23/can-blockchain-restore-trust-to-the-fund-management-and-audit-industries/

Chapter 13

Conclusion

True blockchain-led transformation of business and government, we believe, is still many years away. That's because blockchain is not a 'disruptive' technology which can attack a traditional business model with a lower-cost solution and overtake incumbent firms quickly.

Blockchain is a foundational technology: it has the potential to create new foundations for our economic and social systems. But while the impact will be enormous, it will take decades for blockchain to seep into our economic and social infrastructure. The process of adoption will be gradual and steady, not sudden, as waves of technological and institutional change gain momentum.

In this book, we have been very pragmatic when it comes to use cases of blockchain, and avoided jumping on the bandwagon of 'blockchain will save the world'. It will not, and at the moment, it's actually harming it with excessive power consumption for bitcoin mining – but that is another story.

But what we strongly believe is the need to remove dependencies on centralised authorities that have total control, including governments. It's not about not trusting them, actually the opposite. As human beings, we tend to trust authorities more than peers. It's about scale. Centralised control is a single point of failure. It's a bottleneck in the process. Scale can only be reached with distribution and redundancy of services. Distributed ledger technology (DLT) has these attributes by design. Moreover, its immutable nature (or at least, hard to break) sees its perfect application in independently verifiable audit scenarios, essential for reliable supply chains.

But there is a catch, or maybe a limitation, just now. Identification of parties in a supply chain, or any process in general, is still centralised.

DOI: 10.4324/9781003132592-13

Authentication depends on identity servers. We need to go beyond central identity systems and introduce decentralised identities, an identity that we own and that removes any forged credentials and central control that are typical of traditional identity systems which are more and more often subject to cyber-attacks and frequent violation, with loss of data and breach of privacy of their users. And this, along with proof of provenance, credentials and traceability, is one of the key areas of impact of blockchain technology, which will shape its future.

There is no doubt that blockchain and DLT are here to stay. In this book we have tried to present the 'real life' history, development and implications of this, and to explain to the reader the true face of the technology.

We've also focused on blockchain use cases in real-world applications, and in industries that already use some form of traditional ledger and/or paper records. These examples are the most accessible way to explain how blockchain is different, and help the general reader see how the changes that blockchain can bring about might first take root.

Blockchain is the first major development in 'ledger tech' for several hundred years. Our view is that the next few decades will see the real deployment of blockchain in all our lives, and we hope you look forward to seeing this fine new technology grow and change as much as we do.

Glossary

We've decided, rather than try to offer and maintain our own glossary of blockchain terms, to direct and refer readers to online blockchain glossaries.

The benefit of this approach is that of accuracy and timeliness: we don't want to create a 'silo' of glossary terms, frozen in time within the confines of the book – we'd much rather refer to the constantly updated and maintained online glossaries instead.

Please note: these glossaries are outside our control, but at the time of writing were all working and in apparent good order. Readers are of course recommended to find and bookmark their own glossaries for future reference.

https://objectcomputing.com/expertise/blockchain/glossary

https://blockchaintrainingalliance.com/pages/glossary-of-blockchain-terms

www.comptia.org/content/articles/blockchain-terminology

https://academy.binance.com/glossary

Index

Note: Page numbers in *italics* indicate figures and in **bold** indicate tables on the corresponding pages.

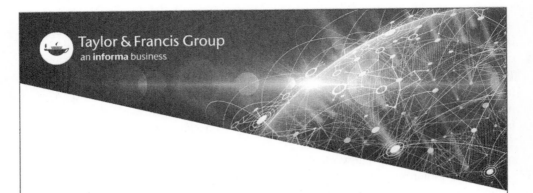